ORDER AND REBELLION
IN TRIBAL AFRICA

ORDER AND REBELLION
IN TRIBAL AFRICA

Collected Essays
with an autobiographical introduction
by

MAX GLUCKMAN

Professor of Social Anthropology in
the Victoria University of Manchester

LONDON
COHEN & WEST

First published 1963
by Cohen & West Ltd.
Broadway House, 68–74 Carter Lane
London, E.C.4
Printed in Great Britain
by Staples Printers Ltd., Rochester

TO MARY,
this record of shared
work

CONTENTS

PREFACE

I HAVE AGREED to my publishers' suggestion that they collect some of my essays in a book, because I have learnt that there is a demand for these essays among students to whom they are not easily accessible. It also seemed worth while to collect the essays together because it gives me an opportunity to clarify my own arguments and indicate their underlying assumptions in an introduction. Comments from colleagues have shown me that my views have not always been understood in the sense in which I wrote these, and if I can clarify my arguments we should be able to discuss them more profitably.

I do not, of course, think of my 'theories' as peculiarly my own. I am but one of many anthropologists, and the essays collected here were written at specific stages in the development of our discipline. They are the product of a set of 'collective representations', operating through a student trained by certain teachers in the anthropological tradition, and controlling his attempts to 'make sense' of a mass of data, compiled under the influence of 'collective representations' as well as of certain personal idiosyncracies. Some of the essays, or parts of them, in turn influenced the development of our subject: these ideas became in their turn 'collective representations'. Why were some selected for attention by my colleagues, and others not taken up? Why, indeed, were some of the ideas which I myself thought to be important neglected, while other points, theoretical or ethnographic, which I had not valued highly, were thought to be significant by younger anthropologists? Collecting the essays together gives me an opportunity to examine my own position in the growing theory of anthropology. It is obviously not easy for me to do this myself; but I think that, however much I overrate or undervalue my own role, this examination will be useful for students. Though I consider that anthropology is a science, we all know that both in

vii

the collecting and in the interpreting of our data, social and personal interests are deeply involved. Hence the subject itself requires that we understand something of the situations in which particular practitioners worked and wrote. In examining myself, I examine the subject; and I can draw attention, albeit briefly, in introductory notes and connecting paragraphs to similar or discrepant work by others going on at the same time, or appearing afterwards.

On consideration, my publishers and I decided that some of my essays on political problems would make a book of reasonable size.

When I was studying anthropology at Oxford, I had the good fortune to become friendly with E. E. Evans-Pritchard and Meyer Fortes, at a time when they were working out their analyses of the political systems of the Nuer and the Tallensi, who lack governmental institutions. 'Political anthropology' emerged with Evans-Pritchard's studies of the Nuer in essays in *Sudan Notes and Records* (1934–5), pulled together in *The Nuer* (1940). These essays, and stimulating discussions with Evans-Pritchard and Fortes before I went to study the Zulu in the field, had prepared me to find more than a straightforward governmental apparatus among the Zulu: they had sharpened my insight into the significance of conflict and cleavage, fusion and fission, in political systems. They had also finally prepared me for field research by increasing the exciting interest in social life I had derived during my training at the University of the Witwatersrand under Mrs A. W. Hoernlé and Isaac Schapera. I have already paid tribute to the way in which Evans-Pritchard's and Fortes' studies of 'stateless' societies influenced social anthropology in an essay on 'The Peace in the Feud' in my *Custom and Conflict in Africa*; and I begin this collection with an acknowledgment of my personal debt to them, my review of Fortes' *The Dynamics of Clanship among the Tallensi* (1945).

I omit the main part of my essay from *African Political Systems* (edited by M. Fortes and E. E. Evans-Pritchard, 1940), my first essay on political problems, in which I put forward the theory of the rebellious cycle of African states, because this thesis is advanced further in later essays. It is summarized in my essay applying it to the very different situation of the Bemba of Northern Rhodesia: this was written in 1946 but only published in 1954. Third comes my Frazer Lecture of 1952, 'Rituals of Rebellion in South-East Africa', which deals with the first culmination of my ideas on many political problems and on interpretations of ritual. I should have liked to include an essay on the first-fruits ceremony of the Zulu, based on reports by missionaries and travellers ('Social Aspects of First-Fruits Ceremonies among the South-Eastern Bantu', *Africa*, xi, 1938, pp. 25–41), partly because it deals with an historical change among the Zulu of general interest, but mainly because it illustrates, in contrast with 'Rituals of Rebellion', the great change in the data for our analysis brought about by modern fieldwork methods. These early records of the ceremony appear useless when compared with Dr Hilda Kuper's account of the Swazi ceremony (in *An African Aristocracy*, 1947) on which I drew for my analysis of 'rituals of rebellion.' For lack of space, I had, with regret, to omit this essay.

To contrast the significance of ritual in a stationary repetitive social system with my views on the role of ritual in conditions of severe change, I have included a broadcast on the Mau Mau movement in Kenya.

I have placed next the symposium on the position of 'The Village Headman in British Central Africa' which I and two of my younger colleagues at the Rhodes-Livingstone Institute, John Barnes (now Professor at Canberra) and Clyde Mitchell (now Professor at Salisbury, Southern Rhodesia), presented to a meeting of the Royal Anthropological Institute and the International African Institute in 1948. It develops the theory analysing intercalary roles (to follow a terminology used in another context by Fortes), and of the significance of ritual in dealing with the conflicts which centre on these roles. For the sake of logic it comes out of chronological order: my own insight into this problem emerged with my study of the roles of native commissioner and chief in Zululand, first put forward briefly in a section of my essay in *African Political Systems* (1940). I reproduce this section with the analysis of the village headman's position, since he has an analogous, dual, intercalary, role. I am grateful to John Barnes and Clyde Mitchell for allowing me to reproduce their sections of this symposium here.

To complete the political essays, I present a broadcast summary of my *The Judicial Process among the Barotse of Northern Rhodesia* (1955), under the title 'The Reasonable Man in Barotse Law', since this is an example, and an all too rare example, of a study of how a tribal political system works in one of its specialized functions.

This book therefore mainly covers my reflections on the theories of my colleagues who studied segmentary societies, and my own theories about African states and how they work. But I have included also some essays on Malinowski. The first, an extended review of Malinowski's *The Dynamics of Culture Contact: An Inquiry into Race Relations in Africa* (edited with an Introduction by P. M. Kaberry, 1946), was originally published in the journal *Africa*, and subsequently re-issued and sold out as Rhodes-Livingstone Paper No. 16 (1948). Continuing requests for copies of this critique have encouraged me to take this chance of re-publishing it. I also include a shorter essay on Malinowski's general theory, and an unpublished broadcast reviewing a book assessing his contribution to the development of our science, in order to balance my severe criticisms of his approach to problems of social change.

Some essays on political problems could not be included: (1) my analysis of the political system of the Lozi, published in *Seven Tribes of British Central Africa* (edited by E. Colson and M. Gluckman; 1951; 2nd impression 1960), was too long, and this defect – for present purposes – of length applies to other essays on Lozi politics and law; (2) my *Analysis of a Social Situation in Modern Zululand*, dealing *in extenso* with the problem of modern political relations raised at the end of the essay included from *African Political Systems*, has just been re-published from *Bantu Studies*, 1940, as *Rhodes-Livingstone Paper No.* 28, and it would not have been fair to include it here, though it is important to me; (3) some of the themes of the essays here presented, together with others, both in the political and the domestic and the ritual fields, were discussed by me in a series of broadcast lectures and then published as *Custom and Conflict in Africa* (1955), and none of these have been included since the book has just gone into a second impression.

Finally, I have omitted all essays on what are ostensibly problems arising from domestic relations. Among these, the one which has made the biggest impression on later work is my comparative study of 'Kinship and Marriage among the Lozi of Northern Rhodesia and the Zulu of Natal' which was published in *African Systems of Kinship and Marriage*, under the editorship of A. R. Radcliffe-Brown and C. D. Forde (1950). In that essay, I put forward a hypothesis to relate variations in the divorce rate in a number of African tribes, to the kinship structures of these tribes. The form in which the hypothesis was presented has been discussed and criticized by Schneider (*Man*, liii, 1953, No. 75), and by Leach in several notes (*Man*, ibid, No. 279; *Man*, liv, 1954, No. 153); and its validity in terms of new ethnographic research has been tested by Barnes, Colson, Mitchell, Turner and Watson in Central Africa; Fallers and Winter in East Africa; Pehrson for the Lapps; Djamour in some Malayan societies; and others. The essay itself is 15,000 words long, and it would require detailed re-analysis in the light of all this comment. It had to be excluded or it would have swollen this book prodigiously. In any case, I hope that my friend, Professor J. Clyde Mitchell, will shortly examine the whole problem of divorce rates anew (see his essay in report on the seminar of the International African Institute, held at Kampala, January 1959 and published in *Social Change in Africa*, edited by A. W. Southall, 1961).

I have designated this essay on divorce rates as 'ostensibly (concerned with) problems arising from domestic relations'. In fact, though it deals with kinship and marriage, I myself class it as a study in the field of political science, since it does not analyse internal relations in the family, or between spouses, but suggests that the *rate* of divorce in any tribe will be influenced by the overall kinship structure, with strong agnatic groups producing stable marriage, and unstable marriage accompanying matrilineal and omnilineal (Barnes' term which I prefer to 'bilateral') descent systems. My essay on 'The Role of the Sexes in Wiko Circumcision Ceremonies', which was published in *Social Structure: Studies Presented to A. R. Radcliffe-Brown* (ed. M. Fortes, 1949), is more directly in the field of domestic relations, though not entirely. This is not included here because some of its arguments will be presented in a book I am working on together with Dr Victor Turner, in which we plan to analyse circumcision ceremonies in North-Western Rhodesia and to consider general problems of *rites de passage* in relation to social structure and to ritual symbolism.

I wish to thank the following people for permission to reprint papers:

(i) The Editors of *African Studies* (formerly *Bantu Studies*), of the University of the Witwatersrand, Milner Park, Johannesburg, South Africa, for 'An Advance in African Sociology';

(ii) The Director of the International African Institute, the

Oxford University Press, and the Editors of *African Political Systems* (Professors M. Fortes and E. E. Evans-Pritchard), for 'The Kingdom of the Zulu of South Africa';

(iii) The Director of the Rhodes-Livingstone Institute, for 'Succession and Civil War among the Bemba – An Exercise in Anthropological Theory';

(iv) The Director of the International African Institute, and Professor J. A. Barnes and Professor J. C. Mitchell, for 'The Village Headman in British Central Africa';

(v) The Manchester University Press, for 'Rituals of Rebellion in South-East Africa', especially as the Press still holds unsold copies;

(vi) The Director of the International African Institute, for 'Social Aspects of First-Fruits Ceremonies among the South-Eastern Bantu';

(vii) The Director of Publications of Her Majesty's Stationery Office for 'The Reasonable Man in Barotse Law', which appeared in the *Journal of African Administration;*

(viii) The Editors of *African Studies*, the Director of the International African Institute, and the Director of the Rhodes-Livingstone Institute, for the two essays on Malinowski's theories;

(ix) The Editor of *The New Statesman and Nation*, for 'Malinowski – Fieldworker and Theorist'.

I am grateful to John Barnes and Clyde Mitchell for allowing me to include their contributions to the symposium on 'The Village Headman in British Central Africa' in a collection of my own work. They have also read and commented on my 'Introduction' to this collection, as have Elizabeth Colson, Meyer Fortes, Isaac Schapera, Peter Worsley, and my colleagues at Manchester University. Worsley has helped me particularly with the drafting of the summary reference to Marxist-Leninist writings on rebellions.

Finally, I thank the Ford Foundation for a generous grant to aid my own research, part of which I employed in preparing this 'Introduction'.

MAX GLUCKMAN

University of Manchester,
February 1962

INTRODUCTION

IN HIS *Mirror for Man*, at the very beginning, Clyde Kluckhohn sums up the origins of anthropology by citing a nineteenth-century wit who described the subject as the study of oddments by eccentrics. The facts treated by our discipline's founders were indeed oddments in two sorts of ways. First, they were odds and ends of facts that were not studied by other disciplines: by such medical experts as there were, by jurists and political scientists, economists, classical archaeologists and so forth. Secondly, when assembled together they made a collection of oddments: folkways and folktales, the out-of-the-way customs of the Western world, the artifacts and other material products of tribal societies, the customs of these societies and their ways of reckoning time, bone and skull shapes and the surface appearances of the stocks of mankind, the position of man in relation to the other mammals, the implements and other remains of prehistoric man, etc. It was a great achievement of our ancestors that, out of studying this illogical assortment, they should have given birth to the well-established discipline – or, now, the several disciplines – of anthropology. For though their original theories, cast first in evolutionary form and then in a series of historical reconstructions, may seem to us to be Procrustean in their forcing of facts, and though they may seem to have searched in what Goldenweiser called 'a chronological vacuum', they nevertheless drew attention to many neglected aspects of social life and they cleared the way for a more systematic treatment of that life. It was perhaps inevitable that as scholars pursued their analyses of these oddments, each category of oddments should have become the field of study of a more specialized discipline – as, for example, physical anthropology has done. Inevitably, also, each of these specialized branches has linked up with other disciplines attacking facts in like manner: as, again, physical anthropology has linked up with comparative anatomy, physiology, and zoology.

I

With the accumulation of more penetrating and comprehensive data on social life itself, other branches of anthropology have emerged. Two of these are represented dominantly in the United States: cultural (or culturological) anthropology, and psychical (or psychological) anthropology. They draw for ideas and aid, and in turn stimulate, psychology, psycho-analysis, and psychiatry. A third branch is social (or sociological) anthropology: it dominates anthropology in the British Commonwealth, is strong in France, and is also strongly represented in the United States. I cannot here discuss why and how these divisions of anthropology emerged: for my purpose it is sufficient to note that I myself was raised in the sociological stream. When I studied anthropology in 1928–34 at the University of the Witwatersrand in South Africa, the sociological current had already begun to run. It sprang from A. R. Radcliffe-Brown, who had 'taught' both Mrs. A. W. Hoernlé and I. Schapera, my own teachers. He in his turn had drawn largely on the work and ideas of the Durkheim school in France, which, though it dealt largely with 'anthropological facts', was itself a product of the separate tradition of 'sociology'.

In those years, in South Africa as in Britain, anthropology was still a united discipline studying 'oddments'. I too was required by the regulations to study these several oddments, taught by several specialists. But already Mrs Hoernlé was warning us against committing 'the psychologists' fallacy' when she criticized, for example, Frazer's theory of the development of magic, religion and science, or Tylor's theories of the origin of beliefs in the soul or of sacrifice. She stressed that it was fatal to use a psychological theory, stemming from an analysis of individuals, to explain a social and cultural phenomenon. Mrs Hoernlé was not denying that psychology was a valid science, of equal status with sociology and social anthropology; but she was putting strongly the argument which opens Durkheim's *Les Règles de la Méthode Sociologique*: that social facts have to be explained by reference to other social facts. And, like Durkheim, who has here sometimes been misinterpreted, she insisted on the importance of psychology's contribution to a *total* understanding of the whole complex reality of any specific human situation. But, she argued, psychology is a highly organized discipline of its own, requiring trained competence both in acquiring and interpreting facts. Hence it is out of respect for psychology, and not in contempt of it, that I deliberately eschew psychological analysis. I stress this point here, since I shall show later that my own theories have been mistakenly both interpreted as psychological, and also criticized for their psychological inadequacy. The shadows of this controversy are thrown across the years from Durkheim's day to the present: for me they were settled by the lectures I heard from Professor Radcliffe-Brown at Oxford in 1938–9. I found that these immediately cleared away for me the difficulties and doubts about what is 'society' or 'culture', by stressing that we study the inter-relations between events, and that several sciences may study the same events in different sets of inter-relations, and that the crucial thing is to be clear about what kinds of inter-relations we are seeking for at any one time. I have set out my taking over of Radcliffe-Brown's view of the nature of a social system in an essay not republished here – 'The Difficulties, Achievements and Limitations of Social Anthropology', (Rhodes-Livingstone *Journal*, I, 1944) – and in my *Analysis of a Social Situation in Modern Zululand* (pp. 53 f.); but since then Professor Fred Eggan has edited our common teacher's clarifying analyses of these difficulties (*A Natural Science of Society*, 1958). There remain, of course, major philosophical problems: but if we compare Radcliffe-Brown's philosophically realist approach with the difficulties raised by Durkheim's Cartesian formulation, I think that our own position, as research workers, is sufficiently clarified for us to proceed without further worry to tackle our field problems.

As the separate branches of anthropology emerged, inevitably they remained involved with their own past, and hence they were prevented from drawing as they might have done on other humanistic disciplines. In a broadcast review of the book *Man and Culture* (1957) in which twelve of Malinowski's pupils assess his work (see below 'Malinowski, Fieldworker and Theorist', Chapter X), I argue that Malinowski, having collected far richer data on tribal life than anyone before him, largely used these data to attack the simple views of tribal life presented by earlier anthropologists, and also by economists and lawyers. Firth says that Malinowski failed to scrutinize the concepts of economics with the same care as he scrutinized the concepts of other social sciences. Firth was by original training an economist: I studied law, and I would say Malinowski failed to scrutinize with adequate care the concepts of jurisprudence. Certainly, Malinowski never

3

turned to economics for the kind of help in handling his data which Firth thus obtained (*Primitive Polynesian Economy*, 1938, and *Malay Fishermen*, 1946); nor did he use jurisprudence in the way that Schapera (*A Handbook of Tswana Law and Custom*, 1939), E. A. Hoebel (*The Law of Primitive Man*, 1954), or I myself (*The Judicial Process Among the Barotse of Northern Rhodesia*, 1955) have done. Trained as we anthropologists were in the study of oddments, even with some specialized eccentricity, we had laboriously, and belatedly, to learn that scholars in other disciplines had long been writing about and illuminating the problems which we were, for the first time, tackling in the so-called primitive societies. When I went to study modern political and economic organization in Zululand, in 1936, I knew something about brachycephaly and the *coup-de-poing*: I knew virtually nothing about sociology or political science. This was not due to bad teaching, for my teachers were excellent, and it was not a personal weakness; this distribution of knowledge inhered in the subject at that stage. No early anthropologist, not even Maine if we can claim him as an ancestor, had dealt with political problems, perhaps because all early research in anthropology was done on the small-scale societies of America, Australasia, Oceania, and India and its islands. It was only with the publication in 1940 of *African Political Systems* that political anthropological science was established.

Professor Fortes has recorded the inception of the idea of this book (*Africa*, xxvi, 1956, p. 295). On reading the proofs of Schapera's *A Handbook of Tswana Law and Custom* (1938), Fortes was 'stimulated to describe to him [Schapera] the strikingly different political and legal institutions of the Tallensi. . . . Out of these talks was born the idea of bringing out a comparative survey of African political institutions.' But these Africanists were selecting political problems for study, problems which had been overlooked by earlier anthropologists. Fortes has told me he thinks the policy of indirect rule, and the work of Miss Margery Perham, were influential in this development. It may be also that in the larger societies of Africa the differentiation of 'political' from 'domestic' relations stands out more sharply than in smaller societies, though both types of relations may still be expressed in the idiom of kinship.

In their political analyses, as in studies of economics, or law, the new generation of anthropological writers used their new richness of data to attack the views of earlier writers. In his Preface to *African Political Systems* Radcliffe-Brown (p. xxiii) summarily dismisses 'writings on political institutions in which there is a good deal of discussion about the nature and origin of the State, which is usually represented as being an entity over and above the individuals who make up a society, having as one of its attributes something called "sovereignty", and sometimes spoken of as having a will (law being defined as the will of the State) or as issuing commands. The State, in this sense, does not exist in the phenomenal world; it is a fiction of the philosophers.' The Editors of the symposium, Fortes and Evans-Pritchard, open a section of their Introduction on 'Political Philosophy and Comparative Politics' (pp. 4–5):

We have not found that the theories of political *philosophers*[1] have helped us to understand the societies we have studied and we consider them of little scientific value; for their conclusions are seldom formulated in terms of observed behaviour or capable of being tested by this criterion. Political philosophy has chiefly concerned itself with how men *ought* to live and what form of government they *ought* to have, rather than with what *are* their political habits and institutions.

In so far as political *philosophers*[1] have attempted to understand existing institutions instead of trying to justify or undermine them, they have done so in terms of popular psychology or of history. They have generally had recourse to hypotheses about earlier stages of human society presumed to be devoid of political institutions or to display them in a very rudimentary form, and have attempted to reconstruct the process by which the political institutions with which they were familiar in their own societies might have arisen out of these elementary forms of organization. Political *philosophers*[1] in modern times have often sought to substantiate their theories by appeal to the facts of primitive societies. They cannot be blamed if, in doing so, they have been led astray, for little anthropological research has been conducted into primitive political systems compared with research into other primitive institutions, customs, and beliefs, and still less have comparative studies of them been made.

[A footnote excepts Professor R. H. Lowie from this stricture, and pays tribute to the work of great legal and constitutional historians like Maine, Vinogradoff, and Ed. Meyer.]

This passage of course immediately provoked a reply from a philosopher, the late Professor R. F. A. Hoernlé, of the University of the Witwatersrand (in *Bantu Studies*, 1940). After pointing out that attacks on unnamed philosophers were difficult to comment on and that there was a distinction between political science and political philosophy, he justified the case for political philosophy as an independent and different subject, and indicated (and approved of) the teleological statements in the anthropological analyses themselves. A reviewer of the book using the initials 'J. L.' (presumably Dr Julius Lewin, the specialist on 'Native' Law and Administration at Witwatersrand University), in the same issue of *Bantu Studies* praised the new contribution of the book, but commented on these passages: 'The editors . . . scorn any assistance that might be derived from other social sciences, and allow themselves a gratuitous criticism of political science which serves only to indicate that they have not really looked into the modern literature on the subject' (I have emphasized that the editors criticized political *philosophers*).

Both Fortes and Evans-Pritchard had studied societies with political institutions very different from those known to the political philosophers, and even the political scientists, of the Western world – different even from the ancient Greek institutions analysed by Aristotle. The stateless, segmentary societies, which they distinguished from the states covered in their symposium, were exhibiting to them the real rudimentary forms of political systems, if we can place systems along a line of morphological development of form, without thereby accepting that more developed forms of the state (not necessarily as complex in political institutions as the segmentary forms of society) have inevitably evolved along a single line. Hence what Durkheim would have called 'introspective speculations' about the origins in time of political institutions would have appeared further removed from reality to them than the reflections of philosophers on the nature of the state later appeared to me, who had studied African states. Indeed, as I try to show in a chapter on 'The Peace in the Feud' in my *Custom and Conflict in Africa* (1955), researches by anthropologists on segmentary societies should compel a serious reassessment of early European political institutions (as has been done by J. M. Wallace-Hadrill on 'The Blood Feud of the Franks', *Bulletin of the John Ryland's Library*, 41, 1959).

Even allowing for this, the brief and casual dismissal of political philosophy in the Preface and the Introduction to *African Political*

Systems has to be considered as possibly another example of the evangelizing zeal of a new subject, determined to stake its claim in the academic world. There was possibly here a real issue to be decided: for undoubtedly some of the empirical findings of the new disciplines of sociology, various forms of anthropology, psychology, and pyscho-analysis, were bound to call in question at least some of the methods and the conclusions of older established disciplines dealing with social relations and human behaviour. This shows clearly in Durkheim's *Les Règles de la Méthode Sociologique*. In addition, every new subject may have to elbow its way into the academic corridors; and this is likely to have been more difficult in the older, well-established countries and their universities than in 'new' countries whose very fluidity of life might draw attention to social problems. Hence the Malinowskian model of beginning a work with an attack on other disciplines – which led him to theoretical sterility when he attacked his own pupils (see essay below on 'Malinowski's "Functional" Analysis of Social Change'), and which we may see here in Radcliffe-Brown's, Fortes', and Evans-Pritchard's attacks on political philosophy – may be deeply rooted in the total academic situation of the time. Unhappily, as shown in Professor Hoernlé's retort, it led anthropologists to assert their own skill against other disciplines when they might have been examining with more care what other subjects had to give them, as well as pointing out what they had to give to other subjects.

My first analysis of field data was published in *African Political Systems* – an essay on the rise of the Zulu state, its structure, and its absorption by Whites. I have outlined the stage at which British social anthropology stood at the time, in order to set the situation in which I wrote this essay. I now discuss the development of my own ideas about the Zulu and other African political systems. This means that the plan of the following discussion is determined by the way in which other research influenced my ideas through the succeeding years, so that I constantly amended my analysis of Zulu politics. Hence I shall pass from considering secular matters to ritual, and back again, from drawing attention to new findings on political rituals to the organization of states, and then to evaluating criticisms of my own treatment of that political ritual. The purpose of this *Introduction* is to expound the development of ideas, not to set out how I conceive all the problems involved at the present moment. I shall do so at the end of my statement on my own ideas in the light of my colleagues' comments.

We have seen that the students of segmentary societies were in fact producing accurate knowledge of previously misunderstood forms of political relations. This did not similarly apply to those of us who were analysing states. Many great scholars had through the centuries been reflecting on the problems arising in states. But the preceding paragraphs emphasize that I was not entirely responsible for my ignorance of what had been written on political problems by those scholars, when I tackled the analysis of the Zulu political system. While I was in Zululand in 1937, I was asked by Fortes and Evans-Pritchard to contribute to their symposium. I wrote an essay on 'The Kingdom of the Zulu of South Africa' in the field. When I dealt with the indigenous political system, my main original contribution to anthropological theory was my perceiving that in the Zulu state there could occur rebellions, to replace the king, but not revolutions to destroy the kingship itself and to establish some new kind of political organization. This crucial point was driven home to me by the history of the Zulu nation. This nation was established between 1818–24 by Shaka, the head of the small Zulu tribe, through conquest of some hundreds of small tribes. In 1828 he was murdered by two of his brothers: one of them, Dingane, killed the other and ascended the throne, and no-one outside of Shaka's agnatic family attempted to seize the throne. In the ensuing uncertainty only one of the subject tribes sought independence. Twelve years later, in 1840, another brother, Mpande, led some 17,000 Zulu in flight to the Boers; and then returned with Boer help and seized the throne. Mpande lived and ruled till 1872; but in 1857 two of his sons split the nation in two and fought a civil war for the heirship to the throne. Cetshwayo won and succeeded in 1872. In 1879–80 he was defeated by the British, and during this war some sections of the Zulu under a prince did not join in the fight; but only one county under an Englishman was renegade to the British. In later reigns, though British overlordship eliminated major fighting, every king's death has produced its rival contenders. Thus no prince in Zulu history had sought power by leading his own followers entirely out of the national hegemony, without thought of return, though as far back as 1824 Mzilikazi, a subject chief, had done so to found the Ndebele nation. Clearly, the process of politics in

Zululand involved struggles between princes for the throne, and apparently not for independence. The throne remained untouched and kingship unaltered.

The Editors made the same point in their Introduction (at p. 13), but it was not made the centre of the analysis of the other four African states dealt with in the book. Schapera cites in detail quarrels, intrigues and revolts within the Ngwato chief's family, and concludes that 'all these disputes split the tribe into factions whose continuous agitations against one another obviously made the Chief's position very difficult' (pp. 79–80). Richards writes: 'Thus for ritual purposes, in spite of quarrels and jealousies between different lines of the royal family, the whole Bemba country can be said to act as a whole and to be conscious of its unity' (p. 112). She speaks (p. 100) of 'difficulties' arising because the heirs to positions are not clearly defined. Oberg in various places (pp. 129, 133, 137, 143, 147, 159) discusses rebellion as a possible danger to the Banyankole king, and stresses the value of accession wars in which all claimants to succession save one are eliminated, so as to serve 'the purpose of eradicating likely rivals' (p. 159), but he does not arrive at any systematic theory about rebellions. Finally, Nadel concludes that

a more equitable balance of power among the Kede could only be achieved by illegitimate means – that is, by feuds and factional splits within the hereditary ruling class. . . . Attachment to one of the rival factions is also the only means by which the subject classes, the commoners with no rank and office, could exercise an indirect influence upon the political management of their country (pp. 177–8).

The whole problem of the legitimacy and illegitimacy of rebellion has of course been discussed at great length by mediaeval historians, by political philosophers, and indeed by politicians.

I think therefore that it is fair to say that the theory that African states contained within themselves a process of constant rebellion, but not of revolution, even though not clearly stated in the 1940 essay, was a new contribution to anthropological theory. As an isolated idea, it had been stated as far back as Aristotle. In the fifth book of his *Politics: A Treatise on Government* he considers 'from what causes and how alterations in government arise. . . . ' (translation by William Ellis, in 1776: 1888 edition used). Later he speaks of:

The alterations which men may propose to make in governments are two; for either they may change the State already established into some other, as when they propose to erect an oligarchy, where there is a democracy, or a democracy or free State, where there is an oligarchy, or an aristocracy from these, or those from that; or else, when they have no objection to the established government, which they like very well, but choose to have the sole management in it themselves; either in the hands of a few, or one only. . . .

He does not refer to this fundamental difference again until Book X, when he speaks 'Of plots: some aim at the life of those who govern, others at their government; the first arises from hatred of their persons, which hatred may be owing to many causes' – and he gives five examples of these causes, three sexual misdemeanours by the ruler (two against women related to the 'rebels'), and two personal insults to the 'rebels'. Aristotle's treatment of these two fundamentally different kinds of revolts thus does not begin to be systematic, and he presents only the germ of the idea.

The distinction has also received bare attention from modern sociologists. Marx himself was primarily concerned with the progression of revolutions through history, culminating in the proletarian revolution which would solve the problems of the class society. By implication, he raises the question of degrees of radical change in revolution, and in discussing Asian society he talks of the unchanging village society, and of palace and other political changes of overlordship which occur without altering the fundamental structure of productive and social relations. But more usually he saw rebellions as actions which, even if unsuccessful, served to show the rebelling social groups that the limited aims for which they had striven could not be achieved without a fundamental overthrow of the whole social order. Rebellion was thus a step on the road towards total revolutionary class-consciousness and action, and was seen as part of a cumulative process. Later Marxist writers in the post-Lenin era, however, came to treat rebellions not as steps on the road towards the ultimate achievement of self-awareness on the part of oppressed social classes, but as mechanisms which served to channel off discontent and thus hinder the emergence of revolutionary consciousness. If such diversionary mechanisms were eliminated the revolutionary alternative would inevitably present itself as the only way out. Thus Trotsky, in the Preface to his *The Russian Revolution* (ed.

F. W. Dupee, 1959), stated that 'for decades the oppositional criticism is nothing more than a safety valve for mass dissatisfaction, a condition of the stability of the social structure.' Developing this notion to its logical extreme in the late 1920s, Marxist-Leninist writers attacked reformist 'Labourist' parties as integral and even necessary parts of a total capitalist social system in the last stages of crisis. They were now 'safety-valves' which in fact contributed to the ongoing of the capitalist order. In the era of the world-crisis of capitalism, reformist parties now played a complementary role, on the left wing, to the fascist movements on the right wing, in preserving 'last-stage' capitalism from final overthrow – hence the term 'social-fascist'.

Meanwhile as Soviet ethnographers have turned their attention to indigenous African states, they have followed this line in applying Engels' generalizations in *The Origin of the Family, Private Property and the State*: since a state has emerged, there must be at least proto-classes with one exploiting the other; and the economic and other social relations of rulers and subjects have not, as far as I can judge from English translations, been examined by these scholars to illuminate the nature of rebellions.

Simmel curiously did not use 'rebellions' to illustrate his analysis of *Conflict*, but Max Weber saw the situations in which rebellions occur very clearly in his analysis of 'The Types of Authority and Imperative Co-ordination':

The exercise of traditional authority is normally oriented to the question of what the chief and his administrative staff will normally permit, in view of the traditional obedience of the subjects and what will or will not arouse their resistance. When resistance occurs, it is directed against the person of the chief or a member of his staff. The accusation is that he has failed to observe the traditional limits of his authority. Opposition is not directed against the system as such. (published in German in 1925: quoted from translation by A. R. Henderson and Talcott Parsons, *The Theory of Social and Economic Organization*, 1947, p. 314).

There has been a similar general recognition by other sociologists, and by historians, of the fact that in some circumstances risings are against the incumbents of superior positions who have violated what we would now call the values of their roles, and that these risings are not directed to overthrowing the established system. Thus Robert Redfield wrote in his *Peasant Society and Culture* (1956) that in preparing his analysis he

was struck by statements that in European history in very recent times no peasant revolt had revolution for its goal, and that the prevailing relation between the peasant and his gentry had not been one of oppressor and oppressed, but rather that the peasant has thought that the rich should be generous and the powerful should not abuse their power. The occasional resentment of or hatred of a rich and powerful man seemed to [him] on the whole to represent cases where someone had failed to preserve the traditional and approved roles and statuses of gentry and peasantry (p. 35).

This statement must stand for a whole range of references I lack space to give: and it shows that here again, as with Aristotle and Marx, there has been little systematic analysis of the structure of a 'rebellious' system itself, beyond perception of the restricted objectives of revolts.

Weber's and Redfield's formulations correspond closely with Fortes' and Evans-Pritchard's (*African Political Systems*, p. 13):

It should be remembered that in these states there is only one theory of government. In the event or rebellion, the aim, and the result, is only to change the personnel of office and never to abolish it or to substitute for it some new form of government. When subordinate chiefs, who are often kinsmen of the king, rebel against him they do so in defence of the values violated by his malpractices. They have an interest greater than any other section of the people in maintaining the kingship. The ideal constitutional pattern remains the valid norm, in spite of breaches of its rules.

My own formulation ran thus (p. 42):

The people depended for leadership against an oppressive leader on their nearer political officers. The Zulu had no idea of any political organization other than hereditary chieftainship and their stage of social development did not conduce to the establishment of new types of régime. Their only reaction to bad rule was to depose the tyrant and to put someone else in his place with similar powers, though individuals could escape from Zululand to other nations' protection; that is, the people could take advantage of the princes' and chiefs' intrigues for power, and the latter in intriguing sought to win the backing of the people. The king's policy was therefore to prosecute any one who threatened to be able to take his place; he had to meet rivals, not revolutionaries. . . ;

I have not cited Aristotle, the Leninist writers, and Max Weber in order to confess that, when we anthropologists formulate ideas as original that have in fact been advanced by earlier writers, we are lacking in scholarship. My examples indicate that political scientists and sociologists and social anthropologists have been dealing with the same problems; and it is reassuring to find that similar theories are independently advanced to solve these problems. An anthropologist's scholarship has to be assessed in his own discipline, and he can only draw on other subjects to tackle its problems (see symposium on *Closed Systems and Open Minds: The Limits of Naïvety in Social Anthropology*, ed. by M. Gluckman, 1963). Indeed, though immediately it seems that these other disciplines can be helpful to us, we should be alert lest their formulations lead us away from developing our own analyses. Too much scholarship can be sterilizing: a great scholar once told me that it was very difficult for him to write, because whenever he set anything down, he knew all the times it had been said before, and all the arguments that had been brought against it.

In this light I incline to think that we might have been obstructed from developing the implications of this conception of a rebellious cycle in certain types of political systems had we relied too much on its treatment by these other earlier writers. I myself, in fact, was in the field when I wrote my first ideas on the Zulu 'cycle of rebellions', and hence could not have looked up Aristotle, Weber *et al.*, and acknowledged that they had anticipated this idea. I am sure that Fortes and Evans-Pritchard knew of this earlier work, though they made no reference to these writers in their Introduction. But it is very possible that had they and I spent our time in pursuing these references, and adopting others' formulations, we might not have proceeded to analyse our own facts and to extract from these further implications. Indeed, Weber's formulations particularly, as shown in other work, might have prevented us from making new contributions to the analysis of the central idea, out of the rich variety of African custom and political struggle. Three of the essays in this collection cover some of these contributions: and I set out their development.

In my first report on the Zulu (written in 1938 for *African Political Systems* and not reprinted here in full) I saw that the king feared rivals, from within the royal family, and not revolutionaries, and that the people exploited the dynastic struggles in the royal family to control their rulers. In about 1946, I was shown a manuscript analysing the problem of who should be the successor to the Bemba paramountcy, made by a Government officer, Mr V. W. Brelsford. He put forward a certain set of rules of succession; and I noticed that his statement of these rules did not accord with his evidence on past successions. I checked his rules against those reported by Audrey Richards in her essay on the Bemba in *African Political Systems*, and found not only that she gave rules different from those given by Brelsford, but also that her statement of these rules conflicted with her own evidence. The difference between the rules as stated by these authorities could be explained because each had worked mainly in the area of the opposed branches of the royal family, which were laying claim to the paramountcy. But in addition, I thought that these differences between Richards and Brelsford, and the internal contradictions in the account of each of them, were unlikely to be incorrect reporting, since both were skilled observers. Hence I proceeded to try to analyse the story of Bemba succession on the assumption that the rules of succession, which were obviously based on independent principles, might also be in fundamental conflict one with the other. Proceeding on this assumption, and applying the theory of the cycle of rebellions and civil war, I considered that I made better sense of the facts of Bemba royal history than either of the learned authorities on the Bemba. Indeed, I was in fact able to write to Brelsford and put three suggestions to him, about events which were not covered by either account. In every case I was correct: and Brelsford replied that I had guessed luckily, where I had in fact predicted theoretically. My analysis was written up in a document which I could not publish until after Brelsford's account was out: Professor J. C. Mitchell, then Director of the Rhodes-Livingstone Institute, subsequently published it (II – 'Bemba Succession and Civil War'). I conclude that major civil wars will be fought in the Bemba system every third to fifth generation, with only minor 'civil wars' in the first and second generations.

This analysis of the Bemba persuaded me that I ought to look more carefully into the rules of succession to other chieftainships in Africa, to see whether similar discrepancies and conflicts existed there. Indeed I had missed the significance of this point among the Zulu; for though in principle the rule is clear in Zulu law – the heir is the eldest son of the great wife – in practice it was often impossible to know in advance who was the great wife; and the rules fixing her status were discrepant and conflicting. I found that other tribal rules were similar: there was a range from rules like those of Ankole which after the death of a king called for an accession war until all contenders for the throne except one were eliminated, and the constant threat of attack by another prince on the Shilluk king, to election of a prince among the Barotse, to the Bemba and Zulu type of situation in which pretenders could constantly assert, with claims valid in law, that they were truly entitled to the throne. Or a somewhat different situation was presented by the Nupe type of polity, in which the Emirate circulated through three dynasties of the royal family. It thus seemed that the very rules of succession, and of claim, to the chieftainship, out of their discrepancy and conflict raised a number of rightful pretenders, and thus forced civil war and rebellion on the tribes. I note here that Aristotle did not make this point about the Greek states, where he cites only individual spurs to attack on the incumbent of rule (e.g. insults, sexual misdemeanours). Nor was it contained in Weber's very brief treatment.

This 'conflict' in the rules of succession also drew my attention to other complexities in the system of political institutions – as among the Bemba to the role of the chiefs' sons, excluded from succession by the rules of matriliny, but acquiring power under another set of rules, and able to influence the succession. I looked again at the Zulu data: and saw more clearly there how the county chiefs were powerful in a different set of relations from those within which princes acquired power. I analyse the conclusions I draw from this in *Rituals of Rebellion* below, and in my *Custom and Conflict in Africa* (Chapter II).

My conviction that we were here dealing with a process inherent in the structure of this type of state – a process of civil war accentuated and increased in its incidence by the accepted rules of chieftainship itself, and by different systems of authority – was strengthened by work done by colleagues on the ritual of chieftainship. Ritual of course is a field of study in which anthropology has always been interested; and here our research has brought out many implications not seen by other types of social scientist. In 1940 Evans-Pritchard had published an analysis of the political system of the Eastern Anuak of the Anglo-Egyptian Sudan. He discusses developments in the nature of this system: here I have space to mention only one phase. These Anuak lived in widely scattered villages which were organized into a system by a common interest in certain royal emblems. Whoever held these emblems was 'king'. But only members of a noble 'class' who were, beyond that, sons of men who had held these emblems, could try to seize the emblems and become king. A contender sought for support in the village of his maternal uncle to help him get the emblems and become king. There was constant fighting between the villages to get the emblems for 'their prince'. The king had neither ritual nor secular powers. That is, the Eastern Anuak villages were 'linked' together politically at that stage of their history only by their battles with one another for the royal emblems and the kingship these signified.[2] The overall polity consisted only in a constant civil war for possession of a circulating kingship, signified by the emblems, and without power. I am not here weighing up this analysis – or Evans-Pritchard's later paper on the Anuak; I cite it only for its influence on my thought.

In 1948 Evans-Pritchard followed this analysis with his Frazer Lecture on the divine kingship of the Shilluk of the Nilotic Sudan. I again lack space to do justice to the subtlety of this analysis, but I quote the conclusion:

I would suggest that it [the divine kingship] is an institution typical of, though doubtless not confined to, societies with pronounced lineage systems in which the political segments are parts of a loosely organized structure without governmental functions. In societies of this kind the political organization takes a ritual or symbolic form which in polities with a higher degree of organization gives way, though never entirely, to centralized administration.

I would further suggest that the acceptance of regicide in one form or another as customary can be explained in the same structural terms. The moral density[3] is great enough for the segments to be represented by a common symbol in the kingship but not great enough to eliminate the powerful tendencies towards fission in the structure they compose. These tendencies are expressed in relation to the symbol, and either the kingship itself, or the king himself, circulates through the competitive segments, as among the Anuak and in past times also in Shillukland, or the segments struggle for royal representation in the capital. In either case their particularistic sentiments operate through dynastic rivalries. The Shilluk kingship, that is Nyikang [mythical founder of that kingship], is changeless and acknowledged as a supreme value by all Shilluk. In that permanence and in that acknowledgement the unity of the nation is manifested. In the rebellions against the kings and in the regicides the segmentary structure with its opposed local loyalties is equally present to the view of the observer. The kingship tends in such societies to become identified, by the attachment of the king's person to one locality, with sectional interests and when this happens other sections assert their rights, and by their action the common interest of all the Shilluk, in the kingship at the expense of the king's person. The kingship embodies a contradiction between dogma and social facts, in a sense between office and person, which is produced by a combination of centripetal and centrifugal tendencies in the national structure and this contradiction is solved by customary regicide.

In Shillukland the people believe that their prosperity and fertility, etc., depend on the kingship, in the spirit of Nyikang, its founder. Hence it is said that Shilluk believed that the ruling king should be in a state of physical perfection and ritual purity: if he became sick or senile 'he should be killed to avoid some grave national misfortune. . . . The king must be killed to save the kingship and with it the whole Shilluk people.' There was also a rule that any prince could at any time challenge the king to mortal combat. Evans-Pritchard does not believe that any Shilluk king was killed ritually, but 'the unpopularity which national misfortune brings on a king enables a prince to raise rebellion.' Looked at in this way, beliefs in divine kingship seemed to aggravate the effect of the rules of succession, which (as among Anuak and Shilluk) produced rival rightful claimants to the throne, and through them constant civil war.

When I was invited by the University of Glasgow to deliver the Frazer Lecture in 1952, Professor Schapera encouraged me to take up again my theory that there were rebellions, and not revolutions, in Zululand. By this time I was thinking in terms of discrepant and conflicting rules of succession, and I looked at beliefs that failing kings were responsible for 'natural' misfortunes as mechanisms which 'forced' civil war constantly on to tribes. It seemed to me that one would have to do more than accept civil war as an inherent part of tribal polity: at the risk of being accused of teleological analysis, one had to think of civil wars as ocurring constantly in the polity, and involving contenders in a fight to seize the kingship, rather than in a struggle for independence from it. In these tribes, with their widely dispersed segments

17

pursuing subsistence husbandry, the sections, each with its own army, fought around the kingship, rather than to get away from the king – though of course I knew too much African history to believe that this was the only process at work, and that no sections would ever break out of the polity. But the process of civil war to maintain the kingship (seen most clearly among Anuak because of the very secular weakness of that kingship), as a central process in the political system, might be present even where the king or chief had substantial secular power. This argument seemed to me to fit in with an emerging new treatment of ceremonial and ritual by anthropologists, who were beginning to see ritual not simply as expressing cohesion and impressing the value of society and its social sentiments on people, as in Durkheim's and Radcliffe-Brown's theories, but as exaggerating real conflicts of social rules and affirming that there was unity despite these conflicts. Bateson's *Naven* (1936), with his theory of schismogenesis, was a big step in this development; but my own insight into these processes was inspired by Fortes' work on ritual. He had advanced and illuminated this thesis in two early articles: 'Communal Fishing Magic in the Northern Territories of the Gold Coast' (*Journal of the Royal Anthropological Institute*, lxvii, 1937) and 'Ritual Festivals and Social Cohesion in the Hinterland of the Gold Coast' (*American Anthropologist*, xxxviii, 1936). It was further advanced in his full study of *The Dynamics of Clanship among the Tallensi* (1945), where he connected the great festivals with the organization of Tallensi hostile lineages and residential units and political relations in congregations maintaining overlapping circles of ritual peace.

I myself observed this ritual process when I made a cursory study of 'The Role of the Sexes in Wiko Circumcision Ceremonies' in Northern Rhodesia (published in *Social Structure: Essays Presented to A. R. Radcliffe-Brown*, ed. M. Fortes, 1949); but for my present purposes the important work was Hilda Kuper's brilliant description of Swazi first-fruits ceremonies in *An African Aristocracy* (1947). In her account of these ceremonies, she stressed that the theme of the sacred songs chanted is 'hatred of the king and his rejection by the people'. This hatred and rejection are shown also in some of the rites, though there are also many rites and songs to affirm his unique power and his identification with his people. In short, what Kuper called 'a drama of kingship' directly exhibited the whole process of the cycle of rebellion and re-strengthening of the kingship which was so apparent in secular political life. Hence in *Rituals of Rebellion* I tried to connect together the following series of facts: the Swazi and Zulu had a stationary subsistence economy, without good communications or highly productive tools, widespread trade, or luxuries to enable the ruling group to establish themselves as a 'class' distinct from commoners; the economy necessitated widespread dispersal of the population, and the division of the nation into counties; all men owned their own weapons, so every county had an army;[4] these counties developed strong loyalties to their leaders and hence local autonomy; leaders had to support followers for their own power and they and their own kin intermarried with these followers; there ensued a tendency towards hostility against the central government and hence towards independence; but Zulu and Swazi history showed that these provincial loyalties very, very rarely led to movements for independence, and in practice the different sections of the nation (as among Anuak and Shilluk) supported different princes in their struggles to gain the throne, and thus were involved in fighting for the kingship, and not against it, even though they might be against a particular king; and this struggle was one of the important themes of the great national festivals.

Here the new slant on Swazi ceremonial given by Kuper illuminated the records on Zululand: I had hoped to republish in this book – but lacked space – an early essay of mine,[5] considering these records and written before I went to Zululand, to show the radical difference between Kuper's observations among Swazi and the descriptions by early observers of the Zulu festivals, or the accounts Bryant and others were given by Zulu after the ceremonies ceased to be performed. In these records, those who hated and rejected the king were thought to be external enemies: Kuper saw that for the Swazi they were internal enemies, and this revolutionized any analysis of the ceremonies. It is necessary here to enter one caveat: I think that we can reasonably assume that the obsolete Zulu ceremonies were organized in the same way as those of their Swazi neighbours; but of course Kuper's observations were made under British rule, when the Swazi were no longer militarily fighting external foes. Hence there is a possibility that the ceremonial was turned against internal enemies, off from external armed enemies: I do not think this happened, since, as I show, there are many other ceremonies organized thus (Shilluk,

Tallensi, etc.). I have developed this interpretation of ritual further in my *Custom and Conflict in Africa* (Chapter V), making use of the essays in *African Worlds: Studies of the Cosmological Ideas and Social Values of African Peoples* (1954) and of the Introduction by the Editor, Daryll Forde. The whole thesis has been pushed much further by V. W. Turner in his *Schism and Continuity in an African Society* (1957).

This analysis has been criticized on various grounds. In his *Government and Politics in Tribal Societies* (1956, p. 175), in which he makes a survey of South African tribes, Schapera concludes that the evidence, even for Zulu and Swazi, does not support my 'main thesis' that: 'I [Gluckman] am tempted to go further and suggest that a periodic civil war was *necessary* to preserve that national unity: sections fought for the kingship and not for independence from it.' I made this statement in a broadcast lecture in the series on *The Institutions of Primitive Society* (edited by Evans-Pritchard, 1954). Schapera agrees that among Zulu and Swazi and other Bantu 'rebels or conspirators usually aim at usurping the chieftainship, and not at breaking away to found tribes of their own. But,' he proceeds, 'as shown by our examples [cited in his book], the outcome of their attempts almost always was the flight or secession of one section, and there are even instances of men who seceded without making a bid for the chieftainship.' I do not agree with Schapera that a careful examination of his examples leads immediately and obviously to his conclusion rather than to mine; but I accept his criticism of my one formulation at least as valid. Looking back on the broadcast in which I said I was tempted 'to suggest that a periodic civil war was *necessary* to preserve . . . national unity', I feel I was carried away by the wish to startle any listening historians into taking notice of our anthropological analyses (note the phrase 'I am tempted' above); but I fear that the statement does reveal that I was still thinking in crude functional terms of institutions – even civil war, which after all can be an institution – contributing to the maintenance of a rather rigidly conceived social structure (Cf. Oberg's somewhat similar statements about the 'function' of poisoning an ageing king and of the accession war in the Banyankole kingdom, *African Political Systems*, pp. 137 and 159). I would withdraw this phrasing.

But I still stand by my other statement cited by Schapera with the above, that among Zulu and Swazi 'territorial segments developed, on the basis of local loyalties and cohesion, strong tendencies to break out of the national system and set up as independent. But in practice the leaders of these territorial segments often tended to struggle for the kingship, or for power around it, rather than for independence. Periodic civil war thus strengthened the system by canalizing tendencies to segment, and by stating that the main goal of leaders was the sacred kingship itself' (in *Rituals of Rebellion*, p. 35). In short, besides the cyclical process of civil war for the kingship, there is also present always a tendency to segmentation and fission; and if I have over-emphasized the former, Schapera has over-emphasized the latter. Thus (at his p. 186) he says that after Shaka's death several of the tribes Shaka had conquered escaped from his rule to the south: in fact only the Qwabe did so, and this was under a threat from Shaka's successor Dingane. Looked at in detail, I consider that Schapera's summaries of Zulu and Swazi history confirm my statement of what has happened in that history.

Schapera's analysis suggests two important points for a study of these kingdoms. First, a prince who feels that he is threatened by the king as a suspect rival may flee with his following, as Mpande did. Mpande returned to conquer the kingdom with Boer help: without that help from the Boers, he might have been too weak to drive out Dingane, and hence there might have been a split in the nation. That is, we have to bring in the military power of rivals in assessing the process. Second, after a civil war the defeated party might in fact flee and set up independently, or seek refuge with a neighbouring power. These are the events Schapera stresses most for the Nguni kingdoms, and I do not see how they counter my analysis of the system itself.

But I consider that Schapera's criticism, and his main analysis, like my own, do not take sufficient account of the fact that we are dealing with different types of political systems. For example, I have never considered that the rebellion-cycle process was dominant among the Xhosa, who split nearly every generation, as he describes here. The Xhosa, expanding south-westwards, had the struggle for the established chieftainship, but the process of segmenting was obviously dominant: i.e. there are systems where the probable outcome of civil war is secession of the defeated party. Indeed, the 'Zulu' – Northern Nguni – political system was of this type before Shaka welded them into a nation (see my *Analysis of a Social Situation in Modern Zululand*, p. 28 f.). Again, similar systems occur among Nyakyusa and other peoples with small chieftainships. Schapera's main examples are taken from the Sotho and Tswana tribes, and though many of these tribes split frequently, a few seem to have had the cycle of rebellions without splitting. As far as the Tswana are concerned, we have to remember that they dwelt mainly concentrated in large towns, cultivating in a circle environing their habitations and grazing their cattle beyond that circle, within an arid environment. If they were increasing in population, it seems likely that ecological necessities would compel them to spread out more widely, and to divide. It is perhaps significant that Tswana rules of succession do not produce that same doubt over who is the main heir, the occurrence of which in other tribes I have emphasized.

We have also to look more carefully at what happened when parties defeated in a civil war fled elsewhere. It is important here that among both Zulu and Barotse, whose history I know well, the commoner who followed his prince or chief in rebellion was not guilty of treason; and though he might be slain in the heat of battle and pursuit, according to law he ought to have been pardoned if he returned and made submission again. This means that men in those states had mediated allegiance to the paramount chief, through subordinate leaders, and not only direct allegiance (see Fortes, 'The Structure of Unilineal Groups', *American Anthropologist*, lv, 1953, p. 26, and my essay on 'The Technical Vocabulary of Barotse Jurisprudence', *American Anthropologist*, 61, 1959, p. 743 f.). It is important to note that the law of treason was similar in mediaeval England (Jolliffe, *The Constitutional History of Mediaeval England*, 1948, pp. 155–65), but ceased to be so later. There must surely be other systematic changes to produce a law under which all who revolt, and not only leaders, are guilty of treason.

Since some form of my statement about Zulu-type states brings together the aims of rebellion, the fact that members of the royal family lead revolts, the conflicts in the law of succession, the form of the law of treason, beliefs in divine kinship, the form of great national rituals, I think it needs very careful scrutinizing before it is abandoned. It carries also the weighty support of Evans-Pritchard's superb analysis of the Shilluk. I would prefer now a formulation, made a year later, which more closely follows Evans-Pritchard's (cited above, pp. 16–17):

The result of the several rules of succession in a tribe was that almost every succession could raise rival claimants, and after the king's death, when national strength was at its weakest, [cf. Oberg on the Banyankole in *African Political Systems*] unifying war for the kingship between the claimants and their supporters might follow. Strikingly, this conflict of rules, or alternative interpretation of rules, leading to war which in time reunites the nation, did not occur among the Bechuana (Tswana) tribes who dwell concentrated in large towns. Otherwise the very structure of kingship and its rules thrust struggles between rival houses, and even civil war, on the nation; and it is a historical fact that these struggles kept component sections of the nation united in conflicting allegiance about the sacred kingship. A clearly marked true heir would not allow competing sections to put forward equally legitimate claims for the throne. Early Germanic law had the same conflict of rules of succession: perhaps a clear legitimist principle with one heir accompanies only a high degree of local concentration, or a high degree of economic interdependence between the sections of the nation. . . . I don't say that the forces are always perfectly balanced, so that no change occurs or no state breaks up. We have plenty of evidence of change and the break-up of states in Africa. But these processes work through elaborate institutional arrangements, which have clearly evolved through long periods of time; and I am suggesting only that they inhibit quarrels from destroying the system: they cannot always prevent that destruction (*Custom and Conflict in Africa*, pp. 46–7 – *note:* published before Schapera's criticism).

In short, I would no longer speak as if civil war had a function in maintaining the system: I see the process of 'unifying civil war' as one of number of discrepant and perhaps conflicting processes at work in an area of political action. But, as noted above, the 'solution' of the working out of these processes, depends on actual, *ad hoc*, distributions of power, in terms of land and followers, and hence on variable increases and decreases of population in different sections of the nation due to demographic chance. I will discuss this view further below (see pp. 35–9), and I hope to assess these formulations anew in a full-scale study of Zulu history.

I have discussed these analyses with Professor Schapera, and he has asked me to stress the strength of tribesmen's loyalties to the chieftainship and to the 'true heir' which he has found throughout his study of South African Bantu history. He drew my attention to one remarkable instance of these strong loyalties in the 1850s. Khari, the Ngwato chief, was killed in a battle with the Shona. His first wife had no children, so he was succeeded by Kgama I, the son of his second wife. Kgama died leaving no children. Sekgoma, son of Kgari's third wife, became chief, and quarrelled with Kgama's mother, who meanwhile had borne another son, Matsheng, under the levirate to her dead husband. She fled to another tribe with this posthumous, leviratic son, and there he was captured in a Ndebele raid. He was then about ten, and he was raised as a Ndebele warrior until he was twenty-six years old. The missionary, Robert Moffat, secured his release as a favour from the Ndebele king, and he was acclaimed by notables of the Ngwato, including the reigning chief, Sekgoma, who had at least to pretend to welcome back his father's 'true heir'. Matsheng was installed chief in Sekgoma's place, with the support of Sechele, a neighbouring chief. Matsheng ruled as a Ndebele, with 'ruthless discipline', and a powerful tribesman intrigued against him with this other chief, Sechele, with whom Sekgoma found refuge. Sekgoma was again installed as chief, while Matsheng in his turn found refuge with Sechele. Matsheng was again installed in a further revolt, with Sekgoma's help, before being finally driven out by Sekgoma's own sons. What is striking in these events is the welcome given to Matsheng, though he was not a biological son of the dead chief Kgari and though he had become a Ndebele alien and barely resided in the tribe (see *The Matabele Journals of Robert Moffat, 1829–60*, edited by J. P. R. Wallis, 1945, ii, p. 140 f.; Sillery, A. *The Bechuanaland Protectorate*, 1952, p. 118 f.; I. Schapera, *A Handbook of Tswana Law and Custom*, 1938, p. 303).

Schapera has been the pricipal person to consider the secular implications of my arguments. Anthropologists have paid greater attention to my treatment of the associated ritual. In her Frazer Lecture on *Divine Kings and 'the Breath of Men'* (1959), Monica Wilson describes an annual 'cleansing of the country' by Nyakyusa and Ngonde, in which men carrying out the ashes from hearths lunged at one another with spears. She quotes one of the priests: 'They said: "Let us dance, let us fight, that the homesteads may be peaceful." "Let us throw out the ashes that death may leave the homesteads and they be at peace." It is to bring out war from within.' Wilson herself comments on this:

Only if the symbolism of rituals of kinship [cited above and discussed in her book on *Rituals of Kinship among the Nyakyusa*, 1956] is ignored could this be interpreted as an expression of rebellion, rather than a confession, and, indeed, I suggest that much of what has been cited as evidence of rebellion in rituals elsewhere in Africa is in fact the formal admission of anger, the prelude to reconciliation. The body politic is purged by the very act of 'speaking out'. (See footnotes to my own Frazer Lecture on rituals of rebellions below.)

It is of course difficult to discuss this point, made in a short aside to comment on a long and careful analysis, since Wilson does not state clearly enough what it is in my analysis to which she is objecting. On the surface, it seems that she is asserting that 'confession' explains better than does 'rebellion', the Nyakyusa rites she cites, and that she thinks this also applies to the whole month-long Swazi and Zulu national ceremonies. If this is what she is saying, then she is arguing that my attempt to connect the Swazi and Zulu rituals with the whole political process is misleading and wrong, and that the whole of the ceremonies can be explained by a process of 'confession' and thus 'purging' of anger, and thus of 'catharsis' (a word I myself used). To argue thus would in my opinion be to commit a serious logical fallacy: so restricted a process as 'confession' cannot explain large-scale national and district ceremonies, for a complex whole cannot be explained by one of its parts. Wilson takes no account of the relations between this type of ceremonial on the one hand, and on the other hand the nature of the economy, the territorial dispersion of population, poor communications, simple weapons of war, the organization of subordinate political units, the law of succession and the law of treason, etc., etc.; while my analysis does attempt to relate national rituals to these features of national political organization.[6] My interpretation may be incorrect: but any valid interpretation must take into account the same phenomena as I have tried to embrace. I do not accept Wilson's implied point in favour of her statement that, because she finds 'confession' in both kinship and communal rituals but no rebellion in kinship rituals, therefore her hypothesis explaining all rituals as 'confession' is inductively more embracing and hence stronger. On the contrary, 'confession' as I have said is embodied in much more comprehensive rituals and therefore cannot account for the wholes of which it is a part. It is more important to examine why African rituals of state can exhibit and tolerate the open statement of conflict (whether as rebellion, licence or protest, as I phrase it, or whether as 'confession' as she does), while African domestic rituals and our own ceremonials of state do so to a much smaller degree. I put forward reasons to explain this difference both in *Rituals of Rebellion* and in *Custom and Conflict in Africa* (Chapter V). Wilson does not explain why 'confession' of this type does not occur in our own state ceremonies, a fact to which Kuper draws attention, or in Barotse state rituals, which I emphasize and relate to the secular exhibition of political conflict in the Barotse political organization.

I have said that I *phrase* the statement of conflict in these rituals as 'rebellion' (and as 'licence' and 'protest' in my *Custom and Conflict in Africa,* Chapter V); and I ask that readers look carefully at my wording. I used this phrasing to emphasize what I see as a connection between the main form of the rituals and the tendencies to rebellion which I see as inherent in the political system as a whole. I was not in doing this insisting that every rite was only and entirely 'rebellion', and that all other processes were excluded. Kuper's description of the Swazi ceremonies emphasizes beyond question this 'rebellious' element. I did not see any of the ceremonies I analysed in *Rituals of Rebellion*, but the people with whom I discussed the Wiko ceremonies of circumcision, which I did observe, emphasized the 'fighting' between men and women involved in them. Fortes on the Tallensi Great Festivals, and Evans-Pritchard on the Shilluk coronation ceremonies, make clear that these exhibit political conflicts. These analyses would clearly allow specific elements of the ceremonies to be 'confessions', culturally defined. In addition, I am certainly inclined to agree that if a psychologist examined the feelings of participants in the Swazi rituals he would find some catharsis through a general 'confession' of anger. Indeed, I included confession as an element in *Rituals of Rebellion* (see penultimate footnote).

My own opinion is that here Wilson has raised against me an argument based on my use of the word 'rebellion' without considering carefully how I applied it to the data. Where I intended to refer to the whole relation between ritual and the structure of political system, she has thought I referred to the process by which culturally defined ritual action affects individuals' psyches and relations between individuals. Professor Wilson focuses on the content of ritual acts, I concentrate on the 'function' of these acts in the political field; and once we clarify this point, I do not think we are at odds.

I consider that this clarification also disposes of two contradictory interpretations of my analysis: namely, that a weakness of my argument is 'the failure to understand conflict in psychodynamic terms', and that this arises from the general opposition of British anthropologists to psychological interpretation; and, on the other hand, that my analysis is psychological with 'mere avoidance of such terms as Oedipus complex'.[7] I hope I have now made it clear that I do not attempt to deal with psychological problems. I state in the essay reprinted here, as on all occasions, that I cannot carry out analyses in 'psycho-dynamic' terms because we have no evidence appropriate for this treatment and because I am not competent as a psycho-analyst. I believe indeed that this competence is difficult to acquire and cannot be picked up by the way: hence I do not 'guess' at psychological mechanisms, though I could make 'guesses' as well as any other anthropologist who lacks adequate training in depth psychology. I would regard research on and interpretation of these rituals and their political relations by a psychoanalyst as complementary, and not hostile, to my own work: and I am pleased when G. D. Gibson says of my analysis of *Rituals of Rebellion* that the 'revealing sociological treatment of some aspects of the old problem of the divine kingship opens the door for the study of correlative questions concerning the occurrence, mechanism, and effect of catharsis by ritual rebellion. These and the problem of the role reversal in the Zulu women's rite may, however, require a more searching psychological analysis' (*American Anthropologist*, lvii, 1955, p. 1074). I maintain strongly, however, that though a psychological analysis would help greatly the sociological analysis, a large-scale political ritual can never be reduced to explanation only by psychological processes (see V. W. Turner, 'Symbols in Ndembu Rituals' in *Closed Systems and Open Minds: The Limits of Naïvety in Social Anthropology*, ed. M. Gluckman, 1963).

In short, I hope I have now made clear that I was not dealing with psychical conflict, but with social conflict: conflict arising from discrepancy and conflict of laws, conflict of interests and social processes, conflict of state unity and territorial dispersion, etc. This is why I did not use the term Oedipus complex. I note here that my study of modern Zululand, which, despite its many unresolved and irresoluble conflicts, 'worked', forced my attention to the problem of how social systems could contain the deep conflicts which are present in all of them.

Since this introduction was written, I have read two analyses which help to explain why some readers have taken my treatment of 'rituals of rebellion' to be psychological. In an article on ceremonies among the Kuma of New Guinea, Dr Marie Reay ('Two Kinds of Ritual Conflict', *Oceania*, xxix, 1959, at p. 294) writes: 'Gluckman, discussing rituals of rebellion, says that "to act[8] the conflicts, whether directly or by inversion or in other symbolical form, emphasizes the social cohesion within which the conflicts exist." I [i.e. Dr Reay] am concerned with the direct dramatization of conflict, both in the spear dance, in which men act in a stylized way as if they were going to war, and in the ritually prescribed games. We might say that the nettle game has the important function of re-integrating the clan after the ritually prescribed conflict of the *tagba boz* game wrenched it into opposing solidary groups. But how does *acting out*[9] the tensions between subclans in the *tagba boz* contest emphasize the social cohesion within which these tensions exist?' By reading the word *out* into my text, behind *act*, Reay changes my sociological analysis into a psychological statement, and thus is able to say (at p. 290) that she does not 'dismiss the idea of such rituals of rebellion having a cathartic value for individual actors, though [she] considers this to be irrelevant to their structural significance or social function', as if I had made the former type of analysis. Since I found this same inclusion of *out* behind *act* in an unpublished work by Dr C. Jayawardena (who has allowed me to refer to it), I suggest that this slight alteration of my text may be common, if not always stated, and may lead to a misleading interpretation. Of course, this slip does not in any way invalidate either of these authors' own analyses, with which I am substantially in agreement: but I give notice that I shall in future use 'perform' instead of the simpler 'act'.

I have left over, for brief mention, the work of students of mediaeval historians upon this kind of problem. I cannot for lack of space deal with their analyses in detail. They have seen that peasant revolts, and risings of the city mobs,[10] did not aim at major revolutions, but were directed against persons and malpractices, or particular shortages and sufferings. What I have not yet found, in an admittedly limited reading of secondary sources, is a systematic treatment of the whole problem. Studies like Kern's classic on *Kingship and Law in the Middle Ages* (translation by S. B. Chrimes, 1948) deal primarily with the fact that the king is supposed to accept the restraints of Law and with the subjects' right to rebel, rather than with the manner in which rebellions, as one of many political processes, are related to such facts as type of economic system, territorial dispersion, type of subordinate units in states, the existence of several claimants to the throne, the law of treason. With all respect, even Marc Bloch in his *La Société Féodale* does not sufficiently relate these factors to the institutions of vassalage and the problem of how kingship survived over divided loyalties and through rebellions, because he is inclined to explain anomalies by saying that the feudal mind did not object to holding discrepant ideas at the same time. In his brilliant vision of the development of feudalism out of its past and into the future structure of Europe, I consider he overlooks the seeming stability within constant strife caused by something like a series of civil wars which defended the main institutions, and did not aim to subvert them. In short, I believe that an application of the thesis that civil wars may be regularities involved in the very structure of mediaeval kingdoms, might illuminate their history. I am encouraged in this view since an historian of the 17th century told me he found it fruitful in approaching that period.

This general thesis, without which I do not feel I can begin to understand Zulu or Swazi or Barotse history, has not been taken up, except where it touches on rituals, by most of my own colleagues in their monographs on African states. There is no treatment of rebellion, other than as producing factions which are hostile to national unity, in several studies written after the publication of *African Political Systems*, but before the publication of my *Rituals of Rebellion*. Kuper (*An African Aristocracy*, 1947, p. 88) stresses that Swazi rivals for succession do not aim to alter the system. The late Professor S. F. Nadel in his full account of the Nupe state, *A Black Byzantium* (1942), concluded that: 'Loyalty to a personal king is factional; solidarity and loyalty on a national scale rallies round the throne and round the abstract principle of kingship rather than round the actual king' (p. 144). He pushed the argument no further though he saw that the system of succession, rotating the Emirate through three royal houses, 'allowed for balance of power and could satisfy rival claims' (p. 88). But his general conclusion was that the state maintained itself as a unit 'despite revolts' (p. 135) – which is treating the revolts not as inherent in the polity, but as breaches of regular life. The Nupe state was advanced economically beyond the stage of the Zulu and Swazi kingdoms. Dr V. W. Turner has suggested to me that it be classed as a 'tribute-organizing state' in contrast with Bantu kingdoms. Nevertheless I feel that Nadel's treatment (pp. 121–2) of the relation between territorial dispersion and national unity is weak, just because of his 'failure' to see 'revolt' as an integral process in the state, as it is not, for example, in modern Britain.

A few studies have been written on African states by anthropologists who qualified since the war. Watson stresses the rebellious process among the Mambwe (*Tribal Cohesion in a Money Economy*, 1958, p. 166), but my other pupil and close colleague, J. A. Barnes, does not use this idea in his analysis of the migratory Ngoni state, which was continually expanding its population. He is concerned with the process of segmentation and breaking out of sections (*Politics in a Changing Society*, 1954, pp. 61 f. and 'Seven Types of Segmentation', *Rhodes-Livingstone Journal*, 17, 1955, p. 18). The Ngoni do indeed seem to have been a polity in which new segments were formed at the one king's death before conquest by the Whites (see above, p. 21). Another, Ian Cunnison, is concerned more with the role of historical lore and custom, and their effect on relations of royal and other lineages, than with the politics of power (*The Luapula Peoples of Northern Rhodesia*, 1959). Fallers (*Bantu Bureaucracy*, c. 1956) considers the use of commoner and royal subordinates in the administrative system, uncertainty of succession, simple technology including weapons and economy, egalitarian consumption; and he concludes that though the state was unstable in its personnel, 'this very instability was, from the point of view of the system in the abstract, a kind of stabilizing influence'. Revolts checked tyranny, but did not alter the system (pp. 126–43). He does not discuss revolts in detail, or what they implied. Southall's *Alur Society* (c. 1956) deals with types and processes of 'domination' in 'segmentary states', but the role of accession wars in the relations of segments is not handled.

These books were all written, if not published, before I put my thesis most strongly in *Rituals of Rebellion* (published 1954). Southall and Fallers deal with problems of administration rather than with problems of the organization of the state, but in addition I believe the attention of these writers (and, to a lesser extent, Barnes) was distracted from examining the nature of civil war in the polities they were discussing by the dominance of 'lineage theory' in the British anthropology of the 1950s. During these years most young Africanists were attracted by the striking analyses by Evans-Pritchard and Fortes of the lineage systems of Nuer and Tallensi respectively, though the latter dealt with far more than lineage relations – i.e. they were full studies of political action. Nevertheless even when these younger anthropologists were dealing with 'states', they became concerned to examine how lineages could exist, or could not exist, in an authoritative system of state-power. They were undoubtedly dealing with real problems; but I suggest that this preoccupation prevented them from examining more fully how struggles for secular power between members of royal lineages were related to territorial dispersion of people, and the other elements of these African states I have constantly recapitulated above. Only thus can I explain how Southall and Fallers have emphasized from my essay on the Zulu political system in *African Political Systems* the relation of lineages to state, which I consider relatively unimportant, while neglecting what I consider important in that state, the succession of rebellions to seize the kingship. I suggest here that it is important, if one is to proceed further in analysing states, to drop this preoccupation with lineage theory which can blind one to the problems of state power. I remember two draft theses at Oxford which described powerful kingdoms as if they were combinations of lineages: I had to remind the writers that they were dealing with chiefs who could order the death sentence and that this had important effects on social life. And Dr P. Kaberry in a review of Barnes', Southall's and Fallers' books considers that a basic weakness is that none of them deals with 'the tasks of government' ('Primitive States' in *British Journal of Sociology*, viii, 1957, p. 233).

I have suggested that the preoccupation with lineages arises from the leading position of Evans-Pritchard and Fortes in African anthropology after the war; and it is shown in the extent to which their works have been re-analysed by younger anthropologists.[11] I fully and gratefully acknowledge the great creative value of their studies and teaching, but I consider it unfortunate that their work on lineages has thus distracted attention from the problems of state organizations. I think, too, that this dominance has led some of our colleagues to overlook analyses of states by South African anthropologists, like Schapera, the Kriges, Kuper, and myself, and by Herskovits of Dahomey. Only thus can I explain how Kaberry, in the same review (at p. 229), can say: 'Clearly, a state, which is continually riven by civil war in which kinsman is set against kinsman and villager against villager, is more unstable than one in which civil wars do not occur and in which basic social alignments tend to persist.' For every analysis of African states show that they all have recurrent 'civil war', and yet the pattern of the political system at least persists. Kaberry would accept that lineages continually segment; and yet the lineage system endures. Then why should not a state system contain similar processes? Her review overlooks completely the argument of my *Rituals of Rebellion*. Here, I think, there is another tendency at work, a tendency which I notice also in Wilson's criticism of my Frazer Lecture, and in the general treatment of Evans-Pritchard's study of the Shilluk kingship and my study of the Swazi and Zulu national rituals. These studies are taken to be studies of 'ritual': and the connection of the rituals with the political structure is inadequately stressed. I welcome this opportunity to point out that I consider Evans-Pritchard's study of the Shilluk divine kingship, Fortes' of the Tallensi Great Festivals, Kuper's of the Swazi *incwala*, and my own re-interpretation of this ceremony, to be analyses of political relations, and not analyses of ritual. I am sure these colleagues would agree with me.

I have already discussed how Schapera took up and tried to set in critical perspective my main thesis: this is so far the only full published assessment, though A. I. Richards makes some similar points in the review of my *Custom and Conflict in Africa* cited above. I am still convinced that this central thesis is an illuminating one; and I am pleased to have had this opportunity to try to set out its implications more explicitly. I hope that it will induce my colleagues engaged on the study of African states to look more carefully at the institution of civil war. Clearly this disturbs a state at one moment, and divides it into factions: but it may have a more complex effect on the system of the state. Since Evans-Pritchard's analyses of Shilluk and Eastern Anuak have been so important for me in the development of my main thesis, I look forward eagerly to see what he makes of his study of the Zande political system. In a number of preliminary articles he has set out a lot of his basic data, but he has not yet put them together into an interdependent analysis.

So far, it seems that the Zande system was one in which after every generation each kingdom split into sections under various sons of the king ('A History of the Kingdom of Gbudwe', Abstract of *Zaire*, October 1956, No. 8, pp. 470, 475); but there are suggestions of continual reconquest of some sections by others, as among Nyakyusa. Elsewhere it seems that rebellions were recurrent in Zande politics, though there were, exceptionally, few against King Gbudwe (*Anthropological Quarterly*, Catholic University of America Press, xxx, 3, 1957, pp. 68, 78).

The Zande then were one of the states which split repeatedly – what Southall has called 'segmentary states'. We return to the major problem raised by Schapera's comments on my thesis: the question of the conditions in which the rebellion-cycle, without fission (see Barnes, 1954, op. cit., p. 57), is dominant, as against the conditions in which sections of the state will continually be breaking out into independence. This problem is too complex to be treated here, and I can only indicate the lines on which I myself am thinking. It seems to me that the states found in Africa, at least south of the Inter-Lacustrine Bantu kingdoms, contain an inherent instability dictated by their comparatively undeveloped technology and the consequent lack of internal economic differentiation. Hence I would now say, in the light of Schapera's criticisms, that most African states are more likely to have constant secessions than they are to remain united. The Zulu-type of state is probably found less frequently than the fissiparous state, and it will occur in unusual conditions. Most African states are still held together by what Durkheim called 'mechanical solidarity', so that a segment can easily set up in independence without any economic shock. My own view was coloured by the fact that I studied, by chance, two states where the cycle of rebellions without fission was dominant – the Zulu and the Barotse. Barotseland was an unusual system for South-Central Africa, in that there was considerable ecological differentiation between its regions, leading to considerable exchange of various kinds between the heart of the kingdom, the flood-plain occupied by the dominant

Lozi, and the surrounding woodland areas (see my essay in *Seven Tribes of British Central Africa*, 1951). Similar differentiation appears to mark the Lunda and the Kongo kingdoms of the Congo basin, though the Lunda sent out conquering armies which established themselves in all but ritual independence. Similar special action occurs in most Inter-Lacustrine Bantu kingdoms, and in those of West Africa. The Zulu were unusual in that Shaka solved for them a pressing land-problem by wholesale slaughter, and thereafter they had plenty of land into which to expand. He also built up the majesty and ritual of kingship. Among the Zulu, the rebellion cycle was dominant through their short history, before their defeat by the British gave temporary reign to fissiparous tendencies. The Ndebele, who broke out of the Zulu state in its early years, established a similar kingdom: but here there was only one succession before defeat by Whites, and rebellion barely occurred, since the king had few sons to be contenders.

Both tendencies appear to be present among the Ngoni, who fled from Shaka's first major conquest and reached the Lake Nyasa region. Barnes' careful analysis of their history raises comparisons with both Zulu and Tswana (1954). He states (p. 17) that though various writers describe three occasions when dissident sections broke off from the main body of Ngoni marching north under Zwangendaba, his own view 'is that only one of these secessions actually took place, and that it was relatively unimportant'. After their leader Zwangendaba's death in the region east of Lake Nyasa, the state broke into five segments. Barnes comments: 'We might also suggest that because so many men became Ngoni only after they had grown up in quite different cultures, mystical sanctions were less effective than they are in more homogeneous societies; but this can hardly be proved. The fact remains that some segments did break off, that the State attempted to annihilate them, and that sometimes they were successful, probably sometimes not. The transition was sharp between the conditions in which a segment was an integral loyal part of the State and that in which it was itself a new State. Spatially a State was surrounded by a no-man's-land. Everything inside the uninhabited ring of country was in the State, everything outside it was not.' In other words, we have here something like the Tswana situation, of an inhabited zone surrounded by an uninhabited area, and this might raise real difficulties for the maintaining of production with an increasing population.

I emphasize again that the weakness of my whole analysis, aside from the ethno-centrism bred by studying Zulu and Barotse, was that I thought too much in terms of organic analogies, whereby I saw the cycle of rebellions as maintaining the system, with some implication that it strengthened the state. There is present in all these states constant rebellions: rebellions aim to seize the kingship or at independence; the outcome may be a new unity or fissure into two segments. Discrepant and conflicting motives are at work in leaders and followers, and these reflect the discrepant processes which are part of the structure and culture of society.

This brings me finally here to the problem of trying to relate differences between the first fruits, or other major national ceremonies, to the two different types of polities. It does seem to me that the ceremonies are far more elaborately organized and that the rites lay greater stress on the conflicts inherent in the political system in tribes where the cycle of rebellions proceeds without fission, as, if I take only South Africa, among Swazi, Zulu, Ndebele, and Shangana. The ceremonies are less important and less elaborate among Xhosa and other Cape Nguni, and among Tswana, where splitting is more frequent – though we must note that among the Tswana group of tribes as a whole there is an order of precedence by acknowledged seniority in which tribal chiefs eat the first fruits. Again, the first fruits ceremonies seem to approach the Zulu-Swazi type in some South African tribes which, though smaller in size than Zulu or Swazi, appear to have greater stability and fewer secessions than the Xhosa or Tswana do – namely the Mpondo, some Natal tribes, and the Venda. Against this, according to Ashton, *The Basuto* (1952, p. 212) had no national first fruits ceremony, and their kingdom was, from its inception, extremely stable. Detailed analysis of this problem requires lengthy comparison and careful assessment of the facts, so I can only note it here. Other variables also enter to complicate the situation. Thus I consider that the attention of the South African tribes on the inland plateau, where drought is more frequent than on or near the eastern coasts, focuses on an annual rain-ceremony, and not on the first fruits or harvest; while correspondingly the more easterly tribes do not have annual rain-ceremonies, but only perform rituals to procure rain when a drought occurs. They focus attention on first fruits and harvest. Further, the degree of economic differentiation within a tribal system may also be significant. As stated above, there was little of this differentiation to bind together the territorial segments of South African tribes: there is such differentiation in Barotseland, and the Barotse have the cycle of rebellions as a dominant process in their polity, but do not have national first fruits or harvest rituals, though they have large-scale assemblages, without public ritual, at their annual moves out of their plain homeland at flood, and back into the plain when the flood falls.

In short, we have here a series of problems, to be tackled stage by stage. First, we must look at the different types of rebellions which in fact occur in various tribes, and perhaps classify them into two series. The first series ranges from institutionalized civil war, as the total overall polity, of the Anuak, to the periodic succession war of the Shilluk, to the cycle of the rebellions of the Ankole or Zulu type, without any radical change in the political system. The second series covers the tribes whose polities are liable to constant fission. These two series have to be examined to see in what conditions each occurs. Thereafter we have to investigate whether each of the two series produces a particular type of ritual, or is influenced by such a type of ritual.

I stress that I do not think that the 'rebellious structure' of African polities is significant only when a rebellion occurs. The possibility of rebellion is something that king, subordinate rulers, and subjects have to take into account all the time. Thus we have to see 'rebellion' as an ever-present, persistent, repetitive process influencing day-to-day political relations. It is only one of many processes at work. There is always the likelihood of some section breaking out and seeking independence, either because it is too weak to attack the king, or because it or the king's party may flee after defeat. Clearly, as I have said, we need to examine the conditions in which one or other of these processes is likely to be dominant. But in a fuller study of these political systems I would now bring into consideration a number of other, largely independent, processes. We have to see any one state as involved in the total field of relations with neighbouring states, whose heads may try to exploit factional divisions in their own interests, as Sechele did the struggles between Sekgoma and Matsheng (above, pp. 23-4). There is likely to be an oscillation of power between the king and the 'barons' during the course of a reign, especially as a new king tries to win over his former enemies among the barons, while turning against those who brought him to the throne; and there may be a longer-term oscillation in this distribution of power through a number of reigns. This kind of oscillation would be somewhat analogous to that described by Leach for the Kachin in *The Political Systems of Highland Burma* (1954) between what he calls the *gumsa* and *gumlao* systems, of which he says: 'Both systems are in a sense structurally defective. A *gumsa* [aristocratic] political state tends to develop features which lead to rebellion, resulting, for a time, in a *gumlao* [egalitarian] order. But a *gumlao* community, unless it happens to be centred around a fixed territorial centre such as patch of irrigated rice terraces, usually lacks the means to hold its component lineages together in a state of equality. It will then either disintegrate altogether through fission, or else status differences between lineage groups will bring the system back into the *gumsa* pattern' (at p. 204). Leach calls this a 'cyclical theory of social change', but I consider that this is a misleading designation: for this kind of change is repetitive,[12] and it works in a long-time cycle without producing, apparently, any fundamental change of pattern. It is misleading to take this as a model of change of the type investigated when African polities are brought under European domination. It were better compared with, say, the general process of alternating centralization and de-centralization which has been traced through the history of some large firms, or by Rappoport in the swing from authoritativeness to 'self-rule' in a mental hospital (*The Community as Doctor*, 1960). That is, as against Leach, I would see this kind of oscillation as part of an equilibrium, in the sense in which the Oxford English Dictionary speaks of '*a body in stable equilibrium* (tending to re-cover equilibrium after disturbance)'. [13] I think it is clear that British anthropologists have always thought in terms of this kind of equilibrium, even if their implicit model was too 'organic'; and anyone reading Evans-Pritchard or Fortes, for example, must conclude that Leach has misread them.

I have not space to go into this point more fully, but I stress that these processes are to a large extent independent of one another, and that each has its own time-structure (see below, pp. 39–40). The result is a complex which has to be disentangled from an actual history to give us some view of the systematic interdependence of the various processes. And here, in the hope that it may stimulate others' research, I throw in another suggestion. Civil wars from the inception of the Zulu state to its conquest by the British, fell at twelve years, twelve years, seventeen years, and twelve years. I know that historians have failed to show a periodicity in rebellions in Europe: but I think it is nevertheless worth pointing out that these periods between Zulu civil wars approach the fifteen years which elapsed between each transfer of power from elders to warriors, and of duties of fighting from warriors to youths, among Masai, Kikuyu, Kamba, and other East African tribes. This has made me wonder whether the growing of younger men into adulthood in which they found their path to power blocked by their elders, has some influence on the total situation, in that this pressure from below tends to lead to rebellion. We must remember that in this type of simple economy there are only a limited number of positions, and types of position at that, open to the ambitious; and the maturing younger men have forcibly to thrust out the established older men, to achieve anything. [14] This may be a false trail: but the whole question of the effect on wider political relations of the movement of men through grades of age clearly needs investigation even where these grades are not institutionalized.

In addition, of course, each revolt has its unique elements, including the personalities of ruler and rivals, the chances of national good fortune and victory or ill fortune and defeat, the haphazard influence of external events. All these facts may in practice produce important changes in the distribution of power among social positions after a revolt, even though the main pattern of the political system persists through the revolt. Hence I now abandon altogether the type of organic analogy for a social system with which Radcliffe-Brown worked, and which led me to speak of civil war as being necessary to maintain the system. Social systems are not nearly as integrated as organic systems, and the processes working within them are not as cyclical or repetitive as are those in organic systems. Moreover, social systems are open to the influences of changes in environment, and to changes due to relations with other social systems, as organic systems are not. I think therefore much more in terms of series of social processes, operating within an ecological setting and the bio-psychical framework of human life, as well as of the restriction and action of a technology and a culture. These are never perfectly adjusted; and hence processes do not cancel themselves out as in organic systems. We have, as Fortes and Firth have stressed, to think of a field of social action in which we can delineate certain processes set in motion by a series of customary institutions, which do largely 'hang together', but only largely, and not perfectly. The institutions, and the values and laws they embody, are often independent, discrepant, and even conflicting (see my *Custom and Conflict in Africa* and Turner's *Schism and Continuity in an African Society*). The structure of such a field is much less rigid and self-consistent than it was thought to be by social anthropologists from the 1920s to about 1950.

As we examine the working of each process, we are, in a current popular terminology, analysing a 'model', though I would insist that we are dealing with a process that occurs in reality. It is a 'model' in so far as we are delineating only part of the reality we are analysing; and to get nearer to reality, we have to complicate the model by feeding in the influence of other processes.

In reality, too, each process may work over a relatively limited period of time: then external events, or the cumulative working of varied and often opposed processes, may alter the basic pattern of the system. For example, I have evidence to show that the pre-Shakan Northern Nguni had a polity in which the process of rebellion was present, but the process of constant splitting of tribes was dominant, as among Cape Nguni, from at least A.D. 1500 to about 1775 or later. Then there emerged Shaka's kingdom, I believe mainly because of a change in the land – population ratio, but possibly also influenced by an increase or shift in external trade. That Shakan kingdom was firmly established within six years: in it, despite slight secessions, the rebellion process was dominant for sixty years, until the kingdom was defeated by the British. Thus statements about each process are made only for a limited period of time. But I would maintain that, however short the period of time during which we are examining the history of a particular political system, we have to make our analysis as if the whole cycle of the process were being completed. During even a couple of relatively peaceful years in Zululand, politics are affected by the cycle of rebellions; and that whole cycle has to be analysed to make sense of the period we are examining. Similarly, in another context, domestic relations can only be analysed if we write as if we were looking at them through three generations (Redfield, *Peasant Society and Culture*, 1956, pp. 91–2), even though there are going to be radical changes in those generations. Mitchell has made an excellent analysis in these terms of *The Yao Village* (1956). But we must be clear that this analysis is made in 'structural time', and is not an analysis of actual events in a period of real historical time. [15]

Here we have again, as Durkheim stressed in *Les Règles de la Méthode Sociologique*, to investigate not only the 'laws' of working of each type of 'social species' but also what laws are present and how they operate at different 'ages' of each social species. These laws – 'processes' as I have called them – will operate with varied power and incidence in the early, middle and late years of a political system.

Finally, external conditions of the state will have marked influence: the introduction of gunpowder and growth of trade, the varied environs of the state (it is important that the early years of the Zulu kingdom were lived in a depopulated no-man's-land before it was encircled by powerful White states, while the state of Buganda, for example, was bordered by other powerful states.)[16] And we have to look at the total polity of states and segmentary societies of which each African kingdom was only a part, as well as at the adjacent establishments of foreigners, Arabs, Europeans and others. I myself believe that if we look widely enough at the history of Africa, we are looking at a picture in which states like the Zulu rose to temporary power over neighbours, persisted for a time with the dominance of the cycle of rebellions, and then broke up,[17] either under external attack or under the pressure of civil wars aggravated by increasing pressure on land through increase of population, or because they grew in size beyond the limits their technology and economic system would carry. They broke up, or large segments moved out to establish new states or to segment further and disappear among the surrounding segmentary societies. And this total picture is complicated by the evidence, now accumulating, of the existence of stone-city civilizations, working iron and possibly using irrigation. Hence states of the Zulu type may have been 'barbarians' surrounding islands of civilization, which they may periodically have destroyed – like the Zimba and Mbo in East Africa (G. M. Theal, *History and Ethnography of South Africa before 1795*, 1907, vol. I, ch. xiv). This full analysis has to

40

be worked out by anthropologists, historians and archaeologists; meanwhile we must build up knowledge by analyses of individual states, in which external events are treated as intrusions into the political system we are analysing, intrusions which produce important results, but which are not systematically involved in the polity itself. This will involve an increased use of historical analyses, as against the closed sociological analyses which were a necessary stage in the development of our discipline, as we had to make a preliminary classification of the great variety of tribal systems we encountered (see my Foreword to Turner's *Schism and Continuity in an African Society*). Schapera on the Tswana, Evans-Pritchard on the Sanusi, Barnes on the Ngoni, Fallers on the Soga, Southall on the Alur, Watson on the Mambwe, and others have already begun to do work of this kind.

In the Foreword to Turner's book, I have also drawn attention to this as part of a general change which is occurring in the modern ethnographic monograph, as written by younger anthropologists. I have called it a shift from the method of using ethnographic data for 'apt illustration', to an analysis of a series of 'cases' which consist of a succession of events affecting the same group or individuals. Professor J. A. Barnes also commented on this change in his Inaugural Lecture to the University of Sydney (published in *Arts, the Proceedings of the Sydney University Arts Association*, i, 1958), and it is the main theme of Turner's book. I consider that a far more complex view of a social system emerges from this type of monographic method, and that it will in turn influence comparative studies. Here I can do no more than draw attention to this important development.[18]

I can deal much more briefly with the problem advanced in the symposium on 'The Village Headman in British Central Africa'. In 1947, when I left the directorship of the Rhodes-Livingstone institute to become a lecturer at Oxford, three members of the Institute went with me to Oxford. Barnes and Mitchell were invited by the Royal Anthropological Institute to give a joint paper to it, and suggested to me that I should introduce their contributions in order to bring out the attempt we were making to co-ordinate our researches. We selected the position of village headman for our analysis, because we had heard Fortes remark that among the Ashanti a lineage may select the proper elder to administer its internal affairs and represent it in traditional relationships, and some Western-trained young man to represent it in his relations with the Colonial Government. This focussed our attention on certain conflicts inherent in a position of this kind. This thesis has been taken up and analysed by all members of the Rhodes-Livingstone Institute: Barnes on Ngoni, Cunnison on Luapula Lunda, Mitchell on Yao (most notably in *The Yao Village*, 1956), Turner on the Ndembu, and Watson on the Mambwe. It has also attracted general attention in the subject from several anthropologists outside our group who have worked together.

I have suggested that the village headman's position is typical of a whole series of social positions whose incumbents represent the authority of a superior hierarchy to members of smallish groups, of which these incumbents are in other respects full members – e.g. the foreman, the shop steward, the ward sister, the non-commissioned officer, the school prefect (in *Custom and Conflict and Africa*, pp. 51 f.). There is a general problem here – the manner in which different sets of social relations, involving quite different rights and duties, interlock. But I had perceived this problem on a larger scale a decade earlier, in my analysis of the position of the modern Zulu chief (Section VII of essay from *African Political Systems* reprinted below). There I had dealt with the manner in which Zulu chiefs are officers of the South African Government, yet are expected by their people to oppose that Government's proposals. I further contrasted the position of Native Commissioner and chief. The chief is a subordinate official under the Native Commissioner, yet he stands sharply in contrast with the Commissioner, for he represents traditional values and history, he participates in the life of his subjects, etc., as the Native Commissioner does not. This I believe was a most significant observation and analysis, and a new insight for me, though its germs are to be observed in some earlier essays (see other essays in *African Political Systems*, and the studies referred to in my essay on Malinowski's theory of social change, reprinted below). This treatment of modern political problems stands in sharp contrast to Malinowski's approach to these problems; and, for example, to the description by Monica Hunter (Monica Wilson) of the position of the modern Mpondo chief (*Reaction to Conquest*, 1936, pp. 421 f.). I developed this point in my *An Analysis of a Social Situation in Modern Zululand*. Similar analyses were made of the position of 'chiefs' by my colleagues at the Rhodes-Livingstone Institute: E. Colson on Tonga, J. A. Barnes on Ngoni, and J. C. Mitchell on Yao (in *African Studies*, vii, 1948, and viii, 1949). Barnes dealt with the problem in these terms fully in his *Politics in a Changing Society* (1954), and Watson pushed the argument further in *Tribal Cohesion in a Money Economy* (1958), a study of the Mambwe. J. van Velsen has in press a corresponding analysis of the Lakeside Tonga of Nyasaland.

Outside of this group, Kuper independently advanced a similar analysis, though she phrased it differently, of the position in modern Swazi polity (*The Uniform of Colour*, 1947, pp. 92 f.). For the rest, this particular formulation has not been taken up. Southall (*Alur Society*) was again, seemingly, so preoccupied with the problem of how Zulu lineage and state co-existed, that he did not dwell on that section of my essay on modern Zululand. More strikingly, when Fallers was dealing with the conflicts of role involved in Soga political life, under British administration, I would have expected direct comparison. But he, too, apparently was so taken up with the position of the lineage in the Zulu state that he did not notice this treatment of the conflicts in the modern system about the position of the chief. I am naturally pleased to note that in a review in the *American Anthropologist* (lxi, 1959, p. 1122) of my re-printed *Analysis of a Social Situation in Modern Zululand*, he states that he feels guilty for not acknowledging its stimulus. In his *Bantu Bureaucracy*, indeed, he does not devote his analysis to the relations of chief and Commissioner: he is more concerned with a problem arising from Weber's sociology, namely that '. . . the institutionalization of . . . two different kinds of authority – that based upon personal loyalty and solidarity between superior and subordinate and that based upon the impersonal, disinterested conception of bureaucratic "office" – within the same society . . . results in instability and strain, and that integration within the political system of such a society can come only through one of these types giving way to the other' (pp. 19–20). That is, he concentrated on changes in, and conflicts between, the expectations involved in the role of chiefs when they are absorbed into a colonial administration. This was a problem I did not treat fully: it deserves to be investigated in other societies.

As this goes to press, I have found a reference to an analysis of a mediaeval empire (*The Carolingian Empire*, by H. Fichtenau) similar to mine of Africa. The translator, Mr P. Munz, writes in his Introduction:

If . . . one reads Professor Fichtenau's account of the political problems of the age, one cannot but be impressed by the similarity of his findings with the generalizations of the anthropologist. 'Indigenous chiefs,' writes Professor Gluckman, 'are caught between the pressure of the Western Government whose servants they are, and the pressure of the people whom they represent against the Government. Where there are no indigenous chiefs, the Government has no machinery to work through, since it cannot handle the allegiances of kinship groups and religious congregations. Where Governments appointed their own chiefs, these were not restrained by indigenous sanctions and often became rank exploiters of their fellows. . . .' (quoting from my essay in *The Institutions of Primitive Society*, ed. by E. E. Evans-Pritchard, 1954, p. 80)

I want to stress about my thesis here, that at first, while in the field, I saw Commissioner and chief as absolutely opposed: this was how Zulu spoke of them. After reading Bateson's *Naven*, where the process of schismogenesis is so strongly stressed and integrative links are barely touched on, I began to look for the integrating mechanisms in Zululand: and I found these in routine administration and in the divisions among tribesmen and Whites caused by several series of interests. I consider that it is important to look at the elements of cohesion, as well as at conflict: in 'modern' Zululand, conflicts are obvious enough, it is harder to see how the system works at all.

I can see now that Southall's and Faller's interest in problems of administration was part of a general trend, possibly stimulated by changes in field problems, and possibly by an increasing theoretical interest of younger, as well as older, anthropologists in sociological writings which led them to examine particularly the analysis of bureaucracy made by Max Weber. I discuss the second stimulus first.

In her editorial introduction to the symposium *East African Chiefs* (1960), Richards says that 'the book is in every sense of the word a joint effort. L. A. Fallers stimulated much of the work by his interest in Weber's theories as to the evolution of true bureaucracies from patrimonial systems of authority. The importance of his contribution will be realized at once by readers of his *Bantu Bureaucracy*. The experiments he made in the collection of career histories in Busoga certainly paved the way for this comparative study.' All the essays in the symposium thus concentrate on problems relevant to this theme, even Beattie's essay on the Nyoro. I single this out because Beattie is a close colleague of Evans-Pritchard's, and he does not seem to have found the same stimulus as I did in Evans-Pritchard's analyses of Anuak and Shilluk polities. Beattie may have been restricted in this essay by lack of space, but I found the same neglect of the problems set by Evans-Pritchard in his admittedly introductory booklet on *Bunyoro: An African Kingdom* (1960).[19] Southwold, who helped with the symposium on *East African Chiefs*, has since written a short study of *Bureaucracy and Chiefship in Buganda* (n.d. – 1961), in which he concentrates on how the Ganda kings strove to restrict the power of autochthonous leaders and to prevent the power of their own appointed officers from becoming entrenched through hereditary succession and attachment of a permanent group of followers, so that there would be an aristocracy able to oppose kingly power, by periodically creating new sets of officers – a problem frequently discussed by historians.

But I believe that this trend of interest in bureaucracy is general, and not specific to the group influenced by Fallers. For independently Colson has written a stimulating essay on 'The Role of Bureaucratic Norms in African Political Structures' as part of a symposium on *Systems of Political Control and Bureaucracy in Human Societies* organized in 1958 by the American Ethnological Society: she suggests that a 'bureaucratic' type of structure could only emerge in situations where, in lieu of money, the type of land usage enables the king to attach land as an emolument of offices between which officials could be transferred – situations which are found in Buganda and in Barotseland. Again, M. G. Smith, working independently, in his *Government in Zazzau* (1960) concentrated on similar problems, for he emphasizes the difference between two aspects of government, politics which are competitive for power over making decisions on public matters, and hence which are segmentary, and administration which is authoritative and hierarchical; and his treatment of administration is fuller than his treatment of politics. Like the authors of the symposium cited above, he tends to treat rebellions and assassinations of kings merely as 'acts of violence', which, while they reflect actual distribution of power within an apparently straight-forward hierarchial system of administration, indicate failures and breakdowns in that system. He does not consider it necessary to examine these rebellions as 'normal' in these types of political systems, in the way that Durkheim argued that some crime is normal to all societies. This same trend emerges in Richards's recent Presidential Address to the Royal Anthropological Institute on 'African Kings and their Royal Relatives',[20] where she concerns herself mainly with 'the problem of the African king with too many royal relatives', rather than with the relation between such a king and royal family and a political organization in a country with certain kinds of economic and technological equipment.

I now pass to the second stimulus of this interest in bureaucracy, the change in the field situation. Between 1930 and 1940 Indirect Rule was accepted by most anthropologists as a happy form of political organization in British colonies. Problems of the role of native authorities in this system of rule, and how far they were involved in difficulties between the demands of two systems, were indeed analysed by anthropologists.[21] Political developments during and after the war, with increasing emphasis by British Colonial Governments on the social services to be provided by native authorities, raised more sharply the question of how far these authorities could be turned into modern-style bureaucrats, or were prevented from doing so by their traditional upbringing and relations with their people, as well as by their training or lack of training. But it took the interest in theoretical problems of bureaucracy to focus research on this particular aspect, as in *East African Chiefs*, and I fear that it has focussed research here too sharply, excluding from view more general problems involved in the structure of states. In trying to understand the present position of chiefs as 'bureaucrats' of the Colonial Government, the writers have traced their analogous roles in the traditional system: i.e. this particular emphasis, important as it is, has in my opinion over-influenced analyses of political systems as wholes. It appears to me to have led, except in Smith's treatment of *Government in Zazzau*, and Barnes' and Watson's studies of Ngoni and Mambwe respectively (op. cit.), to a neglect of problems of actual power and the ends of power in both traditional and modern systems. Hence in traditional systems rebellions became aberrant. As for studies of the modern situation, *East African Chiefs*, for example, does not deal at all adequately with the effect of the rise of colonial nationalism and parties on the 'chiefs', as a review by C. Leys in the *New Statesman* (19 March 1960) points out. Nor, as I have said, do monographs like Fallers' *Bantu Bureaucracy* treat sufficiently the role of Government officials, and the actual conflicts over specific issues of policy and practice, between Colonial Government, 'chiefs', and people, or their relations to the newly emergent political parties and trade unions, as I had tried to do as far back as 1940 in my *Analysis of a Social Situation in Modern Zululand* (op. cit.) and the section of my essay in *African Political Systems* which is reprinted in this book. I must again say that this study of developing bureaucracy is clearly important: but it must not be divorced from the changing situation of power within an altering economy. I believe that the 'rural anthropologist' is particularly likely to fall into this error,[22] if error it be; and though it may be that it is my own interest in the work in the region which makes me find more illumination in Central African studies, I consider that these have profited from the attempt to co-ordinate research in urban and in tribal areas, as in the programme of the Rhodes-Livingstone Institute. Here work by Wilson in Broken Hill and by South Africans on urban areas, and later by Mitchell in *The Kalela Dance* (1956) and Epstein in *Politics in an Urban African Community* (1958), began to deal with the emergence of trade unions and other urban associations, of classes and political parties, among African still involved in networks of tribal ties; and this stimulated analysis of the significance of those ties and the role of chiefs in modern tribal areas, as in my own study of developments of land-holding in Southern Africa, Watson's of the Mambwe chief, and Van Velsen's of Nyasaland Tonga society.[23] All these studies concentrate on the realities of power, and the bureaucratic roles of chiefs are only one element among these realities.

My main contention is that the emphasis on the relation between office-holders in terms of models of bureaucracy distracts attention from the processes of co-operation and struggle for power which mark both the traditional and modern political systems. The study of bureaucracy, I repeat, is important, and all the studies are significant contributions: but these problems need to be set within analysis of decisions on specific policy issues, and of struggles for specific types of control over men and things.

The manner in which men collaborate and compete in taking these decisions and in striving for power is influenced indeed by their ideas on roles, including bureaucratic roles, but it is also set by the type of land and economy, the mode of production, the type of weapons,[24] means of communication. These, as well as networks of social relations, are the framework within which political roles are played; and if we take them into account, rebellions cannot be treated merely as 'acts of violence' which disturb the even working of administrative systems. Rebellions are, in Durkheim's sense, a normal incident of the political processes of these states, and deserve full analysis.[25]

The reproduction of some of my essays has given me the opportunity to try to clarify the points of difference between myself and my colleagues, and to set out, I hope more clearly, what I have been arguing. I have also seized the occasion to point out that I consider that recent concentration on lineage theory, and then on bureaucratic roles, has blocked the development of analyses into some major problems of the structure of states, and of tribal political systems under colonial governments; and to say what I must obviously feel – that my ideas can make a contribution here. I am encouraged in this hope by the comments of my colleagues when I read this *Introduction* in our seminar at Manchester. They pointed out to me that my thesis of rituals of rebellion, and their connection with social processes, had directly influenced Turner's analysis of Ndembu rituals in his *Schism and Continuity in an African Society* (op. cit.), where he concludes, beyond the point I reached, that ritual 'is not so much a buttress or auxiliary of secular social regularities as a means of restating, time and again, a group unity which transcends, but to some extent rests on and proceeds out of, the mobility and conflicts of its component elements' (at p. 316: see also pp. 122 f.). Dr Emrys Peters said the value of the analysis had enabled him to interpret quite different sets of relations outside the African field. He had himself applied it in relating specific elements in a Lebanese village's performance of the widespread passion play of Husein to the social structure of the village. He says of this play: 'In the processions, it was the peasants who punished themselves, the Sayyids and Sheikhs who looked on and mourned. And after the hollow triumph on the theatrical battlefield, the peasants learned the true nature of their moral defeat in the village square, where the eternal validity of Shiism and the position of the Sayyids and Sheikhs as keepers of the true way of life were announced in one stirring and symbolic recitation. The lesson could not be plainer.'[26] Dr R. Frankenberg had applied the analysis to a changing situation, and not a situation of repetitive equilibrium, in his study of a Welsh *Village on the Border* (1957) of England. He puts forward the hypothesis that his village, whose community life is threatened in several ways, runs a series of recreations which come to symbolize its unity, each recreation breaking down because of conflicts inherent in village life, but at that point being replaced by another. The whole thesis of the balance of conflict and collaboration in social systems, and the role of ritual in dealing with independent social processes all equally validated, is a powerful instrument of analysis: it derives from the work of many anthropologists, including notably Bateson, Evans-Pritchard, and Fortes.

Chapter One

AN ADVANCE IN AFRICAN SOCIOLOGY*

1. *Introduction*

Anthropological studies tend to be repetitive in the sense that they are descriptions on the same plane of analysis of new social regions or new aspects of social life. Rarely do they provide us with a new set of abstractions allowing deeper analysis, and giving us new theoretical concepts and new techniques of fieldwork. I do not decry the merits of the 'repetitive' studies. They are immensely valuable both in their own right and in their contribution to the general advance of our discipline. Periodically, however, we get crucial studies which come as climaxes of previous work and also beget a new trend of research. Fortes' *The Dynamics of Clanship among the Tallensi* falls into this select company.

One of the tests of these books is that they should raise new problems in the very process of analysing others. This was significantly true of Evans-Pritchard's study of the Nuer.[1]

Fortes' book, as he himself says in the *Foreword*, follows with the wealth of detail of thirty month's work, the lead set by Evans-Pritchard on the basis of a year's research. His study crowns the value of Evans-Pritchard's. He has not only followed, he has also set a new lead.

Since Evans-Pritchard first published his analysis on the Nuer and Anuak of the lineage, whose significance in Africa had been initially demonstrated by Radcliffe-Brown and Mrs Hoernlé among the Southern Bantu, the lineage has been the focus of studies of African kinship. Meek and Forde in Nigeria, and Fortes in the Gold Coast, have demonstrated its importance in West Africa, and Schapera, Hunter and Kuper in South Africa. Fortes saves these

---

* Meyer Fortes, *The Dynamics of Clanship among the Tallensi: Being the First Part of an Analysis of the Social Structure of a Trans-Volta tribe*, published for the International African Institute by the Oxford University Press, 1945, 30s.

studies from becoming repetitive. But his work raises much wider issues. He puts forward a theory of ritual, based on Durkheim and Radcliffe-Brown, but constructed more objectively. By implication he refines an increasingly used conception of our field of study, to question such fundamental ideas as: what is a social system? How are the different categories of social relations integrated in a single social structure?

As I worked through the book, I became increasingly aware of problems I had missed in my own analyses: not only of ranges of facts I should have collected for a comprehensive account, but problems of categories, of types of behaviour, of analytic interconnections. For one value of a new theoretical contribution is that it enables us to see the data we already have in new patterns. Evans-Pritchard and Fortes have shown that the lineage system is the morphological framework of stateless societies, and that this system interlinks many categories of social relations. The administrative framework of the state may similarly be more than an organizing mechanism: it may be an element of social structure, durable as the lineage system, and serving as it does to interlock variant and congruent systems of social relations, with ritual values acting as pins at crucial points.

It is interesting to speculate on the interdependence of the research-worker and his field of study. I do not mean by this the old charge that each anthropologist's account of a primitive society is a projection of his own personality. But each field by its objective facts forces on the enquirer a particular line of research. To me it seems more than coincidence that the students of segmentary, stateless polities have posed more fruitful problems of political structure than the far more numerous workers on highly organized states. Anthropologists who work on the latter tend to concentrate on the mechanism of administration: the units that are administratively demarcated, the chiefs and the officials, the rights and duties that inhere in the apparatus of state. These are undoubtedly real problems. But do they lead away our attention from underlying problems, in the relation of fields of behaviour and values, of social alignments that are not so clearly demarcated? Is it sufficient to see the paramount chief as archpriest of the nation in view of his political position? – may it not be that his ritual value arises from the conflicts aroused by his power over subordinate groupings?[2] An African state appears to be pyramidal in form; but the categories of social relations which are knit together at every level vary radically. How is this variant interlocking related to the administrative hierarchy? This kind of problem is forced on the student of a segmentary society if he is even to pose his problems. He has to seek for the fusion which is the other aspect of fission – does the anthropologist in studying a state not miss fission which is the other aspect of fusion, and therefore the character of the fusion itself, which may exist outside of, in conflict with, the administrative framework? In the state, as in a segmentary polity, the varied integrating mechanisms which complement cleavages may not coincide simply in a single administrative office and officer.

We know already that African administrative organizations contain inherent cleavages.[3] On this view the conflicts, the rebellions, the dynastic struggles for power, which periodically rupture the internal relationships within the state become not breaches of norms, but norms themselves, processes inherent in the balance of the equilibrium. Fortes shows that in Tale segmentary polity open conflicts emerge from the structural differentiation within the lineage, and are resolved or reconciled in a new balance, by ritual collaboration. Similarly, in states such as the Zulu the splitting of administrative divisions, the conflicts between claimants to a chiefship, between sub-chiefs of provinces, between sub-chiefs and chiefs, may well mirror a readjustment of the political organization to accommodate structural differentiation at the level of village and neighbourhood relations. This type of analysis is likely to recast our whole approach to the problems of civil and external war and of sanctions. Thus I think anthropological research has already demonstrated additional implications awaiting analysis in the thesis that some rebellions are fought to defend the kingship against the king.

To these themes I return at the end of this essay. I use them here to indicate the stimulus derived from Fortes' book. Before explaining this more fully, I have to set out a bare minimum of his own argument.

2. The Tallensi Lineage and Clan

From the very beginning of his study Fortes was confronted with major difficulties. He could not even isolate the people he was studying, as Evans-Pritchard could isolate the Nuer. The people of the Voltaic region between the Mossi, Dagomba, and Mamprusi states stretch without political unity across the land. Each so-called tribe is sporadically at enmity with its neighbours yet it does not seem to have any distinct internal unity as against them. Rattray discovered that the people comprised two major groups of communities, one claiming to be autochthonous, the other to be immigrant. The two sets of communities are indistinguishable from each other by broad linguistic and cultural criteria, though they have distinctive ritual observances. The immigrants may be regarded as independent outliers of the Mamprusi with whose chief they recognize kinship, but not political ties. The autochthones hold exclusive priestly offices in the cult of the Earth, as Custodians of the Earth.[4] These distinctive communities are articulated in a common polity.

They think of themselves as Tallensi but they cannot be marked off as a distinct group. In order to establish their relative identity, Fortes traces social links from the Tong Hills which he treats as the centre of the region. Here immigrants, Namoos, and autochthones, Talis, live close together, and the line of their collocation forms a social and territorial cleavage which is the central pivot of the segmentary structure. 'The cardinal principle of Tale social structure is that every social grouping defined as a unit in one situation, or according to one principle, dissolves into an association of lesser and differentiated units in another situation or according to another principle.' The basic unit of the social structure is the maximal lineage, a group of people linked by an accepted genealogy through the patrilineal line to a reputed common ancestor. But the lineage is not a mere collection of individuals: it is an organization of lesser but similar parts. 'It grows by the continuous multiplication of its parts, not by the mere accretion of new members. And this takes place by the splitting of its cells, the minimal segments, into new segments in successive generations.' Evans-Pritchard first analysed this process in detail among the Nuer and Forde has written on it among the Yakö.[5]

It is one of Fortes' major contributions to advance this particular analysis.

The maximal lineage, which in theory never divides, consists in an integrated balance of opposed segments, constituted on the same patrilateral principle; and these in turn divide into coordinate segments, similarly constituted, till the minimal lineage, the sons of a living father, is reached. Every man[6] – but not a woman – who leaves living male children founds a new lineage within the system of parts. When he dies, he gets a separate ancestral-shrine and his seminal descendants constitute a separate lineage as against the seminal descendants of his full- and half-brothers and seminal cousins. They unite with these to form a superordinate lineage centred in a common grandfather, as against similarly constituted lineages, co-ordinate at a higher level, which centre in their grandfather's brothers, own and classificatory. Should only one man in a generation leave seminal descendants, the process of segmentation is postponed: at that stage the segment as a whole, divided at a lower level, will stand in contraposition to a union of segments in another line at a more ancestral stage. Fortes, like Evans-Pritchard, has a terminology of degrees to indicate this. The maximal lineage divides into major segments, these into outer medial lineages, these into inner medial lineages, these into nuclear lineages, these into effective minimal lineages, and these into minimal lineages, the descendants of a living man. Evans-Pritchard's terminology was simpler: his clan consisted of maximal lineages, these divided three generations lower into major lineages, and these in turn three generations lower into minimal lineages. Those lineages are respectively the cores of primary, secondary, and tertiary territorial sections. It is perhaps unfortunate that Fortes should not have been able to use the same scale, but judging by the published information, the Tallensi lineage-system is more differentiated than that of the Nuer.

One reason why Fortes imported words of different connotation, denoting degree of comparison and other values (e.g. 'effective', 'nuclear'), is that he wished to denote at what points other categories of social relations overlapped with lineage relations. The latter are always corporate: members of a lineage are undifferentiated in relation to 'outsiders' (i.e. to members of co-ordinate lineages), though differentiated within themselves. At the more ancestral levels of lineage-segmentation the main social ties are realized entirely in corporate activities. At the level of the nuclear lineage the system of domestic relations interpenetrates the system of lineage relations. The nuclear lineage is the core of a domestic family living in one compound: and the *nucleus* within which the next segmentation will occur. The inner lineage 'frequently forms the core of an expanded[7] family; it determines the widest

54

field within which domestic relations prevail. Its members have differentiated person to person relations, based on the recognition of generation differences and proxy-parenthood, as well as corporate lineage relations.' Their moral bonds are stronger: sexual intercourse with a 'clan-sister' is reprobated and adultery with a fellow member's wife grave sin; they work common patrimonial land. That is, this grade of lineage is the point of intersection of these different categories of social relations. It is recognized by the Tallensi, but its span varies from lineage to lineage. From this point down these additional relations become more intense, until they end in the full co-operation within the household of which the effective minimal lineage is the frame. As one ascends from the medial lineage, the bonds between the members change. At this range, for example, fellow-members help each other in collective work, as individuals; heads of these lineages may be helped by members of co-ordinate medial lineages within the maximal lineage in a representative capacity, i.e. some of them attend specifically to represent their segments. A man may not marry into his mother's medial lineage. In the maximal lineage, the chief critical norms are the exogamous rule, the ban on adultery with a fellow's wife or marriage to a fellow's divorced wife, and the leviratic right. These rights also extend to the clan (see below) but here we begin to move in the field of politico-ritual relations. At all stages there are ritual bonds: the injunction of assisting in funerals and participation in a common cult of the ancestors of the segments involved.

Fortes sets out the framework of the lineage order at length, since 'observation in the field showed that every significant social activity among the Tallensi is tied up with the lineage system'. His analysis justifies his assertion that 'it is impossible fully to understand [Tallensi] economic, jural or ritual institutions without a grasp of their lineage system'. I have therefore had to follow him and attempt a summary of the system. For in this society without government, and without history in the sense of a record of specific events, there are two things which give continuity from the beginning of time into the future. The one is the Earth on which men make their lives; and this means the Earth as inhabited by the people. The second is the lineage. Hence the dominant ritual systems of the Tallensi are connected with the Earth and the lineage ancestral-cult. To this I return later: I mention it here to emphasize, as Fortes does, that apart from the lineage Tallensi have neither history nor culture. As he aptly puts it, 'the memories and reminiscences of the old men are parts of their biographies and never contribute to the building up of a body of socially preserved history'.

Near the end of his analysis he writes:

In the course of our morphological analysis of the lineage system from within we have made references to the corporate activities in which this system emerges . . . it has been convenient to speak as if the lineage structure exists and persists apart from the activities in which it emerges. But this is only an analytical device. . . . The implied distinction between the structure of the lineage and its function does, however, bring out the important fact that the lineage structure is more than any of its functions. It is the integral of what is common to all Tale institutions in which the patrilineal line operates as an organizing principle. It is the general factor of consistency, coherence, and continuity in the social structure.

The concept of social structure essentially implies ordered extension *in time* as well as ordered articulation *at a given time.* . . . Among the Tallensi the lineage system enables us to see the operation of the time factor in social structure. . . . We see how the lineage structure at a given time incapsulates all that is structurally relevant of its past phases and at the same time continually thrusts its growing-points forward. The dynamic equilibrium of a lineage is an equilibrium in time.

The history of the lineage is written on the surface of the land: in homesteads and farm-boundaries and shrines in their positions relative to one another. It is written too in the modern positions of the present lineage-heads. Here Fortes elaborates Evans-Pritchard's analysis of structural space and time, particularly in his discussion of the order of segmentation in lineages. In this argument, he makes a definite new contribution in his description of how the lineage functions as a system of parts, and not as a collection of individuals. It operates by the rule that on specific ceremonial and jural occasions every segment of the lineage involved must be *represented*, preferably by its head, but at least by one adult man. If more than one man is present, all rank as a unity. An elder can be head of several segments of different orders of segmentation. Thus at any one moment the whole history of the lineage is contained in the existent segments: and as each must be represented on ceremonial occasions, every ceremony crystallizes both the continuity of the lineage in time, with its culture as ordained by the ancestors who are being tended on, and also its present structural form. In fact, in this homogeneous society, history and form of social structure are almost one.

The long quotation from Fortes above can almost be paralleled from Evans-Pritchard. In his *Some Aspects of Marriage and the Family among the Nuer* he describes how women wander about, live in concubinage, and produce children for men with whom they have never lived. He concludes:

Our survey of Nyueny [village] showed everywhere change and confusion. One enquires how so mercurial a system can work. Has there not been some deep error, some serious misunderstanding, in the investigation? I think not. The change and confusion which are so evident in family and domestic associations are not to be seen in the larger social groups, particularly in the lineages. The dynamic social process is there slowed down and is stabilized into structure. For it is very apparent that there are two kinship configurations of persons among the Nuer: the one consisting of their domestic interrelations and the other of their legal relationships. The domestic interrelations have a relatively low degree of consistency and durability compared with the legal, and in our sense of the word, structural interrelations.

Living among the Nuer it is deeply impressed on one that the lineages are the stable framework of kinship structure and that families, even simple legal families are, in comparison, loose and unstable associations which are the means by which new structural tissues are formed. Individuals and 'family' associations of one kind and another seem to float about, as it were, and have an independent existence. But they are anchored to some lineage, or, if they break away from it sooner or later attach themselves to another lineage, take root in its stem, and become part of its growth.

Fortes and Evans-Pritchard thus emphasize the same point. Evans-Pritchard did not analyse Nuer religion [till 1951–56], and here Fortes gives a new lead. Previously, anthropologists have stated in general terms that there is a close association of the ancestral-cult and the kin-group: this was obvious enough. Fortes shows that this association is far more than that the cult is a mnemonic of genealogical relationships. 'The lineage structure is far more than any of its functions': therefore it has an automony of its own. This gives lineage membership, patrilineage in constituting corporate unity, a value different from the value of kinship ties alone. For the Tallensi, kinship values are axiomatic and they are psychically founded in the sentiments established within the family. On the structural plane, their chief ritual projection is in the cult of the patrilineal ancestors who symbolize the unity of corporate units, and therefore the stability and coherence of Tale life. It appears to me implicit in Fortes' argument, and this is borne out by various incidental references in the body of his work, that the spirits of matrilateral ancestors are essentially different from the patrilineal ancestors though the ideology of beliefs is similar. As an individual outside of the patrilineal lineage system a man may have a matrilateral ancestral-spirit, male or female, as a spirit-guardian, or divining-spirit, or his divinity. Here the spirits act for the man in terms of the web of kinship, which is particular for each individual, and not for him as a member of a corporate unit. Similarly, among the Pondo it is frequently matrilateral spirits who possess diviners.[8] This seems to symbolize the fact that becoming a diviner is essentially an individual attribute, and not a character attaching to a man as a member of a lineage.

Again, throughout the South-eastern Bantu area spirits which are capriciously evil are women. The Zulu say that the spirits of old women are always evil, and bring misfortune. Dr Fortes tells me that the Tallensi consider the female ancestors to be more capricious and vindictive than male ancestors. If the patrilineal ancestors are the symbols of continuity, of the enduring values of the lineage and therefore of moral imperatives, they cannot be held responsible for unmerited punishment. Fortes thus opens a new approach to the whole problems of matrilaterality, and the position of women, in these patrilateral societies. It is already well-authenticated that in them women are frequently sources of ritual evil, as in their periods. Women are witches, men are sorcerers.[9]

Fortes' analysis of the historical, and therefore ritual, value of the patrilineage ancestors for Tallensi segmentary policy, suggests a new approach to parallel problems in highly-organized African states. Clearly as has been frequently stated the cult of the chief's ancestors symbolizes the history of the tribe and therefore its persistence in time. But does it not perhaps relate more closely to the administrative organization than to the relations of chiefly family and subjects as such? Among the Tallensi it is the morphology of the lineage-system which constitutes the framework of Tale society. It holds together individuals in time and space. It serves to enforce rights, both through the sanctions of public opinion and the ancestral-cult, and through quasi-judicial process. Thus a man who has a claim against someone of another clan may raid cattle of anyone in that clan:

The victim of the raid could demand restitution from his clansman, the original debtor; and I know of men who pawned a child or sold him into slavery in order to find the means of repaying a clansman who had been raided, rather than let the affair become a source of conflict in the clan. This is a good illustration, incidentally, of the statement . . . that collective responsibility is not a principle of Tale jural relations. It is not the clan but the debtor himself who is responsible for his debt. Selfhelp is a technique for putting pressure on a debtor through the mechanisms of clan and lineage cohesion [in the absence of judicial organization].

We know similarly that Nuer will not support a kinsman in a feud if he is in the wrong. The lineage-system thus indirectly enables people to obtain their rights and thus sanctions rights and order.

This is the obvious function of a state administrative apparatus. Has the apparatus also functions parallel to the other functions of the lineage? Like the lineage-system in a stateless society, the administrative organization is a body on which the living tissues of the African state are grafted. For the positions of chief, to the sub-chief, to district-head, to village-head, in the web of authority do not exhaust their social values. They stand also for the indentity and unity of the sections they 'rule' as against like segments: the chief against foreign chiefs, the village-head against other headmen. The African state like the lineage is not a mere collection of subjects but a system of parts. Do the sub-chiefs act in relation with the chief not as his subordinates, but as the representatives of the segments that pivot on them? Is there a constant readjustment in relations of these 'segment representatives' which is rooted in the further segmentary differentiation at a lower level, in villages and neighbourhoods?

I pose these problems here, for they are suggested by reflections on state ritual organization, which have been stimulated by Fortes' analysis. Meat of Zulu national sacrifices is allocated to sections of the state, as sections, irrespective of the numbers in each section. The Swazi first-fruits ceremonies in parts hinge on the hostility to the chief of his brothers, and the support he gets from the royal clan.[10] Obviously there are radical differences, and state integration is of a different type from lineage-integration. But it seems to me that similar processes are definitely present. At least, to return to our starting point, ritual values attach to every point of the administrative organization as such, because it is the enduring frame of the state, which is locked in the person of the chief. The cleavages between him and his brothers, between him and his chiefs, between him and his subjects, are bridged by administrative ties which at each level of the organization knit together divergent interests.

3. *Clanswomen, Wives, and Matrilaterality*

Fortes' closely reasoned analysis breaks down at one point. He has a good section on the place of clanswomen in the clan organization. By the rule of exogamy women have to marry out of the clan, but they always remain members of it and subject to its ancestors. There are taboos which symbolize the conflict caused by the women's membership of a group which they cannot perpetuate. At funerals, clanswomen have specific roles as such which are sharply differentiated from the roles of the grouping of wives married into the clan. Women are 'our clan-sisters' to all clansmen, as they call the wives of all fellow-clansmen, 'our wives'. I consider that Fortes has not appreciated fully this polar opposition in terms of the two categories of women, or that every woman in practice falls into both categories in relation to different clans, and that this failure has misled his interpretation of matrilaterality vs. patrilaterality in lineage-segmentation.

In discussing lineage-segmentation he argues that the points of division within lineages are the 'mothers'. He quotes, *mulier finis familiae est*, and cites a similar Tale saying, to expand the principle that women produce children to perpetuate a foreign group. He might have cited the fuller, though possibly later, Roman maxim, *mulier et origo et finis familiae est*, to crystallize his later argument. In this he demonstrates that at the lowest level of lineage-segmentation 'fission takes place in the first instance between matrisegments' (i.e. between the sons of one man by different wives, and not between those by one wife). Full-brothers feel more closely bound to one another than half-brothers. Fortes relates this to the conception of a house (*yir*), as belonging to one man, and a section of a house, a room (*dug*), as belonging to each wife.

He argues that two segments which are united in relation to a common progenitor, may be divided in relation to separate progenitrices (i.e. to two wives of this man).

This however does not justify the manner in which Fortes applies the thesis that 'patrilateral origin and matrilateral origin work in polar opposition to each other', the former uniting segments and the latter dividing them. It is contradicted by his own facts. Basically, it is irrelevant if one segment is divided from another by different matrilateral origin. He himself shows that when a man A, whether he is a monogamist or polygynist, has more than one son, the lineage centring on A always splits into new subordinate lineages centring in each son. And if A was a polygynist, and had sons by each wife, each single son founds a new lineage. Common matrilateral origin merely unites two or more of these lineages as against lineages whose founders were born of different mothers. But the former do not form lineages of a *different order* from the latter: all are co-ordinate.

Origin from a common progenitrix is an *additional* point of fission and bond of fusion between lineages; it is not, in itself, the source of differentiation. This is quite clear from Fortes' own description, in which he constantly uses the comparative degree to describe matrilateral linking of lineages: 'somewhat closer ties', 'greater cohesion', 'more closely united', and so on. We may compare this linkage with those which explain the ties between true agnatic lineages and 'accessory' lineages grafted on to them, in terms of descent of the accessory lineages from a sister's son. Similarly, where maximal lineages are interlinked in clanship (see below) it is sometimes explained by a uterine link. Ultimately, this closer linking can be referred to the fact that kinship as such is cognatic, and that the other part of the kinship system, the web of inter-personal relationships, runs in all lines, in opposition to corporate agnatic kinship.

We have therefore to recast Fortes's interpretation at this point. He finds validity for it in its projection on to the ritual plane. The focal ancestor shrine of an inclusive segment:

is designated 'the [shrine] of the father . . .', a notion which stresses the dominance of the father-figure in the unity of the patrilineal descent group and in the coherence of the family. But when a lineage is visualized as a set of segments, these are differentiated by reference to their separate *progenitrices*, just as in the joint family the offspring can be subdivided in accordance with their maternal origins. The focal ancestor shrine of each segment is then called 'the [shrine] of the mothers [of the segment]. . . '. It is identical in form with the 'fathers' [shrine]' but complementary to it in function. Its name stresses the predominance of matrilateral origin in the differentiation of the segments of a lineage, by contrast with the patricentral lineage as a whole. Tallensi speak of a 'mothers' [shrine]' as being the shrine of the segment's founding ancestor and his mother, by contrast with the 'fathers' [shrine]', which they say is the shrine of the founding ancestor of the lineage only. But they recognize that a 'mothers' [shrine]', will in the course of time become a 'fathers' [shrine]' when the lineage undergoes internal differentiation into subsegments, and may function as a 'fathers' [shrine]', if the segment is already so differentiated. When a segment of a lineage is thus distinguished from co-ordinate segments of the same lineage, it is also implicitly contrasted with the whole lineage. It is thought of as a matri-segment, though named after its founding ancestor, and is described as a 'room', *dug* – 'the children of one mother . . .' – of the house', *yir*, on the model of the joint family in which the matricentral *dug* is a segment of the patricentral *yir*.

Nevertheless, it seems clear that a mother with two sons does not have a shrine to serve as an ancestral focus for the two segments descended from her, in their 'closer unity' against co-ordinate segments descended from the sons of her co-wives. (We are told (p. 52) that a man's spirit can never receive sacrifice from matrilateral kin.) The 'shrine of the mother' as a focus of lineage identity is therefore never in fact the shrine of a woman, but always the shrine of a man, her son. As Fortes says a little later, 'every lineage, no matter what its span or order may be, has only one founding ancester and one progenitrix, this man's *mother*' [my italics]. Note that in lineage production the union of progenitor and progenitrix is of son to mother, and not of husband to wife, which is the procreative union in the family.

For as a man alone cannot reproduce, so an agnatic lineage alone cannot perpetuate itself. It can only do so through the women it marries from other clans. The important link is of son to mother, for while the father in whom sub-segments centre symbolizes their unity, it is through his wife or wives that he reproduces himself, and his corporate personality, so to speak, is differentiated in his sons. This occurs whatever the matrilateral linking of the sons. Can we assume that the shrines of the two full-brothers which are the foci of sub-segments are both 'mothers' shrines'?

From the whole analysis I think we can. In short, the mono-gamist with two sons also produces two lineages of lower order, i.e. two rooms in relation to his house. Is a maternal room be-lieved to belong to the wife and not to the husband? If two full-brothers are married and live with their father, are their homes two rooms or one room?

In short it is only *through his wife* that a man is able to produce sons who found differentiated subordinate segments: in himself alone, he remains single and undifferentiated. Fortes himself be-gins this particular analysis by pointing out that each *house* con-tains 'two sets of cleavages; firstly, a stratification by generations, and secondly, a differentiation by descent'. It is the latter which splits subordinate segments and it is made possible by marriage, leading to a mother-son linkage. In a 'mother's shrine' the pro-genitrix is identified with her son, not with her husband: and this applies even if she has two sons. Fortes is therefore wrong in the emphasis he gives his statement that patrilaterality and matri-laterality work as polar opposites. The situation is better sub-sumed in Evans-Pritchard's formulation for the Nuer that 'the social principle of agnatic descent is, by a kind of paradox, traced through the mother' (*Some Aspects of Marriage and the Family among the Nuer*, p. 64). A mother with several sons thus becomes multi-personal in their differentiation as against their father who is always uni-personal, the symbol of unity. Common maternal origin provides an additional link: maternal origin is always diverse in contra-distinction to the eternal unity of paternal origin.

The polarity of father and mother, which undoubtedly occurs as described by Fortes, then arises from the inability of the patrila-teral group, the corporate unit which endures in time, to reproduce itself without marriage to women of other clans. It is, so to speak, corporately procreative but physically sterile, and it has to acquire women to produce children for it. This is the function of marriage-payment (i.e. bride-wealth or bride-price). I believe this is the source of major conflict, and the reason why clanswomen form an undifferentiated group as against wives of clansmen, who are heritable only in the group and remain married to the dead man,[11] to maintain the order and span of segmentation. Women 'are equal to one another in relation to their natal clan'.

Clan-sisters and wives therefore act as united groupings at

funerals, because this symbolizes the conflict rooted in their own position, as producing for another group than that to which they belong by birth: *mulier et origo et finis familiae est*. This formulation is validated by scattered references in the book to the relation of wives and the lineage. For example, the lineage-head's 'functions are most conspicuous in relation to the wives and children of the lineage, for they stand for the greatest common interest of the lineage. It is the productive powers of the wives and the existence of children that secure the perpetuation of the lineage and the immortality of the ancestors' (p. 229). Therefore it is believed that a woman who commits adultery exposes her husband and children to mystical dangers (among the Nuer the husband only, among the matrilineal Bemba the husband's adultery is dangerous for his wife). She has to enter the 'ancestors' gateway'. As wives are thus 'a common interest of the lineage and clan', so:

disputes in higher order lineages arise over inheritance of widows or marriage with a woman who was formerly the wife of a member of a different segment of the clan. Members of the deceased husband's medial lineage feel they have a prior claim to a widow's hand and some-times object to her marrying a man of a different branch of the clan. And if a marriage is dissolved, no matter what the reason may be, it is regarded as a grave breach of clan solidarity for any other member of the husband's clan to take her to wife (p. 246–7).

The chief critical norms of clanship are connected with marriage: the ban on marriage within it, leviratic rights, the duty not to seduce or abduct a fellow's wife or marry his divorced wife. And 'marriage transactions . . . are always relations between lineage units'. It appears to me that Fortes might have given more weight to the positive aspect of the exogamic rule: for it implies that the right to marry each other's women is held by every lineage against every other non-related lineage. This rule is a source of linking and of friction between the different lineages.[12] Because of the frictions involved, marriages are forbidden during the Golib Festival which brings together the widest linked grouping of Tallensi, and not only to secure a truce in actual fighting (p. 243).

The same conflict is posed if we regard the situation of the wo-man in relation to her natal clan.

The concept of a [clanswoman] implicitly stresses the fact that it is a woman's fate to be married out of the clan and to be cut off from its routine corporate activity; and it contains the idea that a woman thus separated from her parental home is felt to belong primarily to the widest corporate unit that stands in contraposition to her husband's where his relations with her are concerned,

i.e. to the clan, which sets the limits of marriage bans. Clans are also the largest political units.

Thus marriage links together two exclusive agnatic segments, which are corporate units in the political field, and it is therefore also the source of conflict between them. On the rights to wives already married hinge ties and conflicts in intra-lineage relations. Is it *therefore* that wives, at least among the South-Eastern Bantu, are frequently charged with witchcraft? that men inherit witchcraft from the mother? that wives become capriciously evil spirits? that in their periods they threaten evil? that the Zulu conceive of dangerous forked lightning to be female, and harmless sheet lightning to be male? At the same time, they may be the source of good: ritually women are highly ambivalent. Men are evil only by choice.[13]

We have returned here to a problem touched on earlier, and again I have to leave it without elaborating it more fully, but I cite finally a further suggestion from Fortes' analysis. 'There is, in fact, a submerged feeling of rivalry in the relations between the men of the clan and the [clanswomen], deprived by an accident of birth [i.e. by being born as women] of effective jural and ritual membership of the clan.' The oldest living clanswoman may never spend a night in the homestead of the head of the maximal lineage lest either or both of them die. She might have been head in his place had she been a man, and

her presence in the homestead which she might have occupied as a man is a hidden challenge and reproach both to the male head of the lineage and to the ancestors. It would be tantamount to a symbolic rejection of the fundamental principles of the lineage organization. For these reasons she cannot stay with the man who most conspicuously represents the extrusion of women from the full heritage of patrilineal descent.

I suggest that there is another strand in this conflict. The above taboo, as Fortes says, symbolizes that the presence of that clanswoman would question the very principle of patrilineality itself, as a dominant value. The conflict is thus rooted in the affiliation of children, and affective sentiment about them. Fortes cites:

a new-born child is confined to its father's house for some time. When it is big enough to be allowed out of doors it must be ritually taken out for the first time by a [clanswoman of the father]. . . . The child's father consults a diviner to find out who will be a suitable [clanswoman]; for the rite is implicitly a blessing of the ancestors, and it is they who are believed to appoint a woman of the clan to carry their blessing to the child. It can be surmised that a [clanswoman] is chosen for this rite because she is by birth identified with the child's father and its lineage, and by sex identified with the child's mother and the function of motherhood.

Perhaps there is another element present: the clanswoman symbolically asserts her rights to her children, who will belong to her husband's lineage.

This is how I see the structural problems: if they are correctly represented, they relate to psychical struggles in a manner I am not competent to assess.

4. *Clanship and Politico-ritual Relations*

Let us return to the maximal lineage. It is not the ultimate largest unit of Tale society. Two to five contiguous maximal lineages are linked, sometimes by a theory of common descent, into a clan. These lineages recognize common rights and obligations which are the critical norms of clanship. They do not marry within the clan or marry women divorced by fellow-clansmen, they should not seduce or abduct each other's wives but they have leviratic rights over widows, they help each other at funerals and in fights, and they may be raided by outsiders for each other's debts. They observe common totemic taboos.

The clan is on the whole locally defined, but the ties of clanship do not set out an organization of maximal lineages in absolute contraposition to a similar organization. Each maximal lineage may have clanship links with maximal lineages in adjacent clans. These links are also defined by the critical norms of clanship. Not every lineage in each clan has links with the same lineages in other clans. Each maximal lineage has a specific field of clanship, which is particular to itself and only part of which is shared with other maximal lineages: there is overlapping but not congruence. In this manner the ties of clanship run across the country in a complex series of overlapping zones. Fortes calls the lineages which link two clans, intercalary lineages.

The overlap is even more extensive. If a maximal lineage A in a clan of A+B+C lineages has clan links with a lineage X in a clan of X+Y+Z lineages, then B and C, and Y and Z, which are not clan-brothers by the critical norms, call each other 'brothers-by-courtesy'. One of the lineages in X+Y+Z may have clan-links with a lineage in clan P+Q+R, none of the lineages of which have clan-links with A+B+C. Then P+Q+R lie on the borders of A+B+C's zone of clanship. They are friends of A+B+C's friends (X+Y+Z), but are also possible enemies since they are friends of A+B+C's enemies, lineages lying beyond. As fits with Radcliffe-Brown's hypothesis, this conflict is expressed in a joking relationship of privileged aggression. Among the Talis, but not the Namoos, in addition pairs of clans or lineages 'on the margin of the field of clanship of each, but not joking partners, have the privilege of moral coercion over each other's members. . . . No member of one group may refuse a member a request of any member of the other', and this injunction has drastic ritual sanctions. They are very chary of making requests to each other, but if a man is so distressed that he is prostrated with grief, he will rouse himself if requested by a man in one of these linked clans.

This summary does scant justice to the complexity of the organization which Fortes had to unravel; it does not even begin to do justice to the significant weight of his analysis. This is essentially based on the principle that segments emerge in action in contraposition to like segments, and that there is latent opposition across cleavages, balanced by ties which cross them. Every time there is a dispute or clash across a cleavage, the mechanism of clan-linkages swings related segments to aid their linked groups. But the ties of integration, through enjoined ritual collaboration of the clans and their component lineages, require a restoration of the *status quo*. Since all groups and individuals accept a single set of values, and there are no irresoluble conflicts in the stationary undifferentiated economy, struggles for power take place within the existent structure:

Tallensi place an extremely high value on their social order. An individual or a particular corporate group might desire to alter his or its position in the society. A clan might strive to assert its supremacy over other clans, whether or not it is entitled to do so. No one would dream of trying to overthrow the whole social order or of agitating against the existing customs and values.

To repudiate membership of the larger unit would be 'tantamount to repudiating the ancestors'. If norms:

are infringed, as invariably happens now and then, they are not thereby invalidated. The infringement tends to provoke processes which cancel out its effects and either re-establish the invulnerability of the norms or bring about a new alignment of structural ties, which neutralizes the breach.

These processes make possible an equilibrium in which:

every tie between corporate units is counterbalanced by cleavages between them, all loyalties between corporate units are kept within bounds by loyalties towards other units, and all common interests are set off by divergent interests.

The dominant cleavage is that between immigrant Namoos and autochthonous Talis (non-Namoos) who include some immigrants. They are contraposed by locality, kinship corporateness, and ritual symbols with strong emotional values. Here also ties of personal kinship and of ritual collaboration cross the cleavage, and there are intercalary lineages, related mythologically to both sides, which have traditional roles as peace-makers. The Tallensi did not go to war for economic gain and could not conquer land, and, though they admired warriors, killing even in war, shedding blood on the earth, brought mystical retribution. 'Wars' between segments, which were a kind of civil war, flared up over trifling disputes. When they occurred between segments across the dominant cleavage, they pivoted the whole alignment of Namoos vs. non-Namoos into action. After a few days of skirmishing controlled and limited by 'rules of war', the peacemaking lineages initiated ritual reconciliation and integration was re-emphasized. The ties of ritual collaboration between clans demanded that different segments, even across the dominant cleavage, co-operate for the good of the whole community and their own section of it.[14] People can sacrifice together only in amity, even though at ceremonies they show the tensions arising from their opposition in privileged teasing.

Tallensi society is demarcated from the dominant cleavage as a region of overlapping clanship zones centring in it. But Fortes

shows that the clanship ties lead far beyond the borders of Taleland to the Gorisi, Namnam, etc. However, it seems implicit that
clans at the centre of Taleland are not themselves structurally
part of these ultimate extensions of the chain, though they
exist objectively and the Tale are aware of them. Thus, 'by these
chains of clanship ties the Talis are linked on to peoples outside
Taleland who live quite beyond the boundaries of their regular
interests and concerns'. Fortes in describing 'wars' shows that
these were too brief to swing more than a few clans into action.
The range of impact of the dominant cleavage is therefore limited,
though the nexus of ties is 'unlimited'. I consider that Fortes
should have indicated whether there are other similar dominant
cleavages beyond – even if there are none. He himself constantly
implies a limitation of the range of this one, by writing of 'geographical centre', 'frontiers', 'the index of the festivals', etc. (see
pages 17, 19, 28, 60, 92, 119–20, 159). If there are other dominant
cleavages, then they with their ranges of impact afford objective
criteria by which Tallensi can be distinguished from other similarly constituted societies. Then the lineages which are structurally 'midway' between the dominant cleavages could serve as
'borders'. They would be effectively in the range of both cleavages.
Fortes' failure to discuss this, even if it be for lack of detailed
data, is an omission, though I gather it is because he lacks data
on the neighbouring tribes. If there are no other dominant
cleavages, what is there away from the Tong Hills?

We see then that the political system of clanship ties in one
sense differs relatively to each maximal lineage, though there is a
degree of absoluteness about the major cleavage which is 'the
copingstone of the whole complex system of differentiation and
integration of corporate units'. The cleavage achieves this by
breaking the clanship nexus: despite the contiguity of Namoos
and non-Namoos, they have only three intercalary lineages tying
the two communities. Two of these are traditional peacemakers.
Of one, Gbizug, we are told: 'it stands aloof in their disputes, taking
neither side, for it belongs equally to both and wholly to neither.'
Across the cleavage in the clanship ties, which denotes the political area, resides integration in the ritual collaboration of Chiefs of
the Namoos and Talis Custodians of the Earth.

Does not this analysis of a reticulated system of overlapping
zones of corporate ties pose for hierarchical states similar prob-

lems which tend to be obscured by the administrative framework? Do ties between corporate units within, e.g. the Zulu state, link some units in opposition to others and to the state? Does some such process operate through the alignments of parties in civil wars? I have shown[15] that the Zulu provinces stood autonomously against the state and on occasion fought against it, and that the provinces were hostile to each other, just as Fortes has demonstrated that a minor lineage stands in contraposition both to its co-ordinate lineage and to the superordinate lineage which includes them all. The further analysis of alignments I have yet to attempt. For as among the Tallensi (see below), so among the Zulu there was a twofold division. The Zulu were divided into provinces, territorial sections, under chiefs to whom they owed loyalty, and also into military divisions attached to particular princes. The overlapping of these two sets of corporate units sets problems of the type analysed by Fortes. Unfortunately, it is too late to examine these for the nation, but they might be examined within the provinces, which now are 'independent tribes'. These again are divided on two bases: purely territorial, and by attachment to chiefly villages. I may mention here that since the Zulu War the Zulu nation has been cleft into two major divisions: and that at one point on the cleavage there is a small sub-district which acts almost as intercalary lineages do among the Tallensi.

5. Ritual, the Social Structure, and the Earth

Fortes advances notably the analysis of ritual which is associated with Durkheim's school and Radcliffe-Brown. I can only introduce a very brief summary of his thesis by quoting verbatim his compressed introduction on the *Underlying Principles of Ritual Collaboration*:

Maximal lineages are the smallest corporate units that emerge in political action. The social and political relations between maximal lineages are regulated by ties of clanship. These ties constitute fields of social relations in which larger corporate units, which we have called clans, emerge. These are the largest corporate units that act in corporate matters. At the level of social and political relations between clans – that is to say, where the fields of social relations, constituted by clanship ties, overlap one another – clanship ties no longer suffice as the organizing mechanism. Here we meet with the interaction of more complex units and regions of Tale social structure than the maximal lineage. The social interests in response to which these interactions occur are more complex and more diffuse than those that are served by clanship. Consequently an organizing mechanism of a different order comes into play, the mechanism of ritual.

Ritual is the appropriate mechanism of social organization at this level because the interests involved are not of a practical or utilitarian kind but of a moral kind – in fact, the most general moral interests of the natives, the maintenance of their existing institutions and norms of social behaviour We must emphasize that we are dealing here with levels of organization correlated with different grades of social interests, and not with hard-and-fast forms of social grouping. We are dealing with different expressions of the same forces. The same categories of ritual values and forms of association serve as a differentiating and integrating mechanism both at the level of social relations between maximal lineages and at the level of interclan relations. And clanship forms the bridge between the two levels as well as the organizing factor at the lower level. Both factors operate at both levels but with inverse dominance. That this is so can be seen from the natives' habit of conceptually assimilating all their social ties to the pattern of genealogical relationship and evaluating them all by the touchstone of kinship. The basic pattern of organization is that which we have described in our analysis of the clan system.

The ritual configurations and connections at the higher level are obviously modelled on clanship configurations and connexions. The reason for this is simply that the ritual relations we are here concerned with exist between corporate units, maximal lineages or clans, defined by the canon of agnatic descent and by their place in the whole field of clanship.

We can say then that a Talis clan has a field of ritual relations over-lapping but not congruent with its field of kinship ties. The fields of ritual relations of adjacent clans are articulated with one another so as to form a connected system linking all Talis to one another. It is through this system that the major cleavage between the Talis and their con-geners on the one hand, and the Namoos on the other, is transcended; and the cycle of the Great Festivals is the medium through which this ritual system is regularly, obligatorily, and conspicuously brought into action.

Their roles in the Great Festivals differentiate Namoos, Talis, and the non-Namoos who are not Talis, but as they must colla-borate to perform the Festivals, these integrate Tale society in a common dependence on mystical powers for the good things of life.[16]

The good things of life for the Tallensi are plentiful crops, many children, and a peaceful and ordered society. These are common interests for all Tallensi. But individuals and particular groups achieve them on their own land, out of their own lives, and by fulfilling their own obligations and asserting their own rights. In doing this, they become involved in marriage disputes, quarrels over slain game, etc. Therefore the common interests give rise to divergent interests – these two aspects, the particular utilitarian and the common values, interpenetrate in every Tale activity. The first aspect is reflected in the secular economic and social organization, the second in the organization of moral norms and religious imperatives.[17]

Three things are made centres of ritual in Tale thought. The Earth, on which men dwell and make their living, has an utilitarian aspect in which particular men and groups work particular pieces of earth; it has also a mystical aspect which is undivided as the ultimate source of men's prosperity. In this aspect the Earth is 'tended on' by the Talis Custodians of the Earth at special shrines, which are centres of undemarcated areas. Thus though the Custodianship of the Earth is distributed between heads of Talis lineages, the Earth itself remains undivided, and Custodians collaborate in the ritual nexus.

But the Earth is lived on by men who use land in terms of their membership of lineages. The whole concept of a lineage depends on the ancestors who founded it and who established Tale culture. No one can contract out of membership of a lineage: he is born irretrievably into it. By that membership he gets right in land, enters into social relationships, inherits totemic avoidances, acquires culture itself, and the sentiments on which it is based are formed in the family itself. Here arises 'the crucial function of the ancestor cult as the ideology around which lineage relations are organized'. Lineage solidarity has not only great practical utility as reflecting the social bonds, which give a Tallensi his place in society. It is rooted in the deepest moral values of the culture, kinship, which is binding in its own right, and it exists in the ancestor cult as 'the objective embodiment of social conscience.' These values are beyond question and they are mystically sanctioned. Breach of the rules precipitates not only material disaster, but may so overwhelm a man that his line itself becomes extinct. The ancestor-cult is therefore far more than a mnemonic of lineage relationships. *Ancestorship* as such has mystical value. This is reflected in the Talis cult of the External Ancestor-shrine, which, like the Earth-shrines, is distributed among different lineages linked in ritual collaboration. The congregations of Earth-shrines and External Ancestor-shrines overlap neither with fields of clanship nor with one another. In practice, Fortes shows that every maximal lineage is a bridge between an Earth congregation and an External Ancestor-shrine congregation. Since a linked lineage 'represents its whole field of clanship in its cor-porate ritual relationship', we see that ritual ties counterbalance potentially conflicting clanship ties. Ritual bonds however are not dependent on clanship ties; the two systems 'are interlocked but not congruent': they operate by counter-balancing each other.

Ancestor-cult and Earth-cult thus represent separate sets of values in Tallensi life, but their ideologies inter-penetrate one another. Fortes demonstrates, for example, how the affective attachment of Tallensi to their localities is woven into the ancestor-cult which symbolizes the values of many systems: of the corporate lineage, of the web of kinship, of locality, of economic prosperity, and even of the individual's fortune which is reflected in the third centre of Tallensi mystical thought, *Yin*, personal destiny. Never-theless, the ideologies are distinct. The External Ancestor:

is more precisely a symbol of the continuity and perpetuity of the clan and its constituent lineages. . . . The Earth, on the other hand, though its cult is also intrinsically bound up with the agnatic line, stands rather for the common interests and common values embodied in the customary norms and sanctions of collective life.

Therefore Fortes calls the two types of shrines 'polar principles of a single religious system'. When clan ritual is performed at one, it is also performed at the other.

In accordance with the segmentary social organization, the equilibrium maintained by ritual collaboration is rooted in the lateral dispersal of shrines among lineages. In both cults, private shrines identify the autonomy of segments apart from the many congregations to which they belong. Fortes has the first clear analysis of the extent to which the ancestor-cult is an index and focus of differentiation as well as of cohesion. Each ceremony, such as a funeral or installation of lineage head, crystallizes social relations through the principle by which each corporate unit in a particular structural context must be represented to aid its linked units. One of Fortes' most important contributions is to show for the Tallensi at least, that there are two types of kinsmen present at a sacrifice: (1) representatives as such of the constituent, co-ordinate and linked lineages of the sacrificing segment; and (2) men drawn by special ties, cognatic and affinal. Other accounts which I know have described the attendants as if they were all drawn by personal, not corporate, ties. Fortes mentions an incident in which a man in joking relationship with the sacrifying lineage 'stole' sacrified meat by privilege. Does this at last enable us to understand Junod's recording in his classic, that in distant Thongaland the uterine nephews or grandsons, 'darlings of the gods', regularly interrupted prayers and stole the sacrifice?

There is an undercurrent of tension in every clan and lineage arising from its segmentary structure. This breaks out in conflicts, but in the long run lineage solidarity prevails. It does so because if men are to prosper they must be in *right* relationship with their ancestors, and to achieve this they must sacrifice to them with representatives of other segments in their fields of lineageship, clanship, and political order. Thus these distinctions raise and reconcile intra- and inter-lineage conflicts. The ancestors, like public opinion, are always on the side of 'corporateness'. Ritual is not to control nature, but to establish a good relationship with mystical powers, and this is effected through a recognition of the common interests of linked groups in an ordered social structure, in the observance of jural rules, and in the maintenance of peace, which between them make possible the continuity of agnatic line.

Corporate links are reaffirmed because people must act as if they were in amity, since they have to collaborate with contraposed segments in burying their dead, installing their leaders, and so on. Ritual offices are dispersed among the segments. Across the major cleavage, Namoos and non-Namoos must collaborate ritually for the good of all and each. The integration of the society is thus achieved at a higher level, but again by a lateral dispersion of interdependent offices vested in contraposed segments, within overlapping fields of clanship.

This is not the total of Fortes' analysis. He states: 'though religion springs directly out of the social structure, it is fed by streams whose sources lie beneath and beyond the social structure'.

I cannot here set out this part of his analysis, but draw attention by reference to a new contribution to the study of totemism. Tallensi is 'a single culture with sectional particularism'. Namoos and non-Namoos have distinctive customs and totems, and there are totems of clans and External Ancestor congregations. There are Earth taboos of animals. Fortes says 'the common thread is the notion of the ancestors as a living mystical force, symbolized in living creatures'. In totem avoidance, the emphasis is on the 'notion of moral obligation . . . directed . . . to the ancestors and not to the totem animal in its own right'. Those who avoid a totem animal, will sell it to others who eat it. In a suggestive sketched hypothesis, Fortes vividly describes how relations between ancestors and men reflect a constant struggle: so the ancestors are frequently symbolized by animals whose teeth are symbols of aggression. The totemic taboo is simple and unquestioned: it images for the individual his own private membership of the lineage. As such, it is the moral imperative of lineage membership itself.

This summary cannot begin to show the skill with which Fortes has analysed the network of ritual ties and cleavages and expounds his thesis of ritual values. Always his argument is rooted in observation, and he postulates no supposed undifferentiated emotion. This part of the book alone gives it great merit: we must await impatiently his full study of the Ancestor-cult and the Cult of the Earth. His greatest achievement here, perhaps, is to demonstrate the integrative value of ritual without false personification and without once importing a teleological phrase. One weakness is, there is no summary of the distinctive rituals of Namoos and non-Namoos in relation to their structures.[18]

6. *The Form of Society*

Fortes' analysis of Tale society is couched in terms which are being used increasingly in sociology. He defines Tale society 'as a socio-geographic region, the social elements of which are more closely knit together among themselves than any of them are knit together with social elements outside that region. We must substitute a relative and dynamic concept for an absolute and static one.' Fortes explicitly uses this concept to demarcate Tallensi society from the surrounding socio-geographic region as an area of interlinked ties of clanship and ritual collaboration ultimately balanced about the major cleavage between Namoos and non-Namoos. This cleavage also is crossed by ties of politico-ritual collaboration.

A more complex conception of social structure is implicit in this total analysis. He states that the aim of the book is a descriptive analysis of Tale social structure at the level of corporate group organization, since this is the framework of the political system. But he does more than describe a socio-geographic region in terms of 'zones of clanship [relationship between maximal lineages] of increasing amplitude and diminishing importance'. This is only the framework of the structure: it is set for all time in a society whose 'history is not a progression but a continuity'. In theory,[14] there can be no splitting of maximal lineages and the names of lineage founders persist forever. Fission of the minor segments does not alter the equilibrium of the major segments. The lineage framework and the land, as we have seen, are the enduring principles of Tale society.

But Tale society consists of far more than these principles. There are very many different categories of social relations. A total field of social relations consists of interpenetrating systems of different categories of social relations: ecological, economic, territorial, lineage-clan (corporate-group kinship), inter-personal kinship, domestic, political, ritual, etc. These different systems are interlocked with one another in a series of cleavages and ties. For example, 'a settlement is only a relatively autonomous community. One might perhaps define it as the region of maximum overlap of all the categories of social relations found among the Tallensi'. Lineage relations and relations of groups to land make stability and continuity essential characteristics of a settlement, whose borders – the 'social circumference' – are fixed by social relations. Neighbourhood ties are *ipso facto* lineage ties, and therefore economic, religious, jural and moral ties. Among the Tallensi spatial and social affiliation coincide, so that 'a man's central field of social relationships is integral with his central field of spatial relationship'. Within this field, for example, I think we can deduce from Fortes' remarks on land tenure, there is an overlap of lineage ties and the web of kinship on patrimonial land.

Territorial segmentation is a function of lineage segmentation and clanship ties are a function of local ties. But the two systems are coincident. Territorial sections of their own autonomy have a competitive orientation to each other. Possibly therefore in Tongo, though the undifferentiated section Kuoreg is co-ordinate with a segment divided into three sub-segments, it is forced to the level of the sub-segments because it is small in numbers.

The high consistence between these categories of Tallensi systems is possible, Fortes suggests, because 'economic factors are neutral'. It is a non-competitive, little differentiated, self-sufficient, stationary, subsistence economy, and therefore does not produce ties and cleavages cutting across those established by genealogical, local and ritual principles. Environment is a fundamental part of Tale social space and the utilitarian and economic elements are fundamental to all relations. But they do not differentiate social groupings on a basis of inequality: it is an honour for one lineage to give land to another which has surpassed it in numbers. In this egalitarian system, all social ties tend to be assimilated to clanship. Though ritual ties and clanship ties themselves are interlocked, they reinforce each other by counterbalancing each other. Nevertheless, both can be translated into a genealogical idiom.

Thus if the social structure consists of interpenetrating systems, a group or social personality may occupy positions in each of these systems. In the Tallensi settlement, the region of maximum overlap, all males occupy similar positions *relative to* one another in all the systems (lineage, territorial, economic, etc.) This is my explication of what Fortes means by 'maximum overlap'. It gives Tale society its high degree of homogeneity despite the great complexity of social ties.

This conception of social structure to some extent justifies Fortes' unorthodox conception of 'clanship'. In the past, a clan has usually been defined as a group of people linked by putative unilateral descent. Fortes here applies the term maximal lineage to groups defined thus, and he uses 'clanship' to denote a category of relations between lineages and their members. Clanship is distinguished by certain critical norms such as the rule of exogamy and the leviratic rights which frequently inhere in clans throughout the world. He thus in effect adds a new term to our vocabulary.

The structure of Tale society is therefore a product of tensions between corporate units in a system of balanced ties and cleavages. Ties and cleavages may reside in different units in the variant systems (clanship, ritual,, etc.), but are so ordered that there are both 'regions of high tension where groups are coupled in polar opposition, and regions of low tension where the units of structure are articulated in complementary relations to one another'. Tie balances cleavage because these are inherent aspects of all social relations. As Evans-Pritchard put it, fission and fusion are complementary aspects of one another. These are basic principles in Freudian ambivalence and in dialectics. Thus in Taleland, the major cleavage is most marked where there are clanship ties across it, i.e. fission is most marked where fusion on the political plane is greatest. Similarly, in the new struggle for European goods and power, rivalry is most acute between clans with close social ties. On the other hand, where some Hill Talis are exploiting their shrines to get money from pilgrims all over the Colony, the Namoos regard the money as 'tainted'. 'In this matter Namoos and Talis have not got a sphere of common interest in which they might be rivals. 'As the Tallensi themselves see, nearness of relationship as well as distance excludes a joking relationship: teasing cuts too near the bone.

It is this principle which lies behind the dynamics of Tallensi clanship. It is the basis of the relative nomenclature of groups and of lineage differentiation. More than this, it is this principle which enables groups to emerge in action, in which they pull corresponding units into action. Specific activities in the round of men's lives – the course from life to death, making a living, coping with misfortune and celebrating good luck – become social events mobilizing certain social relations and groups. Tallensi society is so homogeneous that these temporary associations recur in many events. But Tallensi society as a whole is a synthesis that emerges chiefly in the context of the Great Festivals.

Once again we must repeat, the enduring framework in these variant structural contexts is the lineage system. This is also true of Nuer society. Evans-Pritchard there, in a less detailed analysis, showed that the Nuer ecological, lineage, territorial and political systems, have a high and associated consistence. I have quoted him as saying that in the lineages 'the dynamic social process is . . . slowed down and is stabilized into structure'. I have suggested that in African states a similar frame is provided by the administrative organization, which, despite its autonomous element, is a system of ties between segments of the state. The framework itself alters constantly as the differentiation in each system sets up movements in all the interpenetrating systems. But in primitive society the framework retains its form. The activities which produce differentiation set in train recurrent processes which restore the previous alignments, or create new ones within a similar structural context. A rebellion against a bad chief instals his kinsman as chief.

However, it is too simple to conclude as Richards does that the Bantu state has developed out of the kinship group, is in a sense the kinship group writ large.[20] I doubt if this could be historically validated in a single instance. The ruler-subject relationship is indeed often described in the kinship idiom of the people – it is even with us – and in the stationary economy of pre-European Africa, the ruler-subject relationship had values like those of kinship. But even among the Tallensi there is a point where the systems of social relations abruptly change their character: kinship ties are insufficient, and ties are of a new type, politico-ritual.

It seems to me that Fortes' analysis offers a new method for posing the whole series of problems involved in the incorporation of kinship units within a state administrative apparatus. For example, in describing the Zulu political pyramid[21] I suggested that there was a change in the sanctions operating at the different levels of political organization. Force decreases in relative importance as a sanction when one considers allegiance to king, to district head, to village-head, to family-head, respectively. The power of the ancestors increases. Though the king invokes his ancestors for national good in the first-fruits ceremonies, he has to be magically protected against any subject who may transgress his rights to eat first. The transgressor is not threatened by the king's ancestors, but, if caught, is punished secularly. The transgressor against the kin-head's prior rights is punishable by the ancestors. Again primary rights to land are conferred by membership of nation and district, but the actual land a man gets largely depends on his bonds within the family and patrilateral group. Here other positive bonds, with their negative sanctions, become important: a man on the whole depends on his kin, and not on his chief, for help in working his gardens and caring for his herds, in acquiring bride-wealth and rearing children, in debt and dispute. This is descriptive generalization on the institutional level. I suggest that a reformulation in Fortes' terms will enable us to pose the problems in a form allowing further analysis, and above all comparative analysis – even with the segmentary societies.

If we pose the problem I have described above in these terms, we get a far more fruitful analysis. Then the system of domestic relations becomes a separate one, though it is one into which effects from the political system will intrude. But domestic relations operate by processes peculiar to themselves. One of the most important conclusions that emerges is that there is a radical distinction between kinship as such, in which the web of relationships is peculiar to every individual, and the organization of corporate groups on a kinship-linkage. Fortes emphasizes the difference in separating his studies of *The Dynamics of Clanship* and *The Web of Kinship* (which is now the second half of his study of Tallensi social structure). Above we have seen that these two systems overlap in the inner lineage, where 'the members have differentiated person to person relations . . . as well as corporate lineage relations'. Similarly, Evans-Pritchard made separate analyses of the corporate kin-group relations of the Nuer (in his *The Nuer*) and of the domestic relations (*Some Aspects of Marriage and the Family among the Nuer*).[22] He showed in the latter that great instability in domestic groupings such as the family existed side-by-side with social stability, which inhered in the continuity of lineage-groups as the cores of territorial segments. Forde made a similar distinction in his *Marriage and the Family among the Yakö*. Then the operation of different movements in these different spheres implies that I formulated a false problem: for the sanctions in a group with the time-continuity of the Zulu state must inevitably be different from those in such a temporary organization as the family. I could describe the difference, but not proceed beyond using it to define the difference between political and domestic relations. The problems rather are: the sphere of domestic relations reveals certain processes; how far are these recurrent, how do they alter the constitution of particular domestic groupings, how do cleavages and ties interact in the history of the groupings – and hence, how are domestic relations sanctioned. On the other hand: the sphere of political relations reveals certain other processes; how far are these recurrent, how do these alter the constitution of particular political groupings, how do cleavages and ties interact in the history of these groupings – and hence, how are political relations sanctioned. The two sets

of sanctions can be described to differentiate political and domestic relations: but I repeat, they are different by assumed
definition. Analytically, in this form they are incommensurable.
What we may find is that there are identical, or similar, or different, types of movement in each system: these we can compare.

But the omnipresence of both domestic and political systems
in all societies has been demonstrated. Then we have a further
set of problems involved in the interaction of the processes of
both systems. For example, I am working at the moment on an
hypothesis that the divorce rate is higher in societies with matrilineal and bilateral kin-groups than in those with patrilineal kin-
groups. Assuming this to be factually true, we must interrelate
movements in the domestic sphere with movements in the political and kin-group sphere. I must point out that this set of problems is entirely different from the intrusion of political action into
domestic relations in any actual society. For example, a Zulu
father can get the chief to take forceful action against a son who
breaks certain laws of domestic relations. So that though the father
does not himself use force, as in the Roman *jus vitae necisque*, force
becomes a sanction in the domestic group.

There is implicit above a very important methodological principle: namely, that we can never compare with one another the
complex sets of behaviour which constitute cultural realities in
either a single society or a range of societies. They are too overladen with reality. I find a very striking significance in the two
types of comparison made in Fortes and Evans-Pritchard's comparative *Introduction* to *African Political Systems*. Whenever they
compare societies on the basis of real differences, nothing emerges.
Take their distinction between states and stateless societies.
They test correlations of the distinction with phenomena such as
mode of habitation, demography, and mode of livelihood. The
results are negative; and necessarily so, because these are such
complicated institutions that they do not bear comparison. It is
even difficult to fit them into categories. The Zulu, Tswana,
Ankole, Kavirondo, and Nuer are grouped as pastoral-agriculturists. But their whole ecological setting, the distribution of their
settlements, their division of labour, etc., are interwoven into
incommensurable complexes.

On the other hand, they did obtain significant results when they
compared 'social processes',[23] movements in the societies in

time-space. For example, they showed that states' histories are marked by periodic civil wars which resulted in changes of the personnel holding offices but not in the institutional character of offices. They related this to the simple non-accumulating economy, itself a type of process, and to territorial segmentation of the society, another type of process. Again, they argued that in the stateless societies there is a general tendency for a centralized organization to emerge under European occupation. Among the Nuer, this showed in the appearance of prophets who led the temporarily united Nuer tribes against the White man. Is this not a similar process to the rebirth of Zulu nationalism, including tribes which in the 1879–80 War fought for the British against the Zulu king? And passing outside the tribes covered by that book, is it not similar to the unions of Transkeian tribes which followed the prophets Makana and Nongqause?

My suggestion is that if we are to develop as a comparative science we must abandon attempts to work with real units, and attempt to deal with abstract process – i.e. with social movements. Van Gennep's concept of *rites de passage* is the most striking example of how universally this type of formulation can be applied, and of how fruitful it can be. If we can isolate movements of this type, then we can in any one social field attempt to analyse the interaction of different types of movements, as well as compare the types of movement in one social field with those in another. For example, we might take three principles: territorial segmentation, rebellions in a non-changing or repetitive polity, type of succession to the chieftainship. If we work these out in their interaction in a series of fields we might get profitable general conclusions. We might not, it is true. But I argue that it is impossible to compare:

(1) the Bemba, shifting cultivators with an undifferentiated economy, scattered villages, a ritual military kingship, matrilineal;

(2) the Nupe, peasants and courtiers, a differentiated economy, a 'feudal' political structure, patrilineal;

(3) the Zulu, pastoral-agriculturists, a military kingship, patrilineal.

On the other hand it is possible to see that:

(1) the Bemba matrilineal system of succession contains contra-

dictory rules that inevitably, after a while, produce rival claimants to the throne;

(2) the Nupe system of succession makes the Emirate rotate through three dynasties of the royal house, so that there are rival sections about the throne;

(3) the Zulu system of patrilineal succession, in which the heir is chosen by his mother's status, which in turn is uncertain, also produces rival claimants.

I could extend this list indefinitely. Thus in most African states we find that there is a recurrent process by which there emerge rivals in every succession. How does this process interact with the processes of territorial division, of the struggle of people against harsh rulers, of population expansion and migration to new land? Here is comparability.

7. *Conclusion*

There is a wide variety of analyses woven into Fortes' book which I have not been able even to touch upon. It is difficult reading – partly, and here I think Fortes is at fault, because of the number of Tale terms used. The argument is packed and so integrated that it seems repetitive. This it is not; the same points recur in different contexts and the basic theses have to be recapitulated. What appears to be detail of fact is really analysis. The book is also difficult to read because Fortes' style is probably not easy. But he is coping with major difficulties, for he is moving on a plane of analysis deeper than usual in social anthrolopogical literature. Periodic summaries of the development of the argument would have eased his task, and the reader's.

The Dynamics of Clanship among the Tallensi is one of the most important books in our literature. It must be read and read again.

Chapter Two

SUCCESSION AND CIVIL WAR AMONG THE BEMBA

AN EXERCISE IN ANTHROPOLOGICAL THEORY*

IN THEIR INTRODUCTION to *African Political Systems*, Fortes and Evans-Pritchard state:

A relatively stable political system in Africa presents a balance between conflicting tendencies and between divergent interests. In Group A [a group of societies 'which have centralized authority, administrative machinery, and judicial institutions . . . and in which cleavages of wealth, privilege and status correspond to the distribution of power and authority'] it is a balance between different parts of the administrative organization. The forces that maintain the supremacy of the paramount ruler are opposed by the forces that act as a check on his powers. . . . The regional devolution of powers and privileges, necessary on account of difficulties of communication and transport and of other cultural deficiencies, imposes severe restrictions on a king's authority. The balance between central authority and regional autonomy is a very important element in the political structure. If a king abuses his power, subordinate chiefs are liable to secede or to lead a revolt against him. If a subordinate chief seems to be getting too powerful and independent, the central authority will be supported by other subordinate chiefs in suppressing him.

It would be a mistake to regard the scheme of constitutional checks and balances and the delegation of power and authority to regional chiefs as nothing more than an administrative device. A general principle of great importance is contained in these arrangements, which has the effect of giving every section and every major interest of the society

* Reprinted from *Human Problems in British Central Africa*, xvi (1954). This paper was read to a conference of research officers of the Rhodes-Livingstone Institute in Livingstone in 1947. I was then Director of the Institute, and the paper lay in the Institute's files. Mr Epstein, a recently appointed officer, who was making a short field trip to the Bemba unearthed the paper, and I agreed to publish it.

84

direct or indirect representation in the conduct of government. Local chiefs represent the central authority in relation to their districts, but they also represent the people under them in relation to the central authority. . . .

A different kind of balance is found in societies of Group B ['societies which lack centralized authority, administrative machinery, and constituted judicial institutions . . . and in which there are no cleavages of rank, status or wealth']. It is an equilibrium between a number of segments, spatially juxtaposed and structurally equivalent, which are defined in local and lineage, not in administrative terms. Every segment has the same interest as other segments of a like order. The set of inter-segmentary relations that constitutes the political structure is a balance of opposed loyalties and of divergent lineage and ritual ties . . . divergence of interests between the component segments is intrinsic to the political structure . . . the stabilizing factor is not a superordinate juridical or military organization, but is simply the sum total of inter-segment relations.[1]

Fortes and Evans-Pritchard themselves in the same book described the political systems of the peoples they had studied, the Tallensi and the Nuer, respectively. I myself wrote there on the Zulu, and said of the organization of the Zulu nation into sections (which I called tribes):

the tribes and smaller groups [were] part of a pyramidal organization with the king at the top. . . . [The] administrative framework . . . ran through the social groupings, but the position of the head of each group in the series was different, for he was related to the members of his group by different ties from those linking them to the head of the larger group of which it was part. . . . The nation was a federation of tribes whose separate identities were symbolized by their chiefs. The tribes were even autonomous within the national organization for on occasion many tribesmen supported their chiefs in quarrels with the king, though some were swayed by national loyalties.[2]

In a later article I saw more clearly the social processes at work. I described how the Zulu nation was created by a small tribe, the Zulu, coming to dominate all the other small tribes of South-Eastern Africa. The nation was divided into groups (which I still called tribes), which were based on these old units.

Between tribes there continued a balancing of tribal chief against tribal chief; for the chief was not only part of the administrative machinery in which he represented the state power, but also the centre of his tribe's unity for which he stood against the state and other tribes within it. Within a tribe, relatives of the chief, or men in charge of political districts, could still attain independence by winning people away from the chief, subject to the king's intervention. It is suggested that under the conditions of communication prevailing over the vast Zulu territory, the nation was stable as its component units were hostile. A tyrannous king would unite the tribes against him, but they combined under the king to prevent any tribe becoming too powerful. This was also achieved by the continued fission of tribes which was partly due to the spread of the increasing population over fresh arable and grazing land, partly to the conflicting groups within each tribe, and partly to the creation by the king of new tribes under his relatives and other rising important men. In the early Nguni period [the period of small, continually splitting tribes] fission of tribes prevented the growth of a centralized government; here it strengthened the centralized government by keeping down the strength of each tribe.

The divergent interests of groups within the nation were balanced by their common allegiance to the king and the values he symbolized, by the regimental system, and by the administrative machinery which worked through delegated authority, with lessening executive power, in a pyramidal organization from nation, to tribe, to tribal district, to homestead. These separate chains of administration were linked in a council system in which homestead headmen united under their district head, district heads under their chief, and chiefs under the king.

The second important point here is that

any threat to the king came from members of the royal family, some of whom were established as chiefs. . . . Intriguers for power sought popular support and the people turned to those men who were near in power to their rulers to escape from intolerable oppression. The political balance persisted so long as the ruler observed the norms of rule and the values accepted by the subject. When he transgressed these rules, his subjects knew of no other political system, nor could they establish another under the social conditions then prevailing. They could be rebels, not revolutionaries. The king's danger came from rivals who could be installed in his place, with similar powers in a similar organization; he was deposed, but his office remained unaffected, as is shown in the ability of his successor immediately to undertake religious functions, to symbolize the values of the society and to express them in ceremonial.

And a deposed, or assassinated, tyrant after his death became a guardian spirit of the tribe.[3]

The theory underlying this argument is that societies which have a stagnant techno-economy have conflicts which can be

resolved by changing the individuals occupying office or in relationship with one another, without changing the pattern of the
offices or relationships. Politically, it means that a rebellion changes
the king, but does not affect the kingship – nay, may even
strengthen the kingship, against a tyrant who has broken its norms.
Secondly, it means that the territorial sections of a kingdom
struggle against the central power and each other, without dis-
rupting the central authority. The point in the above quotation
which I wish to emphasize is the statement that 'the nation was
stable as its component sections were hostile' to one another.
In this essay I propose to apply this theory to a certain minimum
of facts I have about Bemba political structure. Evans-Pritchard
has analysed these segmentary tendencies in the political systems
of two tribes without a centralized national organization: the Nuer
and the Anuak.[4] Fortes has also dealt with the segmentary tendencies in the Tallensi system, which also is not nationally
organized. I must emphasize that they show that the segmentary
tendency does not mean that the system is characterized by
continual division only. Thus Evans-Pritchard:

A [Nuer] tribe is an exemplification of a segmentary tendency which
is characteristic of the political structure as a whole. The reason why we
speak of Nuer political groups, and of the tribe in particular, as relative
groups and state that they are not easily described in terms of political
morphology, is that political relations are dynamic. They are always
changing in one direction or another. The most evident movement is
towards fission. The tendency of tribes and tribal sections towards
fission and internal opposition between their parts is balanced by a
tendency in the direction of fusion, of the combination or amalgamation
of groups. This tendency towards fusion is inherent in the segmentary
character of Nuer political structure, for, although any group tends to
split into opposed parts, these parts tend to fuse in relation to other
groups. Here fission and fusion are two aspects of the same segmentary
principle and the Nuer tribe and its divisions are to be understood as a
relation between these two contradictory, yet complementary, tendencies.
Physical environment, way of livelihood, mode of distribution, poor
communications, simple economy, etc., to some extent explain the
incidence of political cleavage, but the tendency towards segmentation
seems to be inherent in political structure itself.[5]

On the Anuak he says:

There are two types of Anuak political system. In the one type, there
are isolated villages ruled by headmen with no superior political head

over them. The headmanships are restricted to members of a certain lineage whose fathers held the posts before them. Cleavages within a village community operate through ostracism of a headman and the practice prevents despotism while preserving intact the prestige of the headmanship. In the other Anuak type, the villages are not exclusive as in the first. All the villages in the eastern type recognize a single king and the noble rulers of the different villages all belong to the same clan and can therefore be substituted for one another in any village of the area. . . . All the villages . . . have a common interest in the kingship, and it is this common interest which relates them to one another in a political organization.

. . . We may speak of an inter-village organization with the emblems [of kingship] as its integrative element. The villages are politically independent, but they are not, as in the west, politically isolated. They participate in a polity, a kind of inter-village league. Fighting between villages [for the emblems to make their own noble, king] has not the sole effect of maintaining their exclusiveness in relation to one another, but has also the effect of maintaining the organization as a whole. The struggle for the emblems enhances their prestige, and, since the emblems represent the unity of the organization, it serves to preserve this unity.[2]

Fortes says of the Tallensi:

Jural notions and procedures are in conformity with the elaborately segmented character of the social structure. As there was formerly no completely dominant social unit or association, there could be no constituted legal machinery backed by irresistible force. Every region of Tale society, from the joint family to the whole vaguely delimited aggregate known as the Tallensi, exhibits a dynamic equilibrium of like units balanced against one another, of counterpoised ties and cleavages, of complementary institutions and ideological notions. . . . Tension is implicit in the equilibrium. It might explode violently when the specific interests of a unit were violated. But conflict could never develop to the point of bringing about complete disintegration.

Fortes cites various

factors restricting conflict and promoting the restoration of equilibrium . . . Social relationships fluctuate between unity and discord, co-operation and conflict, for forces engendering both are always active; but in the long run an equilibrium is maintained. The political system of the Tallensi hinges on this principle.[7]

Unfortunately, Evans-Pritchard has not yet published his analysis of the political system of the highly organized Azande.

Most writers on highly organized societies recognize the existence of cleavages in the political system, but I do not consider that they sufficiently appreciate that in this type of political system, in indigenous Africa, the cleavages are an aspect of the integration of the political system. I have stressed this in my study of the Zulu, cited above, and Nadel has emphasized it in a study of the Nupe of Nigeria, where succession to the Emirate passes between three dynasties of the royal family.[8] Recently, when I was requested to look over certain data on the Bemba kingship, I was struck with certain anomalies in the data presented to me, which I considered could best be explained by applying the theory of cleavages – co-operation, of the segmentary principle of fission-fusion. By applying this theory to the facts presented to me, I was able to state that I was certain that in parts of Bemba history on which I had no data, certain recurrent facts would be found. It therefore occurred to me that it would be an interesting test of the theory to set out clearly the manner in which I applied the theory to the facts I have, before testing it on the facts not yet known to me.

The facts available were in Richards' essay on 'The Political System of the Bemba Tribe' in *African Political Systems*, and in a manuscript on *The Succession of Bemba Chiefs* by Vernon Brelsford (District Officer) which I was shown by the Secretary for Native Affairs, Northern Rhodesia Government. It is shortly to be published.[9] Mr Brelsford has sent me some additional notes but I must stress that neither of these writers was concerned with the problem I am setting here, and I am dependent entirely on the data they supply. I begin by setting out the basic points in the data available, and then apply the theory set out above, to them. A major interest in this exercise is that the theory is applied for the first time to an African political system based on matrilineal succession. Nuer, Tallensi, Nupe, Zulu, and others about whom the point has been made before are all patrilineal.

I first set out briefly the history of Bemba chieftainship through the reigns of the last eight kings. Most of the material is shown in the genealogical table (after Brelsford, but cf. Richards in *African Political Systems*, p. 102).* Then I draw the deductions from facts on the basis of the general theory.

* Females in italics; chieftainships in small capitals; which chieftainships held by women in small capitals preceded by a star (*); numbers A1, etc., refer to genealogical chart.

Bemba laws of succession to the kingship and their organization into chieftainships may be summed up as:

(1) the nation is divided into a number of chieftainships on a territorial basis, under a king who himself rules a large area;

(2) the title of the kingship (CITIMUKULU) is inherited by each king, as are the titles of the subordinate chieftainships (MWAMBA, NKULA, NKOLEMFUMU, MPEPO, CHIKWANDA, CEWE, SHIMUMBI);

(3) the king and these chiefs are all members of one matrilineal clan, and succession to the kingship and these chieftainships pass through a generation of brothers by one mother, and then to their 'brothers' (in Bemba terminology) by their mother's next senior sister, after which it drops to their nephews by their own sisters in order of genealogical seniority of the sisters; after passing through the sons of two or three sisters succession again drops a generation to the uterine nephew by the most senior sister;

(4) men thus pass from one chieftainship to another on their way to the throne, but the actual chieftainship held is irrelevant to the right to succeed to the kingship: what counts is genealogical seniority;

(5) there are a number of chieftainships held by sons of chiefs, to which succession is by the sons of the senior male of the royal family;

(6) in addition to these chieftainships, there are two important female chiefs' titles (*CANDAMUKULU and *MUKUKAMFUMU) which are said to give the right to bear kings; succession to these is from sister to sister and then to uterine granddaughter, but failing a granddaughter, a daughter may be appointed.

2

About the year 1850 the king of Bembaland was Cimbola (A7), whose mother held the title *CANDAMUKULU. One of his senior chiefs [title ?] was Cileshe (A2), who ruled in a part of the country where he got much ivory. His mother held the title *MUKUKAM-FUMU. I do not know what the genealogical connection between Cimbola and Cileshe was. The people of Cimbola (A7) envied those of Cileshe (A2) their chief's wealth in ivory, and they informed Cileshe that if he attacked the king, they would shoot fake arrows at him. He attacked, drove out Cimbola, and took the title of CITIMUKULU ('I' in this lineage). Later he recalled Cimbola and gave him a chieftainship, principally with ritual status, with the title CHIMBOLA. He changed the title of Cimbola's mother from CANDAMUKULU to CANDAWEYAYA so that it would be clear that she could not bear a king. We are told that he gave the title of *CAN-DAMUKULU to his mother (previously *MUKUKAMFUMU), but on the table *CANDAMUKULU I is shown as his elder sister, *Cilufya* (A1).

I do not know at present whether other relatives of Cimbola (A7), closer to him than Cileshe (A2), had held the other big subordinate chieftainships, but Cileshe presumably appointed his full-brother, next to him, Citundu (A3), to the big MWAMBAship. Assuming that his next brother, Kalulu (A5), was dead, Cileshe seems to have passed over Bwembya (A6) for a chieftainship, though Bwembya became king as CITIMUKULU II. Bwembya was almost dumb and a fool. Since succession passes from brother to brother, Citundu (A3) must have died as MWAMBA I, before his brother CITIMUKULU I Cileshe (A2) died. Again, Bwembya (A6) was passed over, and the MWAMBAship dropped to the senior nephew, Kapalaula (B3).

For the female titles, I gather from the table that CITIMUKULU I's (A2) mother retained the title *MUKUKAMFUMU, and the title *CANDAMUKULU was given to his older sister, *Cilufya* (A1). I assume that the second sister, *Kanyanta* (A4), in this generation died before her sister *Cilufya* (A1) for she did not get the title *CANDAMUKULU. This passed according to the rule stated to *Cilufya*'s (A1) eldest own uterine granddaughter, *Kangwa Conya* (C4), while the *MUKUKAMFUMUship passed to the eldest (presumably surviving) uterine granddaughter of Cileshe's (A1) mother, *MUKUKAMFUMU I, i.e. to *Kasonde* (B2).

When CITIMUKULU I (A2) died he was succeeded by his presumably eldest surviving brother Bwembya (A6), as CITIMUKULU II, despite his handicaps, 'probably because of [the paramountcy's] spiritual importance', though he had been passed over for MWAMBA.

Reign of CITIMUKULU III (B4)

Citapankwa (B4), a wild fighting fellow, drove out the deficient Bwembya and seized the throne as CITIMUKULU III, so that his elder brother Kapalaula (B3) MWAMBA II did not succeed. Citapankwa created the title NKULA for his younger brother, Sampa (B6). When

Kapalaula (B3) MWAMBA II died, his classificatory brother Cimf-wembe (B7) did not succeed, but instead his eldest living nephew, Mubanga (C2). But it is possible that Kapalaula (B3) died after CITIMUKULU III (B4) and IV (B6) and if a man has been passed over he does not re-enter the lists, so that the succession was regular. It is possible that *MUKUKAMFUMU II, *Kasonde* (B2), may have died in this reign. Presumably she died after her sister, *Nakasafya* (B5), who should otherwise have become *MUKUKAMFUMU after her elder sister *Kasonde*. For some reason the *MUKUKAMFUMUship then did not pass to a granddaughter, but went to the younger sister's eldest daughter, *Mwendecanda* (C8), who became *MUKUKAMFUMU III.

When CITIMUKULU III (B4) died he was regularly succeeded by his next brother, Sampa (B6), as king CITIMUKULU IV. This meant that Sampa abandoned the title NKULA, but for some reason this did not pass to the next senior male, Cimfwembe (B7), but dropped a generation to Mutale (C3), who became NKULA II. As we have seen, Mutale's elder brother (Mubanga, C2) may already have been appointed MWAMBA III, the eldest brother (Canda C1) presumably being already dead.

Reign of CITIMUKULU IV (B6):

When CITIMUKULU IV (B6) died, he was correctly succeeded by his collateral brother (B7) to be CITIMUKULU V, though he had no title before. Note that as there were no daughters among this man's siblings, and his younger brother (Mulenga, B8) was pre-sumably already dead, this house ends with CITIMUKULU V.

Reign of CITIMUKULU V:

This reign brought varied fortunes to the royal family. Mutale (C3) NKULA II seems to have died first (though Richards shows him as MWAMBA IV – but she also shows Kanyanta (D1) as MWAMBA IV). If NKULA II thus died first, he was correctly succeeded by Cikwanda (C6) as NKULA III, since this man was the eldest son of the second senior sister in the preceding generation. CIKWANDA seems to be a title as well as a name, and the holder ruled at Mpika. NKULA III (C6) hankered for the salt-licks of Mpika, so he gave up the NKULA-ship and returned to the CIKWANDAship. But while he was NKULA, Mubanga (C2) who was MWAMBA III had died. Cikwanda (C6) NKULA III refused the MWAMBAship, since the two titles are almost equal, and his younger brother Ponde (C10) was then entitled to the MWAMBAship, since their three other brothers had died violent deaths previously. But the other house accused Ponde of killing the recently deceased MWAMBA (C2). The Administration was called in, Ponde resisted, and was banished. Therefore the title MWAMBA dropped to the senior nephew, Kanyanta (D1), who rose from NKOLEMFUMU to be MWAMBA IV and was succeeded as NKOLEMFUMU by his younger brother (name ? – D3). Presumably Luatila (D2) was already dead. These men were sons of the senior woman in generation C, *Kangwa* *CANDAMUKULU II (C4). When Cikwanda (C6) gave up the NKULAship, his brother Ponde (C10) refused it though he had reinstated himself in the nation; it is said that he had more power behind the throne of CITIMUKULU V (B7) whose favourite he was. By doing this he did not lose his right to the kingship, because for succession to that it is irrelevant what title was held before, or if none was held. Ponde (C10) had sufficient sway with CITIMUKULU V (B7), to wrench the succession to the NKULAship from the then NKOLEMFUMU III (D3), who was the next senior nephew, and to get appointed as NKULA IV his nephew (Bwalya, D12) by his own full-sister *Mwendecanda* (C8) *MUKU-KAMFUMU III.

On the death of CITIMUKULU V (B7), since none of the sons of the senior sister *Kasonde* (B2) were still alive, the eldest son of the second sister, *Nakasafya* (B5), who was Cikwanda (C6), though he had abandoned the NKULAship and refused the MWAMBAship, became king as CITIMUKULU VI. This was in 1911, and when he died in 1917 his brother Ponde (C10), who had refused the NKULAship, became CITIMUKULU VII. When he died in 1922, all the men of that generation were dead, and a dispute ensued about the succession.

The Appointment of CITIMUKULU VIII:

The two claimants for the kingship were Kanyanta (D1) MWAMBA IV and Bwalya (D12) NKULA IV. Kanyanta's argument was that he was the senior son of the senior sister in the preceding generation, and there is a suggestion that his side argued that the holder of the MWAMBAship always became king. Bwalya countered that the succession of CITIMUKULU V (B7), CITIMUKULU VI (C6), and CITIMUKULU VII (C10) had shifted the paramountcy into the house of *Nakasafya* (B5). Bwalya (D12) seems to have been the stronger man, and possibly in the old days there would have been war. Government enquired into the succession, and appointed Kanyanta (D1) as CITIMUKULU VIII, in 1924.

Reign of CITIMUKULU VIII (D1):

CITIMUKULU VIII thus left the MWAMBAship, and was succeeded as MWAMBA by his next brother living (D3), who left the NKOLEM-FUMUship to become MWAMBA V. Their youngest full-brother Mbonkali (D5) left the MPEPOship to become NKOLEMFUMU IV, and the MPEPOship passed to the eldest son of their mother's next full-sister, *Cimbabantu* (C5), who at some time unspecified had correctly succeeded her sister *Kangwa* (C4) to become *CANDAMUKULU III. When Mbonkali (D5) died in 1942 while holding the NKOLEMFUMU-ship, Musenga (D6), who had been MPEPO, became NKOLEMFUMU V and his younger brother Mutale (D10) became MPEPO.

Meanwhile, in the other house of *Nakasafya* (B5), NKULA IV (D12) had died in 1934. His house was successful in asserting a prerogative claim to fill the NKULAship, for the house of *Kasonde* (B2) which was holding the kingship and the MWAMBAship does not seem to have disputed the succession: the next brother to the dead NKULA, in that house, Musungu (D14) became NKULA V. This house also seems to have established its right to the CIKWANDAship and the SHIMUMBIship. Presumably the family was too strongly entrenched in the NKULA area for the CITIMUKULU VIII (D1) to try to put in one of his closer relatives, for by genealogical descent, Mbonkali (D5), then still alive, was senior to Musungu (D14); or else the Ponde's (C10) intrigue in getting his own nephew made NKULA IV (i.e. D12) cast the senior branch out of the NKULA succession.

Meanwhile, *Mwendecanda* (C8) *MUKUKAMFUMU III died in 1930, and she was succeeded by the eldest daughter of her eldest daughter, viz. by *Nkumbula* (E10) who became *MUKUKAMFUMU IV. This was a perfectly regular succession, but there is some confusion since, probably to join her mother's brother, *MUKUKAMFUMU III (C8) left her site in Kasama and went to Chinsali. Her daughter *Nankumbula* (D13) followed her, and there is some story of CITIMUKULU VIII's attempting to make a very junior female in the other house, viz. Sampa (D22), into MUKUKAMFUMU IV. He failed to do so.

Cimbabantu (C5) *CANDAMUKULU III died in 1937, and as the only (grown ?) granddaughter was mad, she was succeeded by her eldest

94

daughter *Cawili* (D7) as *CANDAMUKULU IV, since *Cilufya* (D4), the eldest daughter in that house by the older sister (C4), was presumably already dead.

Death of CITIMUKULU VIII (D1) *and the Succession Problem:*

Government recognized Kanyanta's (D1) right to become CITIMUKULU VIII before Bwalya's (D12) on the grounds that he was the senior son of the senior sister in the preceding generation, and this is borne out by the formulations of the law of succession given to Brelsford and Richards, and by the actual succession within this lineage. The senior living son of the senior woman in the preceding generation has succeeded regularly to the kingship, though succession to the other big chieftainships, MWAMBA and NKULA, has been far from regular. CITIMUKULU VIII (D1) died in 1943, and on this rule the succession should pass to his next brother MWAMBA V (D3), who however is old and unlikely to take it.* The next brother Mbonkali (D5) died in 1942, so there is now a dispute between the sons of *CANDAMUKULU III (C5) on the one hand, and NKULA V (D14) on the other, for the throne. *CANDAMUKULU III was seized by the Ngoni and the father of her sons was an Ngoni. *Mwendecanda* (C8) *MUKUKAMFUMU III was probably older than *CANDAMUKULU III (C5), but there is no doubt that legally the children of *CANDAMUKULU III have the superior claim. Therefore the NKULA V (D14) party is objecting to the succession of her sons on the grounds that they are not pure Bemba, since their father was an Ngoni. This is the position at present, and again there is little doubt that were it not for the presence of the Government, war would have decided the matter.

3

In addition to these chieftainships inherited matrilineally there are a number of chieftainships which are succeeded to by chiefs' sons. The most important is the MAKASAship, for MAKASA plays a dominant role in the inheritance ceremonies of the CITIMUKULU. Others are MPOROKOSO, MUBANGA, MISENGO. In the election of men to these posts, genealogical seniority should count, but there is a

---

* He did take the kingship, but died within the year. NKULA V (D14) succeeded him with Government support, not Musenga (D6), who had become MWAMBA VI! – later note.

constant struggle by important chiefs to get their own sons in, and while this is greatest between the two branches of the lineage, it also occurs within these branches.

4

The problem of the relative status of the *CANDAMUKULU and *MUKUKAMFUMU titles is complicated. Richards (at p. 93) definitely states that 'the mother of the paramount is highly honoured, succeeds to a fixed title – the *CANDAMUKULU – takes part in tribal councils, and has several villages of her own'. Outside of the table (at p. 103) she does not mention the title *MUKUKAMFUMU at all. Her implication that the woman becomes *CANDAMUKULU after her son becomes king is not borne out by the facts; nor is it correct if she means that only a woman who had the title *CANDAMUKULU could bear a king; for both *Kanyanta Bwalya Cabula* (A4) and *Nakasafya* (B5) bore kings without recorded titles, and there is little doubt that if the sons of *Kasonde* (B2) *MUKUKAMFUMU II had lived they would have become king.

On the other hand, Brelsford says that the titles *CANDAMUKULU and *MUKUKAMFUMU are equal in status; there is therefore no promotion from one to the other, for that would be pointless. Both titles carry the right to bear kings (or, as we have seen, no title may be held by the mother of a king, who possibly has died before her turn to succeed comes). Brelsford states, presumably on Bemba authority, that the two senior sisters, *CANDAMUKULU and *MUKU- KAMFUMU, bear kings. Yet in fact *MUKUKAMFUMU III (C8) was already genealogically the third senior sister, with C4 and C5 above her on the table, and there are many women above *MUKUKAM- FUMU IV (E10). In fact, the rule that a uterine granddaughter, and not a daughter herself, should succeed to these female titles, is very significant, because it carries the possibility that daughters without these titles will have the right to bear kings and chiefs before the granddaughters who have the titles, as *Nakasafya* (B5) did before her daughter *MUKUKAMFUMU III (C8). I shall revert again to this confusion in the female descent principles, for in this matrilineal nation it is the crux of the problem.

The three major chieftainships are the CITIMUKULUship, the MWAMBAship, and the NKULAship. Both writers agree that the

MWAMBA and the NKULA are almost equal in temporal, though not in ritual, status with the CITIMUKULU. Thus Richards writes:

Naturally the ritual and political organization of the paramount's capital is more elaborate than that of his inferiors, but even the smallest sub-chief maintains his miniature court and tries to ape the state of those above him, while the bigger territorial chiefs sometimes rivalled the power of the Citimukulu in the old days.

Brelsford says that MWAMBA and NKULA are almost equal in temporal power with the CITIMUKULU, but ritually he is their superior.

5

The lessons of the last eight reigns may be summed up thus:

(1) The CITIMUKULUship has passed regularly according to the rules of succession, from brother to brother in a genealogical generation; and when that horizontal line was exhausted it dropped to the oldest nephew of the senior woman in that generation; and when her sons were exhausted, it passed to the sons of the woman nearest in seniority to her. After that it has dropped another generation, for in this lineage there were not more than two productive full or classificatory sisters in one generation, until the third (C), that which has produced rival claimants to the throne. There is but one exception to this rule of succession to the CITIMUKULU-ship, when Citapankwa (B4) seized it out of turn, but no man has been passed over, even on the grounds of incapacity – not even the fool Bwembya (A6). Those on the table who might have succeeded and did not, had all died before their turn came, except Kapalaula (B3). It is quite clear that the title held by a man previously was irrelevant, for many succeeded without having held a previous title.[10] There is therefore no doubt that the order of succession should now be: The present MWAMBA (D3), then the present NKOLEMFUMU (D6), then the present MPEPO (D10). This is assuming that the fact that they are half-Ngoni does not count legally, though it is important politically. Brelsford and Richards both stress that it is only the womb from which a man comes that counts for his rights to succeed, and his father is irrelevant. Richards implies that even illegitimacy would not bar a man's claim.

Has NKULA V (D14) any claim? Brelsford says 'yes', for he

speaks of his mother *Mwendecanda* (C8) *MUKUKAMFUMU III as the second senior sister, when in fact she is third senior sister, if it is the genealogical position, and not date of birth, of the woman that counts. To this point we shall return later. However, even if NKULA V (D14) has no legal claim, in practice he has a strong one. I must repeat that the problem of the third sister's sons has not arisen before in this lineage; Brelsford says there have been many third senior sisters in other royal lineages in the past and their sons have never succeeded.

(2) Though the CITIMUKULUship has thus gone regularly, the MWAMBAship and NKULAship have not. Most of the irregularities in generations C and D are explained by the machinations of Ponde (C10) and his elder brother Cikwanda's (C6) liking for salt. A6 was passed over deliberately; B4 seized the kingship before he was due to be a chief. It is not clear why B7 held no chieftainship. After generation B the MWAMBAship seems to have run regularly. On the death of Mubanga (C2) MWAMBA III, it was offered to his next oldest 'brother', Cikwanda (C6), who was then NKULA, but he refused the MWAMBAship as NKULA is equal to MWAMBA. His next brother Ponde (C10) tried to get the MWAMBAship, and had entered the MWAMBA country to take it, but was rejected by the other branch of the family on the grounds that he had killed the late MWAMBA (C2) by witchcraft. Therefore it dropped to the oldest nephew, Kanyanta (D1), and from him it went to his younger brother. The same may be said of the NKULAship, once it had passed from the senior branch of C generation to the junior branch when Ponde (C10) got his own nephew appointed instead of his classificatory nephew, D3. Since then it seems accepted that the NKULAship runs in the junior line.

6

The crux of the succession is the status of the royal women, and this gives the territorial cleavage a particular form. Richards and Brelsford are agreed that succession is to the sons of the senior woman in any generation, but while Richards says that the mother of the Paramount becomes *CANDAMUKULU, Brelsford definitely states: 'whether the line passes through only the two elder sisters, Candamukulu and Mukukamfumu, or whether also through any third sister is a point which will be discussed later' – when he says it does not. But he clearly implies that the two senior (not necessarily elder) sisters hold the titles *CANDAMUKULU and *MUKUKAMFUMU, though in fact *MUKUKAMFUMU III (C8) is already a 'third' sister, and *MUKUKAMFUMU IV has six classificatory sisters genealogically senior to her.

I believe that the statements on this point made by Richards and Brelsford are correct recordings of statements of Bemba law, and that the inconsistency between them is the symbol of the line of Bemba political cleavage. There is a definite conflict arising out of three rules rooted in the Bemba matrilineal succession:

(1) The succession through brothers, full and classificatory, born of a group of sisters, in order of genealogical seniority, to a number of chieftainships of ascending status up to the kingship;

(2) the succession to the titles of chieftainesses through full-sisters and then to uterine granddaughters; and

(3) the titles *CANDAMUKULU and *MUKUKAMFUMU carry the right to bear the king.

To these rules, we must add the fact that MWAMBA and NKULA have the power to influence the succession.

If we examine the table, we can see at once how the inconsistency between Richards' and Brelsford's statements arises.

When Cileshe (A2) seized the kingship, he gave the two titles *MUKUKAMFUMU and *CANDAMUKULU to his mother and elder sister and they were inherited according to rule. The *MUKUKAMFUMU-ship dropped from Cileshe's mother to her senior uterine granddaughter, Kasonde (B2). When *CANDAMUKULU I (A1) died, presumably her sister Kanyanta Bwalya (A4) was already dead, so the title skipped a generation according to rule and was taken by her senior uterine granddaughter, Kangwa (C4). If we return to the *MUKUKAMFUMUship, I think we may safely assume* that Nakasafya (B5) died before her elder sister Kasonde (B2) *MUKUKAMFUMU II or she would have inherited the title; and the title could not pass to classificatory sisters in the line of Kanyanta (A4) for she had no daughter. The title then did not pass to an own daughter of *MUKUKAMFUMU II (B2) (say Cimbabantu, who later became *CANDAMUKULU III (C5), but query was she at the time in the hands of the Ngoni by whom she had been captured and not yet re-

* Later I was told that this was correct.

leased?)*. It passed to the daughter of *Nakasafya* (B5) who would have succeeded if she had still been alive, and *Mwendecanda* (C8) became *MUKUKAMFUMU III. My theoretical reconstruction is difficult because I do not know whether C5 did not succeed because she was held by Ngoni (Brelsford, to a letter, said 'yes'), but it seems clear that if *Nakasafya* (B5) had become *MUKUKAMFUMU the title would then have passed to her own granddaughter through *Mwendecanda* (C8); and I assume that if there had been a daughter by Kanyanta (A4) she would have become *MUKUKAMFUMU and been succeeded by her own granddaughter, and the process by which the *MUKUKAMFUMUship drifts away from the main line would have been accelerated. This drift away of the title is clear in the next generation: when *CANDAMUKULU II (C4) died, her own sister (C5) succeeded her. Note that on C5's death, the title did not pass to women in the other line (of *Nakasafya*, B5) in that generation (i.e. to C8 or C11), but went to the late holder's daughter, *Cabili* (D7), since the granddaughter was mad. This may mean that if there had been daughters of *Kanyanta* (A4) they would not have got the title *MUKUKAMFUMU as I suggested above.

When *MUKUKAMFUMU III (C8) died, the title passed to her own eldest uterine granddaughter, *Nkumbula* (E10), who became *MUKUKAMFUMU IV, and not the senior classificatory granddaughters, who are presumably E – 2, 4, 5, 6, 7, 9.

Thus it is clear that the *MUKUKAMFUMU title (and theoretically it could have been the *CANDAMUKULUship) must sooner or later drift away from the main line, and the holder of it lose the right to bear a king under the rule that succession is to the sons of the senior woman. Thus when Brelsford says (and presumably was told) that the *CANDAMUKULU and *MUKUKAMFUMU bear kings, this was true in the earlier generations, but ceases to be true in the later ones; and when Richards says that the mother of the Paramount is always the *CANDAMUKULU this is not true of the earlier generations, but becomes increasingly true later: for when the sons of *CANDAMUKULU II and III (C4 and 5) have died, since *MUKUKAMFUMU III (C8) was only the third sister, the succession should have dropped to the sons of *CANDAMUKULU IV (D7). But if according to the rule the mad granddaughter had succeeded, and not the daughter, then even the title *CANDAMUKULU, though it would still have carried the right to bear a king, would have had that right

* Later I was told that this was correct.

postponed; for the sons of her mother would have had prior rights to her own children.

What is probable is that the statement that the mother of the king is always *CANDAMUKULU is stressed by the house that carries that title; while the rights of both titles to bear kings would be stressed by the other house into which the title *MUKUKAMFUMU has passed.

Clearly, in these rules of succession to the female titles, since they are quite different from the rules of succession to the male titles, lies the source of conflict.

7

But there is a further drift away from the main line. I have assumed on the evidence of the chart, that when Cileshe (A2) seized the kingship, he expelled the closer relatives of his predecessor from the big territorial chieftainships, and placed there his own close relatives. Despite the passing over for chief's office of his own brother Bwembya (A6) who became CITIMUKULU II, all the big titles were held by men who clearly had the right of succession to the kingship. That is, in the general round of promotion which marks any succession, i.e. in the sense that the former second in the line of succession becomes now the first, and the former third now second, people moved steadily nearer to the kingship; and Cikwanda (C6) could even refuse the MWAMBAship and abandon the NKULAship without losing the right to become king. Then Ponde (C 10) was accused of refusing the NKOLEMFUMUship and trying to hasten the passing of the MWAMBAship to his line by killing by witchcraft the MWAMBA III (C2), and the MWAMBAship dropped into the fourth generation of the senior house, where there are already so many sons that the junior house is unlikely to attain the MWAMBAship, in that generation or the next. Meantime Ponde (C10) in revenge succeeded in wrenching the NKULAship into his own house, while he himself refused it, and it is now accepted that the NKULAship runs there, for no one in the senior house opposed B14's claims to succeed B12. But Brelsford says that NKULA V (D14) could still claim the MWAMBAship and though he would probably have refused it in the old days he might take it today since MWAMBA's salary is much higher than NKULA's.

Even if NKULA V (D14), the son of a third senior sister, were considered to have a claim to the throne after the sons of the two senior 'sisters' of his mother (neglecting the structurally irrelevant fact that the husband of the second sister was an Ngoni), if the succession to NKULAship continued in the junior line, clearly the holder of the NKULAship in the future will, under the rule of succession by the sons of senior sisters, cease to have the right to participate in the general promotion towards the kingship. That is, with the female *MUKUKAMFUMUship a major male chieftainship, the NKULAship, with minor chieftainships CIKWANDA, CEWE, and SHIMUMBI, has drifted away from the main line of legal succession to the kingship.

Again, theoretically, I can see no reason why it should not have been the MWAMBAship that drifted away from the main line, while the NKULAship remained; but the important point is that one female chieftainship *had*, under the rules of succession, to drift away, and one major male chieftainship has drifted with it. I cannot say if this was inevitable by the rules of succession, but it seems to me that it was bound to happen as soon as the junior branch, holding a big chieftainship, began to drift out of the line of general promotion to the kingship.

We are now in a position to apply the general theory set out in the introduction to the facts of Bemba succession. I must stress that I do not want to postulate a teleological argument; I am analysing the facts of Bemba history and their effect on the internal organization of the nation.

The first important fact to emphasize is the great temporal power of MWAMBA and NKULA; they are almost equal to CITIMUKULU, the king, though he is ritually superior. Why did these big territorial chiefs not assert their independence of the king and establish independent kingdoms? Because they too were heirs to the kingship in the early stages of the lineage's hold of the kingship and chieftainships. Then NKULA IV (D12), by one legal rule, asserted his claim to the paramountcy, though by another (that the sons of the third sister have no claim), he had lost it. He said that the succession of B5 *Nakasafya's* sons, C6 and C10, had shifted the descent. He lost. His younger brother NKULA V (D14) now asserts his claims above those of Musenga (D6) and Mutale (D10) on the grounds that the latter are half-Ngoni. Could he use the argument that his mother was a *MUKUKAMFUMU (C8)? Will the sons of *MUKUKAMFUMU IV (E10) claim the right on this latter ground, though she has 6 senior sisters to bear kings before her in her generation? My only piece of field research was to get Lady Gore-Browne to ask a Bemba (a supporter of NKULA V, D14) if *MUKUKAMFUMU IV (E10) had the right to bear kings. He replied, most significantly: 'No, she hasn't, but she doesn't know it.'

On contradictory legal grounds, each house asserts its claim to the kingship. In the old days this would have led to war; today it leads to a struggle for the Government's support. That is, NKULA V's (D14) family does not assert its independence of the king; it struggles to win the kingship for itself, by asserting a claim, which has some legal foundation, since the rules of succession denote several possible heirs.

Thus Richards says (*African Political Systems*, p. 100):

In most types of succession whether to the name and spirit of a dead man or to his office, there are usually two or three potential heirs, and although there are certain rules of priority, it is practically never the case that there is one child known as heir to the chieftainship from birth and brought up as such, as occurs in those South African tribes in which the eldest son of the great wife must always succeed. A Bemba chief, or commoner, is succeeded by his brothers in order of age, next by his sister's children, and failing them, by his maternal grandsons. Difficulties arise when there is a choice between an older classificatory 'brother' not a sibling, but possibly a mother's sister's son, or an even more distant 'brother' still, and a young man, a maternal nephew who is the child of the deceased's own sister, with whom . . . his ties are very close. Here the principles of primogeniture conflict with that of propinquity of kinship, in the case of a branch of a family that has been in existence for three or four generations, and it is probable that in these cases the nearest heir is appointed unless he is manifestly unsuitable, when the more distant 'brother' or 'maternal nephew' is selected. I never heard of a regent being appointed for a young man as is commonly done in those Bantu tribes where the heir to the throne is known from his time of birth.

We can thus say: in the history of this particular royal lineage at first the big territorial chieftainships were all held by a limited number of close relatives; within the first three generations there was no dispute about who was the rightful heir to the kingship, though there were irregularities in the succession to, and struggles for, the big chieftainships. When it became time for an heir to be taken from the fourth generation (D), there was a dispute between the senior men in two branches, and Government had to settle this matter. This dispute continues, and the junior line is now advancing its claim on different legal grounds from those it used before. Meantime, for some years the two branches have struggled for the minor chieftainships, especially those of chiefs' sons.

The tendency of the Bemba territorial chieftainships to separatism is here canalized in a struggle to make the chief into the king. At the beginning of the rule of a new lineage, the chiefs are close relatives of the king and in the direct legal line of succession to the kingship. Within three or four generations one junior branch, holding a couple of powerful chieftainships, and one chieftainess title, drifts away from the main line, and loses the legal right of succession, by genealogical position, to the kingship. They then assert that they have the right – on one or other alternative 'legal' ground – and are prepared to fight for the throne with their people's support. If the senior branch wins, presumably it would depose the junior branch from all its seats of power; if the junior branch wins, the senior man in it presumably becomes king and gives his close relatives the big subordinate posts. All the main seats of power are now again held by one small family, and all the sub-chiefs are again in the direct line of succession to the throne. I am prepared to assert that the process now begins again as a repetitive cycle in Bemba history. In terms of the general theory set out above, it seems to me that in this process the territorial sections do not assert their independence of the king and try to establish a second Bemba kingdom, but they struggle to keep or to get the kingship for their head; that is, the separatist tendency is canalized into a struggle to make the head of the territorial section king. Then in the fight for the kingship, every few generations, a civil war unites the nation and does not divide it, since it returns all the chieftainships into one small family, all of whom have rights to the kingship. It is this process which lies beneath what we see as a dynastic struggle for palace power. Thus we see that here, as Evans-Pritchard said of the Nuer,

the tendency of tribes and tribal sections towards fission and internal opposition between their parts is balanced by a tendency in the direction of fusion, of the combination or amalgamation of groups. . . . Here fission and fusion are two aspects of the same segmentary principle and the Nuer tribe and its divisions are to be understood as a relation between these two contradictory, yet complementary, tendencies . . . the tendency towards political cleavage seems to be inherent in political structure itself.

Among the Nuer, the fission and fusion of aspects the process show in the splitting and uniting of groups at various times; among the highly organized Bemba the fission aspect appears in the contradictory rules of succession and the drifting of the seats of power, while the fusion principle appears in the ritual superiority of the kingship (of CITIMUKULU) and the struggle of the subordinate chiefs to get the kingship.

If my postulated theory is correct, then certain facts would repeat themselves in Bemba history. On the data we have, the struggle came to a head in the fourth generation from the founder of this lineage, Cileshe (A2). If his younger sister, *Kanyanta* (A4), had had daughters it might have occurred a generation earlier. We are told that there are 25–32 kings remembered, and I suggest that investigation would show the following facts:

(1) That the usurper, Cileshe (A2), stood in the same relationship approximately to the deposed Cimbola (A7), as the present NKULA V (D14) stands to the late CITIMUKULU VIII (D1). Note that the mothers of both the younger usurper (Cileshe) and the would-be usurper (NKULA V) held the title *MUKUKAMFUMU, while the mothers of the reigning kings (Cimbola and CITIMUKULU VIII) both held the title *CANDAMUKULU. Further, I suggest that every three-four–five generations back in Bemba history there will be records of similar inter-familial struggles. It is irrelevant that the people of Cimbola, the deposed king, co-operated to let in the usurper, Cileshe, because the new value of ivory seems to have been an extraneous complicating factor.

(2) Further, these inter-familial struggles must have been based on a junior branch holding one powerful chieftainship and a female title, so this process too must have been recurrent.

(3) I suggest that it will be found that when Cileshe seized power he had to depose not only the king, Cimbola, but also relatives of Cimbola holding chieftainships who were more closely related to the king than he; and that he then made his own relatives into the big chiefs. This too I suggest has recurred throughout Bemba history, that whosoever won the inter-familial struggle concentrated the minor chieftainships in his own family. Once a man has done this, he need not fear his rival; we see that Cileshe actually brought

Cimbola back and created a new ritual chieftainship for him, and apparently changing Cimbola's mother's title from *CANDAMUKULU to *CANDAMWEYA was considered sufficient to do away with Cimbola's family claim to the throne. This fact in itself is strong argument for my general theory.

All the above facts are capable of confirmation, and I consider that if they are found to be as I have postulated, it is strong support for the general theory about African political systems which I have quoted above.

However, there is one point on which I am not clear and can say nothing. Theoretically the *CANDAMUKULUship should have dropped from C5 to her granddaughter, *Katongo* (E2). This would have kept the right to bear kings with the title, but postponed it far into the future.

8

If this is correct, what happens now? Government backs either NKOLEMFUMU (D6) or NKULA (D14): but whichever line it backs, it will probably leave the other branch retaining its own chieftainship so that the old process of re-integration of the royal chiefs does not occur. Then there may persist strain and jealousy, gradually increasing and culminating in a demand for independence by the junior branch. But if I am correct, whomsoever Government supports, it should support him wholeheartedly. That is, if the present NKOLEMFUMU (D6) is made CITIMUKULU, then on the death of NKULA V (D14) the NKULAship should pass to NKOLEMFUMU's line; and similarly if the NKOLEMFUMU is rejected for the CITIMUKULUship, he should also be rejected for the MWAMBAship. These changes should be made consistently till all the seats of power are again closely linked in one family. Of course, the practicability of doing this depends on how widely based is the power of the rejected man in the nation.

However, there are other possibilities. Government rule may so dominate the whole situation that the Bemba royal family is becoming comparatively insignificant, and the tendency to separation may have ceased to operate. At present it might not appear in modern administration, because NKULA V has a Native Authority and Treasury independent of the CITIMUKULU and MWAMBA. If this is so, it will not matter whom Government backs, for it will be

Government organization which binds the Bemba into a nation; and, assuming the present ruling line is supported, NKULA must accept their paramountcy because he, by Government appointment, is a subordinate official with them in Government's system.

However, it is clear that these possibilities, and the people's reactions, have to be examined before a proper decision can be made in full knowledge of all relevant facts. The academic theory, which I have tried to support, has great practical significance.

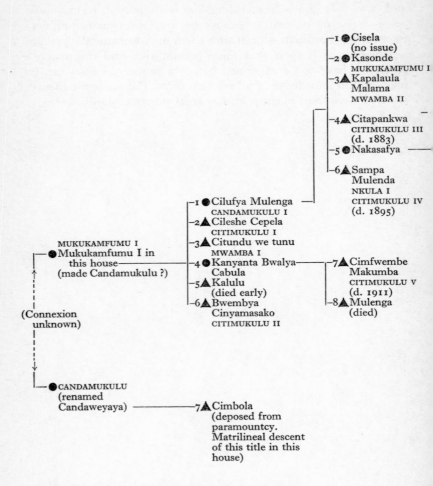

A   B

- 1 ● Cisela
  (no issue)
- 2 ● Kasonde
  MUKUKAMFUMU I
- 3 ▲ Kapalaula
  Malama
  MWAMBA II
- 4 ▲ Citapankwa
  CITIMUKULU III
  (d. 1883)
- 5 ● Nakasafya ——
- 6 ▲ Sampa
  Mulenda
  NKULA I
  CITIMUKULU IV
  (d. 1895)

- 1 ● Cilufya Mulenga ——
  CANDAMUKULU I
- 2 ▲ Cileshe Cepela
  CITIMUKULU I
- 3 ▲ Citundu we tunu
  MWAMBA I
- 4 ● Kanyanta Bwalya ——
  Cabula
- 5 ▲ Kalulu
  (died early)
- 6 ▲ Bwembya
  Cinyamasako
  CITIMUKULU II

MUKUKAMFUMU I
● Mukukamfumu I in
this house ——
(made Candamukulu ?)

↑
|
(Connexion
unknown)
|
|
↓

- 7 ▲ Cimfwembe
  Makumba
  CITIMUKULU V
  (d. 1911)
- 8 ▲ Mulenga
  (died)

—● CANDAMUKULU
(renamed
Candaweyaya) ——————— 7 ▲ Cimbola
(deposed from
paramountcy.
Matrilineal descent
of this title in this
house)

**Abbreviated tree of the present Bemba royal
house showing descent through the female
line. Chieftainships of the Paramount line in
capitals. Children of males not shown.**
(*After Brelsford, with points from Richards or from
text added in brackets and with question marks by
M. Gluckman.*)

**Pecked line runs between the two houses of
Kasonde (B2) and Nakasafya (B5).**

Seven descendants in the sixth generation are omitted for
lack of space: a daughter of E2; three sons of E10; a daughter
of E13; a daughter of E25; and a daughter of E28.

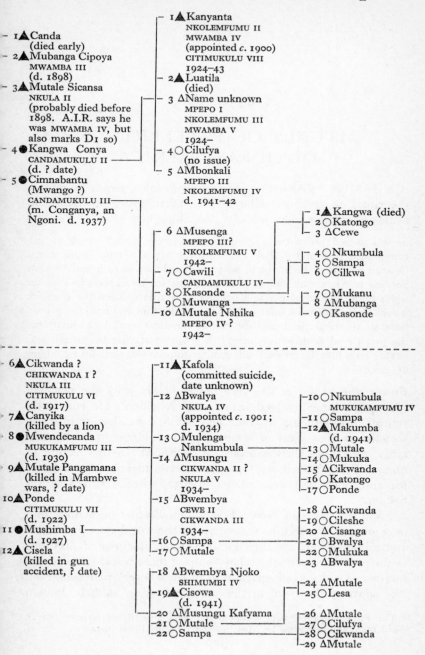

C   D   E

- 1 ▲ Canda
  (died early)
- 2 ▲ Mubanga Cipoya
  MWAMBA III
  (d. 1898)
- 3 ▲ Mutale Sicansa
  NKULA II
  (probably died before
  1898. A.I.R. says he
  was MWAMBA IV, but
  also marks D1 so)
- 4 ● Kangwa Conya
  CANDAMUKULU II
  (d. ? date)
- 5 ● Cimnabantu
  (Mwango ?)
  CANDAMUKULU III
  (m. Conganya, an
  Ngoni. d. 1937)

- 1 ▲ Kanyanta
  NKOLEMFUMU II
  MWAMBA IV
  (appointed c. 1900)
  CITIMUKULU VIII
  1924–43
- 2 ▲ Luatila
  (died)
- 3 Δ Name unknown
  MPEPO I
  NKOLEMFUMU III
  MWAMBA V
  1924–
- 4 ○ Cilufya
  (no issue)
- 5 Δ Mbonkali
  MPEPO III
  NKOLEMFUMU IV
  d. 1941–42

- 6 Δ Musenga
  MPEPO III?
  NKOLEMFUMU V
  1942–
- 7 ○ Cawili
  CANDAMUKULU IV
- 8 ○ Kasonde
- 9 ○ Muwanga
- 10 Δ Mutale Nshika
  MPEPO IV ?
  1942–

- 1 ▲ Kangwa (died)
- 2 ○ Katongo
- 3 Δ Cewe

- 4 ○ Nkumbula
- 5 ○ Sampa
- 6 ○ Cilkwa

- 7 ○ Mukanu
- 8 Δ Mubanga
- 9 ○ Kasonde

- 6 ▲ Cikwanda ?
  CHIKWANDA I ?
  NKULA III
  CITIMUKULU VI
  (d. 1917)
- 7 ▲ Canyika
  (killed by a lion)
- 8 ● Mwendecanda
  MUKUKAMFUMU III
  (d. 1930)
- 9 ▲ Mutale Pangamana
  (killed in Mambwe
  wars, ? date)
- 10 ▲ Ponde
  CITIMUKULU VII
  (d. 1922)
- 11 ● Mushimba I
  (d. 1927)
- 12 ▲ Cisela
  (killed in gun
  accident, ? date)

- 11 ▲ Kafola
  (committed suicide,
  date unknown)
- 12 Δ Bwalya
  NKULA IV
  (appointed c. 1901;
  d. 1934)
- 13 ○ Mulenga
  Nankumbula
- 14 Δ Musungu
  CIKWANDA II ?
  NKULA V
  1934–
- 15 Δ Bwembya
  CEWE II
  CIKWANDA III
  1934–
- 16 ○ Sampa
- 17 ○ Mutale

- 18 Δ Bwembya Njoko
  SHIMUMBI IV
- 19 ▲ Cisowa
  (d. 1941)
- 20 Δ Musungu Kafyama
- 21 ○ Mutale
- 22 ○ Sampa

- 10 ○ Nkumbula
  MUKUKAMFUMU IV
- 11 ○ Sampa
- 12 ▲ Makumba
  (d. 1941)
- 13 ○ Mutale
- 14 ○ Mukuka
- 15 Δ Cikwanda
- 16 ○ Katongo
- 17 ○ Ponde

- 18 Δ Cikwanda
- 19 ○ Cileshe
- 20 Δ Cisanga
- 21 ○ Bwalya
- 22 ○ Mukuka
- 23 Δ Bwalya

- 24 Δ Mutale
- 25 ○ Lesa

- 26 Δ Mutale
- 27 ○ Cilufya
- 28 ○ Cikwanda
- 29 Δ Mutale

Chapter Three

RITUALS OF REBELLION IN
SOUTH-EAST AFRICA*

SIR JAMES FRAZER'S *The Golden Bough* sets out to explain the ritual of the priest-king of the Italian grove of Nemi. He begins his monumental work by describing how

in this sacred grove there grew a certain tree round which at any time of the day, and probably far into the night, a grim figure might be seen to prowl. In his hand he carried a drawn sword, and he kept peering warily about him as if at every instant he expected to be set upon by an enemy. He was a priest and murderer; and the man for whom he looked was sooner or later to murder him and hold the priesthood in his stead. Such was the rule of the sanctuary. A candidate for the priesthood could only succeed to office by slaying the priest, and having slain him, he retained office till he himself was slain by a stronger or a craftier.

Frazer thus raised at the very outset of his work the problem of a priest-king involved in a 'ritual rebellion'. He constantly returns to this theme, as when he describes the election in many societies at New Year of temporary 'mock-kings' or 'scapegoat-kings' who were then banished or sacrificed. In this lecture to honour Frazer's memory I propose to consider in what manner his anthropological descendants interpret similar rituals of rebellion.

From the grove of Nemi, Frazer's intellectual quest took him on a journey in which he ranged across the world among peasants and primitive folk, and through time among the great civilizations of the past. He traced the relationship of these priest-kings with a number of widespread agricultural rituals whereby men conserved 'the spirit of the corn' in the last sheaf, or in animals, human

* The Frazer Lecture, 1952, delivered at the University of Glasgow on 28 April 1953; and published by Manchester University Press, 1954.

beings, or effigies. Sometimes they destroyed these to return the fertility to the soil before sowing. Frazer argued further that these customs lay at the heart of certain rituals, with their associated myths, of the ancient Mediterranean and Near East civilizations. These rituals and myths concern the story of a god, sometimes a deified mortal, who was slain or died, and then resurrected by the love of a goddess who was mother or wife to the dead, or enamoured of him. The best known of these pairs were Adonis and Aphrodite, Tammuz and Astarte, Osiris and Isis, Dionysus and Demeter, Persephone – she alone a daughter – and Demeter. Frazer summed up these myths:

[Men] now pictured to themselves the growth and decay of vegetation, the birth and death of living creatures, as effects of the waxing or waning strength of divine beings, of gods and goddesses, who were born and died, who married and begot children, on the pattern of human life. . . . Under the names of Osiris, Tammuz, Adonis and Attis, the peoples of Egypt and Western Asia represented the yearly decay and revival of life, especially vegetable life, which they personified as a god who annually died and rose again to life.[1]

In these myths Frazer saw men handling dramatically the dying and resurrection of vegetation with the change of the seasons. Typical of these myths is the tale of how the hero was slain by a wild boar or an enemy disguised as a wild boar. In Syria, the blood of wounded Tammuz, or Adonis, poured down the rivers to the sea, as those rivers in their spring spate carried red soil with them that discoloured the coastal waters. This is the ceremony to which Milton refers in his *Ode on the Morning of Christ's Nativity*:

In vain the Tyrian Maids their wounded Thamuz mourn.

Ceremonies were performed to aid the dying hero, and with him the vegetation.

Frazer undoubtedly oversimplified the problem.[2] But there is great value in his relation of the stories of the dying god both with widespread agricultural customs, and with customs connected with priest-kings. In this demonstration Frazer, like most of his contemporaries, was interested in the intellectual patterns which he believed must lie behind all these customs. The modern anthropologist, basing his analysis on detailed observation in the field, is concerned in greater detail with the ceremonial rôles of persons, categories of persons, and social groups, in relation to one another. Frazer could not have pursued these problems for he lacked the relevant evidence; and if I concentrate on a sociological analysis, it is not to deny the importance of Frazer's intellectualist analysis.

I shall therefore consider the social components of ceremonies, analogous to those which concerned Frazer, among the South-Eastern Bantu of Zululand, Swaziland, and Mozambique. Here there are (in some cases, were) performed, as elsewhere in Africa, national and local ceremonies at the break of the rains, sowing, first-fruits, and harvest. In one ceremony the idea of a goddess who is propitiated by the rites is clearly expressed; usually the ceremonies are directed to the ancestral spirits of the tribal chiefs or the kinship groups concerned. But whatever the ostensible purpose of the ceremonies, a most striking feature of their organization is the way in which they openly express social tensions: women have to assert licence and dominance as against their formal subordination to men, princes have to behave to the king as if they covet the throne, and subjects openly state their resentment of authority. Hence I call them rituals of rebellion. I shall argue that these ritual rebellions proceed within an established and sacred traditional system, in which there is dispute about particular distributions of power, and not about the structure of the system itself. This allows for instituted protest, and in complex ways renews the unity of the system.

2

The Zulu had no developed pantheon. Their ideas of the High God were vague and there was no ritual address to him. *Heaven* was believed to be responsible for certain devastating phenomena, such as lightning. It was controlled by special magicians. The only developed deity in their religion was *Nomkubulwana*, the Princess of Heaven, who was honoured by the women and girls of local districts in Zululand and Natal, when the crops had begun to grow. The performance of these agricultural rituals by women on a local scale contrasts with great national sowing and first-fruits rites, which were mainly the responsibility of men as warriors serving the king on whom the ritual centred.

The women no longer perform their ritual to honour the goddess *Nomkubulwana*, so I did not observe it during my own work in Zululand.[3] But the goddess herself still visits that pleasant land.

She moves in the mists which mark the end of the dry season and which presage the beginning of the rains. From their homes on the hills the Zulu look over these mists, which lie in the valleys touched by the light of the rising sun, and they comment on the Princess of Heaven's beauty. A missionary in Zululand wrote:

> She is described as being robed with light as a garment and having come down from heaven to teach people to make beer, to plant, to harvest, and all the useful arts. . . . She is a maiden and she makes her visit to the earth in the Spring of the year. She is also described as presenting the appearance of a beautiful landscape with verdant forests on some parts of her body, grass-covered slopes on others, and cultivated slopes on others. She is said to be the maker of rain.[4]

According to Father Bryant, a Catholic missionary who has been the foremost student of Zulu history and culture,

> she is supposed to have first given man form. The Zulu say she moves with the mist, on one side a human being, on one side a river, on one side overgrown with grass. If no rites were performed for her, she was offended and blighted the grain. From time to time she appeared in white to women and gave them new laws or told them what would happen in the future. The rainbow is the rafter of her hut – she dwells in the sky and is connected with rain.[5]

Nomkubulwana is thus clearly a goddess of the same kind as the corn-goddesses and corn-gods of the ancient world. Father Bryant explicitly compares her with these deities and draws parallels between their respective rites. The most important of these rites among the Zulu required obscene behaviour by the women and girls. The girls donned men's garments, and herded and milked the cattle, which were normally taboo to them. Their mothers planted a garden for the goddess far out in the veld, and poured a libation of beer to her. Thereafter this garden was neglected. At various stages of the ceremonies women and girls went naked, and sang lewd songs. Men and boys hid and might not go near.

Certain of the ancient ceremonies which Frazer analysed were also marked by lewd behaviour, particularly of women, and the planting of special gardens by women. Thus Frazer described 'the gardens of Adonis,' as useless as those of *Nomkubulwana*:

> baskets or pots filled with earth, in which wheat, barley, lettuce, fennel, and various kinds of flowers were sown and tended for eight days, *chiefly or exclusively by women*. Fostered by the sun's heat, the

plants shot up rapidly, but having no root they withered as rapidly away, and at the end of eight days were carried out with the images of the dead Adonis, and flung with them into the sea or into springs.[6]

These similarities can easily be pushed too far.[7] But all I wish to stress here is that in many classical ceremonies at this season, as in Africa, a dominant rôle was ascribed to the women, and a subordinate rôle to the men – 'Bacchantic' is a word we owe to this arrangement. These elements appear in ceremonies throughout the South-Eastern Bantu tribes. Thus we are told of a ceremony to drive away crop-pests among the Tsonga of Mozambique:

> Woe to the man who walks along the paths! He is pitilessly attacked by these viragos, who push him to one side, or even maltreat him, and none of his fellows will go to his assistance. They all keep out of the way, for they well know what would be in store for them, should they meet the savage crowd![8]

This temporary dominant rôle of the women – a dominant rôle that was publicly instituted, indeed approved, and not exercised tactfully in the background – contrasted strongly with the mores of these patriarchal peoples. Hence it is my first example of a ritual of rebellion, an instituted protest demanded by sacred tradition, which is seemingly against the established order, yet which aims to bless that order to achieve prosperity. To understand how this rebellion worked we must contrast the women's behaviour here with their accustomed behaviour.

In the first place, it is important to grasp that the men did not merely abstain from participation in the ceremonial, and regard it as a women's affair. The men were convinced that the ceremony would help produce bountiful crops: old Zulu men complained to me in 1937 that the neglect of the ceremony accounted for the poor crops of today. The men wished the ritual to be performed, and their own positive rôle in the ceremony was to hide,[9] and to allow the girls to wear their garments and do their work while elder women behaved with Bacchantic lewdness as against the usual demand that they be modest.

Secondly, the ceremonies were performed by the women and girls of local districts, while the men as warriors in the king's regiments joined in great sowing and first-fruits ceremonies for national strength and prosperity. The direct interests of women and girls were confined to their home districts, and here they took action to get local prosperity. Their ceremonial actions, marked by dominance and lewdness, were effective in contrast to their usual subordination and modesty. I cannot here describe this contrast in detail,[10] but state briefly that they were in every respect formally under the tutelage of men. Legally women were always minors, in the care of father, brother, or husband. They could not in general become politically powerful. They were married out of their own kin-group into the homes of strangers where they were subject to many restraints and taboos. In ritual their rôle was not only subordinate, but also highly ambivalent and usually evil. They could perform good magic, as when a pregnant woman burnt medicines whose smoke benefited the crops. But they could not become magicians; indeed, if a woman stepped over a fireplace where magic had been prepared, she fell ill. Though the menses were the source of children, so that the menses could be beneficial, usually during their menstrual periods women were a constant threat of danger. In this condition they could spoil magic, blight crops, kill cattle, and rob the warrior of his strength and the hunter of his skill. Terrible ills afflicted a man who had intercourse with a menstruating woman. In religion women were equally suppressed and as potentially evil. They moved to reside under the protection of their husbands' stranger ancestors, whom they could not approach directly. They did not, like men, become ancestral spirits doing good for their children in return for sacrifices. For as spirits women were capriciously evil: male ancestors did not normally continue to afflict their descendants after sacrifice had been made, but female spirits might continue to cause malicious ill. The Zulu vaguely personify the power of Heaven in storms, and they distinguish two kinds of Heaven. The first, marked by sheet-lightning, is good, and male; the second, marked by forked-lightning, is female, and dangerous. Finally, as men could learn to become good magicians, so they could learn to be malignant sorcerers, deliberately choosing to be wicked. But women's inherent wickedness attracted to them sexual familiars who turned them into witches and demanded the lives of their relatives. In Zulu myths it was Eves who introduced killing by sorcery into Paradise. Most Zulu charges of witchcraft were made against women – against sisters-in-law and daughters-in-law, and between the fellow-wives of one man or the wives of brothers.

One path to good ritual action was open to women. They could be possessed by spirits and become diviners: 90 per cent of this kind of diviners were women. However, this possession was an extremely painful illness which might endure for years, and often killed the patient. The symbol of a successful initiation was the right to carry shield and spear, those badges of manhood.

Thus the standardized beliefs and practices of the Zulu stressed the social subordination and the inherent ambivalent position of women. Women potentially threatened evil by ritual means. Yet in practice they not only were useful, as the main cultivators of gardens, but also they were essential for the procreation of society. The agnatic lineage – a group of males descended through males from a male founding ancestor – was the dominant enduring group in Zulu kinship and familial life. Women of the lineage were married elsewhere to produce children for other lineages. As the Romans said, *mulier finis familiae est*. But the men who as a group were socially fertile in that their children perpetuated their existence, were on the other hand physically sterile. Under the rules which forbade men to marry their kinswomen, they had to obtain wives elsewhere in order to get children. For, *mulier et origo et finis familiae est*. Thus the male group depended on stranger women for its perpetuation. When these women married into the group they were hedged with taboos and restraints. For while the group's continuity and strength depended on its offspring by these women, its very increase in numbers threatened that strength and continuity. A man who has two sons by his wife produces two rivals for a single position and property; and his wife is responsible for this dangerous proliferation of his personality. If he has two wives, each with sons, the cleavage, like the proliferation, is greater. Hence the rôle of women in producing children both strengthens and threatens to disrupt the group, and this ambivalence is expressed in the manifold beliefs I have recited. Since struggles between men over property and position, which threatened to disrupt the group, were fought in terms of their attachment to the agnatic group through stranger-women,[11] it is not surprising that charges of witchcraft were brought frequently by fellow-wives, jealous not only of their husbands' favours but also for their sons, and by both men and women against sisters-in-law and daughters-in-law. Moreover, the men of the group, because of their unity, could not attack each other directly with accusations of witchcraft, but one could attack another indirectly by accusing his wife.

Cattle come into this series of conflicts, firstly as the main property, beside position, over which men fought. Land was then plentiful. Another potent source of quarrels was women. However, women and cattle were in a sense identified, though – and perhaps therefore – taboo to each other, since a man required cattle to give as marriage-payment for his wife. Cattle, the herding of which formed, with warriorhood, the admired Zulu rôles, were thus not only taboo to women, but also the apparent symbol for their transfer from the security of their natal home to the uncertainties of a strange village and to the vicissitudes of conjugal life. Though marriage was the goal of all women, in the years of courtship Zulu girls were liable to suffer from hysterical attacks, which were blamed on the love-magic of their suitors. When a girl married, cattle moved into her home to replace her, and her brother used these cattle to get his own bride. The stability of her brother's marriage, established with these cattle, depended on the stability of her marriage and on her having children; for theoretically if she were divorced – though in practice divorce was extremely rare among the Zulu[12] – or if she were barren, her husband could claim the cattle with which his brother-in-law had married. The cattle thus came to symbolize not only the manner in which a girl became a wife, but also the conflict between brothers and sisters, with the brother heir to his sister's marriage as well as to the group's cattle. From this position the sister was excluded by virtue of her sex. For had her brother's and her sexes been reversed, she would have been heir to cattle and social predominance, and he destined to perpetuate a group of strangers and not his and her own natal group.

This is part of the social background in which we must try to understand the *Nomkubulwana* ceremonies with their protest of women's rebellion. They took place when women had embarked on the arduous and uncertain agricultural tasks of the year and promised a good harvest from the one goddess in the array of virile 'gods' and ancestors. The young girls, still in their natal homes, acted as if they were their brothers: they donned male clothing, carried weapons (like the possessed diviners), and herded the beloved cattle. Their brothers remained in the huts, like women. The younger married women,[13] with lewd behaviour, planted the goddess's field: as men at the capital ceremonially sowed a field for the king. A dropping of normal restraints, and inverted and transvestite behaviour, in which women were dominant and men suppressed, *somehow* were believed to achieve good for the community – an abundant harvest. Clearly a wealth of psychological and sociological – even physiological – mechanisms are contained in that '*somehow* were believed to achieve good'. I have not time to enter into these mechanisms, of which indeed as yet we understand little. Here I stress only that the ceremonial operates seemingly by an act of rebellion, by an open and privileged assertion of obscenity,[14] by the patent acting of fundamental conflicts both in the social structure and in individual psyches.

In this interpretation the Princess of Heaven has disappeared into the background, like – as Frazer might have said – her morning mists when the sun has risen over the hills. Yet clearly she lies at the heart of the ceremony. As Frazer pointed out of her sister and brother deities in the ancient world, she symbolizes the vast seasonal change which comes with spring, and that swing of the seasons within which man's life is set. On this swing of seasons – and on the seasons being good and bountiful – depend the crops, and social life in turn depends on these. The goddess, with her privilege of granting or withholding a bountiful harvest, thus relates social life to the natural world in which it is set. She does so in an anthropomorphic form which is appropriate to her rôle in linking a patriarchal society, pressing heavily on the hardworking women, with its wooded, grass-grown, then scantily cultivated, environment. Her figure is only partly human, for it is also partly woods, grass, river, and gardens. She is a woman, but a maiden and unmarried, yet fertile. She makes the rain. She taught all the useful arts and gives laws to women who do not make laws. But when we know something about the social rôles of the participants in the ceremonies – which Frazer did not know – we can push our analysis along paths other than the single intellectualist path which Frazer followed. For him this sort of ceremony was a response to man's thinking about the universe: with more knowledge, we can see that it reflects and overcomes social conflict as well as helpless ignorance.

3

The *Nomkubulwana* ceremony is one of many domestic rituals which exhibit these processes; I have selected it for treatment here because it involves a deity of the type to which Frazer devoted so much attention. Among the neighbouring Swazi and Tsonga, and in the Transkei, these women's rites are associated with the driving away of an insect pest; and there is a similar ritual among the Zulu for *Nomkubulwana*. The Transkeian Thembu women to the south also perform the cattle-herding rite at a girl's puberty ceremony. Some ceremony of this kind seems general to these patriarchal South-Eastern Bantu. Other domestic ceremonies also exhibit the theme of rebellion.[15] However, I turn now to analyse a great national ceremony connected with crops and kingship, in which the theme of rebellion in the *political* process is made manifest.

The Zulu kingship was broken after the Anglo-Zulu war of 1879; but happily the kindred Swazi still perform national ceremonies which are very similar to those the Zulu used to perform. Dr Hilda Kuper* has given us a brilliant description of them.[16]

The Swazi *incwala* ceremony has been taken by most observers to be a typical first-fruits ceremony, and indeed no one should eat of some of the crops before it has been performed. In most South African tribes a breach of this taboo threatened ritual danger not to the transgressor, but to the leader whose right of precedence 'was stolen'. There is evidence that many broke the taboo: if caught, they were punished by the chiefs. The sanction on this taboo itself states the main theme of rebellious conflict with which we are here concerned. The king had thus to race his subjects 'to bite the new year', the passage into which was marked by the sun's turn at the tropic. But the king must also 'race the sun' and begin the ceremony before the solstice itself. This requires some calculation as the king must go into his retirement when the moon is on the wane, and symbolizes that man's powers are declining. The nation resides on the land and is dependent on the cosmic forces, but it must utilize and even subdue them. Here too the king is concerned to prevent other nations stealing a march on him.

The ceremonies vary according to the age of the king: they are

* I am grateful to Dr Kuper, and to the Director of the International African Institute, for permission to quote at length from Dr Kuper's *An African Aristocracy*. Dr Kuper has also criticized my summary of the ceremony and added valuable points. She considered I should stress other points I had to omit for lack of space: these are stated in footnotes 16 and 17.

reduced to a few rites if he succeeds as a boy and blossom in his maturity. But only the king among the royal clan can stage the ritual. When two princes organized their own ceremonies this led, in Swazi historical thought, to great disasters: national armies were sent to punish them for this treason. Certain immigrant provincial chiefs of other clans retain their own first-fruits ceremonies, which they stage later, but they keep away from the king's *incwala*.

Two calabashes are prepared for the ceremony. Each calabash is known as 'Princess' (*inkosatana*), and seems to be connected with the Princess *Inkosatana*, who, according to Dr Kuper, is 'a sky deity whose footprint is the rainbow, and of whose mood lightning is the expression'. This suggests further some relationship with *Nomkubulwana*. The calabashes are prepared by hereditary ritual experts known as 'The People [Priests – M. G.] of the Sea'. A pitch black bull is stolen from the herd of a subject not of the royal clan. 'He is angry and proud', and these conflicting emotions are said to impregnate the ingredients for the ritual. The bull is slain and strips of its skin are twined about the 'princess' calabashes. Then in the evening 'the Priests of the Sea' set off under the royal ancestors' blessing to get the waters of the sea and the great bordering rivers, and plants from the tangled forests of the Lebombo Mountains. This was formerly a hazardous journey into enemy lands but 'the waters of the world [were required] to give strength and purity to the king'. As they go through the country the grave priests practise licensed robbery on the people.

On the day of the night when the moon will be dark, the calabashes are placed in a sacred enclosure in the royal cattle-kraal. Some of the priests pillage the capital. The 'little ceremony' has begun. The age-regiments of veterans from the capital of the king's dead father's queen-mother assemble in the kraal as the crescent of the weak moon. Amid the lowing of the cattle they slowly chant the sacred royal song:

> You hate the child king,
> You hate the child king (*repeated*).
> I would depart with my Father (the king),
> I fear we would be recalled.
> They put him on the stone:
> – sleeps with his sister:

> – sleeps with Lozithupa ([the] Princess):
> You hate the child king.

The words are repeated in varying order over and over again. During the chanting the regiments from the capitals of the king and his queen-mother enter the kraal and the army forms a crescent. Queens and princesses, and commoner women and children, stand in separate ranks, distant according to status. All chant a second sacred song:

> You hate him,
> Mother, the enemies are the people,
> You hate him,
> The people are wizards.
> Admit the treason of Mabedla –
> You hate him,
> You have wronged,
> bend great neck,
> those and those they hate him,
> they hate the king.

This song too is sung again, and is followed by songs 'rich in historical allusions and moral precepts', but which may be sung on secular occasions. Dr Kuper cites one: it too speaks of the king's enemies among the people for it urges revenge on those who were believed to have killed his father, King Bunu, by sorcery.

> Come let us arm, men of the capital,
> the harem is burnt,
> the shield of the lion has disappeared
>   (*repeated*).

Meanwhile the king is in the sacred enclosure. The Priests of the Sea come with medicines to treat him, and women avert their eyes for 'to look on the medicines of the king can drive one mad'. A pitch black bull is killed in the enclosure, and the army moves from the crescent shape to that of the full moon against the enclosure, while a young regiment goes behind it. While the king is treated with powerful magic he is surrounded by his subjects. The army chants a royal song which is sung at all important episodes in the king's life:

> King, alas for your fate,
> King, they reject thee,
> King, they hate thee.

The chant is silenced; foreigners who do not owe allegiance to the king, and men and women of the royal clan and women pregnant by these men, are ordered away. Dr Kuper considers 'that the king at the height of his ritual treatment must be surrounded only by his loyal and unrelated subjects'. The leader of the Sea Priests shouts: 'He stabs it with both horns. Our Bull'; and the people know that the king has spat medicine to break the old year and prepare for the new. The crowd applauds, for the king 'has triumphed and is strengthening the earth'. The people chant the national anthem, now full not of hate and rejection, but of triumph:

> Here is the Inexplicable.
> Our Bull! Lion! Descend.
> Descend, Being of Heaven,
> Unconquerable.
> Play like tides of the sea,
> You Inexplicable, Great Mountain.
> Our Bull.

They disperse. Fire burns all night in the enclosure.

Before the sun rises the men assemble again in the kraal and chant the songs of rejection. They shout, 'Come, Lion, awake, the sun is leaving you,' 'They hate him, the son of Bunu,' and other insults to stir the king to activity. With the rising sun the king enters the enclosure, and it is encircled by the army. Again they sing,

> King, alas for your fate,
> King, they reject thee,
> King, they hate thee.

Foreigners and those of the royal clan are expelled and the spitting ceremony is again performed. The ritual is over.

There remains an essential 'work of the people for kingship'. The warriors weed the queen-mother's gardens, but their work is described by a term for working with little energy, with play and dawdling. The regimental leaders urge the warriors to strenuous effort and scold slackers, but, still, it is called working without energy – I suspect it is at least an unconscious protest against work for the state. The army dances; and then the people are feasted according to rank. This ends the little ceremony, and during the ensuing fortnight the people practise the songs and dances for the great ceremony which is performed when the moon is full, and man's powers with it rise to a new status. People from all over the country assemble for these days of national celebration.

The themes I am analysing have emerged in the little ceremony, so for lack of time I summarize the great ceremony, which Dr Kuper has described with unsurpassed artistry. On the first day young warriors, pure and undefiled by sexual relations, make an arduous journey to get green everlasting and quick-growing shrubs. Then they dance with the king. After they have rested, on the third day the king is treated with powerful medicines. Another stolen bull, whose theft has made its commoner owner 'angry', is killed by the youths with their bare hands: and he who was not pure is liable to be injured. Magically powerful parts of the bull are taken to treat the king. The fourth day is the great day, when, to quote Dr Kuper, 'the king appears in all his splendour, and the ambivalent attitude of love and hate felt by his brothers and his non-related subjects to him and to each other is dramatized'. The king goes naked save for a glowing ivory prepuce-cover to the sacred enclosure through his people, as they chant the songs of hate and rejection. His mothers weep and pity him. He spits medicines so that his strength goes through and awakens his people. Now he bites the new crops; and next day the various status groups of the nation do so in order of precedence. In the afternoon, the king, surrounded by men of the royal clan, dances at the head of the army. They change their song:

> We shall leave them with their country,
> Whose travellers are like distant thunder,
> Do you hear, Dlambula, do you hear?

And the women reply,

> Do you hear?
> Let us go, let us go.

The words and the tune are wild and sad [say the Swazi] like the sea 'when the sea is angry and the birds of the sea are tossed on the waves'. The royal women move backwards and forwards in small, desperate groups. . . . Many weep. The men's feet stamp the ground vigorously and slowly, the black plumes wave and flutter, the princes come closer, driving the king in their midst. Nearer and nearer they bring him to his sanctuary. The crowd grows frenzied, the singing louder, the bodies sway and press against the enclosure, and the king is forced within.

Dr Kuper was given two apparently conflicting interpretations of this rite. The first was that the royal clan wants to migrate again. 'They want their king to come with them, they want to leave the people whom they distrust in the country where they stayed a little while.' The second interpretation was: 'The [royal clan] show their hatred of the king. They denounce him and force him from their midst.' I think both interpretations are correct, for both are stressed in the next act.[17] The song changes:

> Come, come, King of Kings,
> Come, father, come,
> Come king, oh come here, king.

The princes lunge with their sticks against the small doorway and beat their shields in agitation, draw back slowly and beseechingly, try to lure him out, beg him with praises: 'Come from your sanctuary. The sun is leaving you, You the High One.'

The king emerges as a wild monster, his head covered with black plumes, his body with bright green, razor-edged grass and ever-lasting shoots. These and other accoutrements have ritual associations. He 'appears reluctant to return to the nation. He executes a crazy elusive dance.' Then he returns to the sanctuary, and again the princes cry to him to come out, 'king of kings'. 'They draw back, pause, sway forward. At last he responds. At his approach they retire, enticing him to follow, but after a few steps he turns back and they close behind him again.' The warriors dance vigorously, beating their shields, for 'they keep their king alive and healthy by their own movements. The mime goes on with increasing tension . . . [the king] is terrifying, and as the knife-edged grass cuts into his skin he tosses his body furiously in pain and rage.'

The pure youths at last come to the front: they carry special large black shields. The song changes to triumph:

> Thunder deep,
> That they hear the thundrous beat.

The youths pummel their shields as the king dances towards them, but they retreat from him. He retires two or three times more to the sanctuary, and then emerges carrying a gourd, which though plucked the previous year is still green. Foreigners and royalty again leave the amphitheatre. The king again retreats, tantalizing the men: then suddenly he lurches forward, and casts the gourd on to a shield. The men stamp their feet, hiss, and thump their shields: and all disperse.

Some informants told Dr Kuper that in the times of wars the recipient of the gourd, who thus received the powerful vessel symbolizing the past, would have been killed when he went to battle; and she suggests that he may be a national scapegoat, 'a sacrifice to the future'.

The king is full of dangerous magical power. That night he cohabits with his ritual wife, made blood-sister to him, so that commoner and royal blood meet in her to make her sister-wife to the king. All the population on the next day is in a tabooed state and subject to restraints, while the king sits naked and still among his powerful councillors. 'On this day the identification of the people with the king is very marked.' For example, people who break the taboo on sleeping late are reprimanded, 'You cause the king to sleep', and are fined. The queen-mother is also treated with medicines.

On the final day certain things that were used in the ceremony are burnt on a great pyre, and the people dance and sing, but the sad songs of rejection are now taboo for a year. Rain should fall – and usually does – to quench the flames. There is feasting and revelry at the expense of the rulers, and gay love-making. The warriors weed the royal fields, and then disperse to their homes.

The ceremonies themselves exhibit their main symbolism in Dr Kuper's vivid account. One can feel the acting out of the powerful tensions which make up national life – king and state against people, and people against king and state; king allied with commoners against his rival brother-princes, commoners allied with princes against the king; the relation of the king to his mother and his own queens; and the nation united against internal enemies and external foes, and in a struggle for a living with nature. This ceremony is not a simple mass assertion of unity, but a stressing of conflict, a statement of rebellion and rivalry against the king, with periodical affirmations of unity with the king, and the drawing of power from the king. The political structure, as the source of prosperity and strength which safeguards the nation internally and externally, is made sacred in the person of the king. He is associated with his ancestors, for the political structure endures through the generations, though kings and people are born and die. The queen-mother links him with past kings, his queens with future kings. Many other elements are present, but again we see that the dramatic, symbolic acting of social relations in their ambivalence is believed to achieve unity and prosperity.

4

First, I must again pay tribute to Sir James Frazer's deep insight. He stressed that these agricultural ceremonies were connected with the political process, and that the dying god was often identified with secular kings. He drew attention also to the rebellious cere-monial, for he described the widespread installation of 'temporary kings' who were sacrificed or mocked and discharged after a few days of ostensible rule. He could not draw, from his inadequate material, the conclusions which we are drawing. It might be possible to test the hypothesis I have advanced on the classical material, but I doubt if the data are available. Professor Frankfort's learned analysis of the Egyptian ceremonies can tell us only that

the Royal Princes, and also the Royal Kinsmen, participated in force. In addition some reliefs show figures designed as 'men' or 'subjects'. They represent the crowds of onlookers who, though certainly excluded from the comparatively restricted area in the temple, watched the pro-cessions to the harbour and perhaps participated in other ways which we cannot now reconstruct.[18]

Untrained observers and native accounts in primitive societies have generally failed to record these important elements in cere-monial. Hence I venture to suggest that Near Eastern and classical ceremonies may have been similarly organized to exhibit social tensions.

5

We are here confronted with a cultural mechanism which challenges study by sociologists, psychologists, and biologists: the analysis in detail of the processes by which this acting of conflict achieves a blessing – social unity.[19] Clearly we are dealing with the general problem of *catharsis* set by Aristotle in his *Politics* and his *Tragedy* – the purging of emotion through 'pity, fear and inspira-tion'. Here I attempt only to analyse the sociological setting of the process.

I would chiefly stress that the rebellious ritual occurs within an established and unchallenged social order. In the past the South-Eastern Bantu people may have criticized and rebelled against particular authorities and individuals, but they did not question the system of institutions. Zulu women undoubtedly suffered severe psychical pressure in their social subordination and their transference by marriage to stranger-groups, but they desired marriage, children, well-cultivated and fertile fields to feed their husbands and families. In the *Nomkubulwana* ritual they became temporarily lewd viragoes, and their daughters martial herdsmen; but they accepted the social order and did not form a party of suffragettes. Here I think is an obvious pointer – and it is not necessarily wrong because it is obvious – to one set of social reasons why these African ceremonies could express, freely and openly, fundamental social conflicts. They possessed, not suffragettes aiming at altering the existing social and political order, but women seeking for good husbands to give them children.

Similarly, in African political life men were rebels and never revolutionaries. King and rival prince and subject all accepted the existing order and its institutions as right. Contenders for power against established authority sought only to acquire the same positions of authority for themselves. Professor Frankfort describes a similar structure in Ancient Egypt. Pharaoh 'maintains an established order (in which justice is an essential element) against the onslaught of the powers of chaos'. This order was *maat* – usually translated as 'truth', but 'which really means "right order" – the inherent structure of creation, of which justice is an integral part'. It was so 'effectively recognized by the people, that in the whole of Egypt's long history there is no evidence of any popular rising', though there were many palace intrigues.[20]

The acceptance of the established order as right and good, and even sacred, seems to allow unbridled excess, very rituals of rebellion, for the order itself keeps this rebellion within bounds. Hence to act the conflicts, whether directly or by inversion or in other symbolical form, emphasizes the social cohesion within which the conflicts exist. Every social system is a field of tension, full of ambivalence, of co-operation and contrasting struggle. This is true of relatively stationary – what I like to call *repetitive* [21] – social systems as well as of systems which are changing and developing. In a repetitive system particular conflicts are settled not by alterations in the order of offices, but by changes in the persons occupying those offices. The passage of time with its growth and change of population produces over long periods re-alignments, but not radical change of pattern. And as the social order always contains a division of rights and duties, and of privileges and powers as against liabilities, the ceremonial enact-ment of this order states the nature of the order in all its rightness. The ceremony states that in virtue of their social position princes and people hate the king, but nevertheless they support him. Indeed, they support him in virtue of, and despite, the conflicts between them. The critically important point is that even if Swazi princes do not actually hate the king, their social position may rally malcontents to them. Indeed, in a comparatively small-scale society princes by their very existence have power which threatens the king. Hence in their prescribed, compelled, ritual behaviour they exhibit opposition to as well as support for the king, but mainly support for the kingship. This is the social setting for rituals of rebellion.[22]

Here is one answer to Dr Kuper's discussion of the songs of hate and rejection with which the Swazi *support* their king:

The words of the *Incwala* songs are surprising to the European, accustomed at national celebrations, to hear royalty blatantly extolled, the virtues of the nation magnified, and the country glorified. The theme of the *Incwala* songs is hatred of the king and his rejection by the people. [A Swazi wrote]: 'The [one] song or hymn is an indirect allusion to the king's enemies not necessarily from outside, but may be from members of the royal family, or among the tribesmen. The line, 'he hates him! ahoshi ahoshi ahoshi' – is intended as a thrust against all who may not join in the *Incwala*, whose non-participation is regarded as an act of rebellion, hostility and personal hatred to the king.' Of the [rejection song he wrote]: 'It is a national expression of sympathy for the king, who, by reason of the manner of his choice, necessarily provokes enemies within the royal family. . . . The songs show the hatred evoked by the king, but they also demonstrate the loyalty of his supporters. The people who sing the songs sing with pain and suffering, they hate his enemies and denounce them.' [Another Swazi] said: 'I think these songs are magical preventives against harm coming to the king.'

When the king walks naked to the sanctuary through his people,

the women weep and the song of hate rings out with penetrating melancholy. Later, when [Dr Kuper] asked the women why they had wept, the queen-mother said: 'It is pain to see him a king. My child goes alone through the people', the queens said: 'We pity him. There is no other man who could walk naked in front of everybody,' and an old man added: 'The work of a king is indeed heavy.'

It is the particular king who is hated and rejected by some that has to be pitied and supported by those who are loyal. People may hate the kingship in resenting its authority, but they do not aim to subvert it. For, 'it is the kingship and not the king who is divine'.[23]

In Europe we can no longer ritually reject the king alone, for there are too many among us, even in this United Kingdom, who reject and hate the kingship and the social order it defines: therefore, to quote Dr Kuper, 'royalty [is] blatantly extolled, the virtues of the nation [are] magnified, and the country [is] glorified'. There may be a few among us who accept the kingship but believe another should occupy the throne. Generally, in various parts of the Commonwealth, as in my homeland of South Africa, it is the Crown itself, and not its incumbent, which is resented. Some South Africans desire independence from the Crown: throughout the Commonwealth there are revolutionaries who wish for republics organized in quite different orders. On the whole no one struggles against a particular sovereign.

This simplified contrast illuminates the social setting of the Swazi ritual of rebellion. Swazi polity was a system in which there were rebels, not revolutionaries. Should a particular king be a tyrant, his people's redress was not to seek to establish a republic, but to find some good prince whom they could establish as king. They were constrained both by belief and custom, and by the structure of groups in which they united for rebellion, to seek for their saviour leader in the royal family. For it was firmly believed that only a member of the royal family could become king. In these circumstances of a rebellion against a bad king for not observing the value of kingship, the rebellion is in fact waged to defend the kingship against the king. The people have an interest in the values of kingship and fight for them. In short, since the rebellion is to put a prince, who it is hoped will observe these values, in the king's place with the same powers, a rebellion paradoxically supports the kingship. Further, as the leader of a rebellion is a member of the royal family, rebellion confirms that family's title to the kingship. Therefore a prince can invite commoners to rebel and attack his kinsman king without invalidating his family's title. In this situation rulers fear rivals from their own ranks, and not revolutionaries of lower status: and each ruler, in fear of his rivals, has a great interest in conforming to the norms of kingship. Every rebellion therefore is a fight in defence of royalty and kingship: and in this process the hostility of commoners against aristocrats is directed to maintain the rule of the aristocrats, some of whom lead the commoners in revolt.[24]

All these alignments are dramatized in the ritual of rebellion, together with unity against nature and external foes. The king is strengthened as king: and the kingship is strengthened in his person, through association with kingly ancestors, with the queen-mother, and with inherited regalia which symbolize the throne's endurance. But his personal isolation, and the conflicts that centre on him as an individual incumbent of the throne, dramatically express the real alignments of struggles for power in the system, and intensify actions and emotions expressing loyalty. While the king is a minor few ceremonies are performed; the men do not assemble and the songs of hate are not sung. The king's personal position is too weak to allow conflict to express dramatic unity in complementary opposition.

The rebellious structure of this type of stationary society has long been noted by historians.[25] But this ritual of rebellion suggests that we may push the analysis further. The great ceremony which was believed by the Swazi to strengthen and unite their nation achieved these ends not only by massed dances and songs, abstentions and festivities, but also by emphasizing potential rebellion. If this emphasis on potential rebellion in practice made the nation feel united, is it not possible that civil rebellion itself was a source of strength to these systems? I cannot here present all the evidence that supports this bold statement. These were states based on a comparatively simple technology with limited trade connections. They had not goods to raise standards of living and the rich used their wealth largely to feed their dependents and increase their followings. Hence the societies were basically egalitarian. They also lacked a complex integrating economic system to hold them together and their system of communications was poor. Each territorial segment was on the whole economically autonomous and lightly controlled from the centre. The territorial segments therefore developed, on the basis of local loyalties and cohesion, strong tendencies to break out of the national system and set up as independent. But in practice the leaders of these territorial segments often tended to struggle for the kingship, or for power around it, rather than for independence. Periodic civil wars thus strengthened the system by canalizing tendencies to segment, and by stating that the main goal of leaders was the sacred kingship itself. Hence when a good Zulu king had reigned long and happily two of his sons fought for his heirship during his lifetime. In other nations (e.g. Ankole) there was a free-for-all civil war between potential heirs. In others (e.g. Zulu) a peaceful king would be attacked by someone claiming he was a usurper. Frequently segments of the nation would put forward their own pretenders to the throne, each segment ready to die behind its true prince.

This suggestion is strengthened by the fact that rarely in Africa do we find clear and simple rules indicating a single prince as the true heir. Frequently the rules of succession are in themselves contradictory in that they support different heirs (e.g. Bemba), and more often still they operate uncertainly in practice (e.g. Swazi and Zulu). Almost every succession may raise rival claimants. Or the heir is selected from the royal family (Lozi). Or else the kingship rotates between different houses of the royal dynasty which represent different territorial segments (e.g. Shilluk and Nupe). Another device is the dual monarchy with rule split between two capitals, one of which may be ruled by the king's mother or sister (e.g. Swazi and Lozi).[26] The very structure of kingship thrusts struggles between rival houses, and even civil war, on the nation; and it is an historical fact that these struggles kept component groups of the nation united in conflicting allegiance around the sacred kingship. When a kingdom becomes integrated by a complex economy and rapid communication system, palace intrigues may continue, but the comparatively simple processes of segmentation and rebellion are complicated by class-struggles and tendencies to revolution. The ritual of rebellion ceases to be appropriate or possible.

6

Certain points remain to tie up our argument. First, why should these ceremonies take place at first-fruits and harvest? I suggest that there are real socially disruptive forces working at this season, which require physiological and psychological study. In all these tribes the first-fruits come after a period of hunger. Quarrels may arise because of the sudden access of energy from the new food, for it is after harvest that wars are waged and internecine fighting breaks out. Even before that the expectation of plenty, especially of beer, undoubtedly leads to a violent outburst of energy in the men, who are quarrelsome at this time. Some people in fact eat the new food before the ceremony is performed. There is, if crops are good – and many South African tribes held no ceremony if they were bad – the jubilant ending of uncertainty. In this background difficulties arise where one family's crops are ripe while another family lives still in hunger. The taboo on early eating allows each family to move into plenty at roughly the same time. The very move into plenty observably produces a charge of emotion in the society. As food supplies are drawn on in these subsistence economies, each household tends to withdraw into itself. After first-fruits and harvest wider social activities are resumed: weddings, dances, beer-drinks, become daily occurrences and attract whole neighbourhoods. This great change in the tempo of social life is accompanied by relief because another year has been passed successfully, while the heavy demands of the ritual, and its slow and ordered release of conflicting emotions and pent-up energy, control behaviour by the programme of ceremonies and dances, stressing unity. All are performed under the sanction of deities or royal ancestors. The Lozi have no hunger period and no great ceremonies.[27]

The women's ceremony, and the king's ceremonies at sowing and first-fruits, are clearly agricultural rituals. Some of the social and psychical tensions they cope with are associated with stages of the agricultural cycle, and the food which it is hoped to produce or which has been produced. But these tensions are related through the ritual actors to the social relationships involved in food production. Agricultural success depends on more than the fickleness of nature, though fickle nature is personified in all the ceremonies. The goddess *Nomkubulwana* is a nature-spirit who may grant good crops or not. She is a nature-spirit for women not only because she is connected with crops, but also because women act as a body in neighbourhoods. These neighbourhoods contain women from many different kinship-groups of diverse ancestral origin, and in any case women cannot approach the ancestors who are primarily held responsible for prosperity. The *Nomkubulwana* ritual is thus a land-cult, and her garden is planted far out in the veld. Like this garden, *Nomkubulwana* herself remains outside the ring of society: she does not enter the ceremony. She is propitiated when the crops begin to grow and when they are attacked by pests, so that the women and their goddess are associated with the most uncertain[28] stages of agriculture, when the women's work is heaviest. Here celebrants reverse their rôle drastically. This suggests for psychological study the possibility that the marital situation of women produces great strains and that these are never well subdued. They show in women's liability to nervous disorders, hysteria in fear of magical courting by men, and spirit-possession.[29] Sociologically, the ritual and the nature-spirit seem to be related to the potential instability of domestic life and groups.

The first-fruits ceremony is a political ritual organized by the state which is an enduring group: hence it exhibits different beliefs and processes. The Bantu believe that the ancestral spirits of the king are in the end primarily responsible for the weather, and for good crops. These spirits have been in life part of the society, and they are always about certain sacred spots inside men's habitations. They may be wayward in their actions, but they are inside society. The ruling king is their earthly representative who supplicates them in a small-scale ceremony at sowing; and again the first-fruits ceremony to celebrate a successful season (the Zulu called the ceremony 'playing with the king') involves the king and his ancestors. The ritual is organized to exhibit the co-operation and conflict which make up the political system. After this ceremony there follows a series of separate offerings of the first-fruits by the heads of all political groups, down to the homestead, to their own ancestors. But the women make no offering from the harvest to *Nomkubulwana*, who, by another set of beliefs, granted fertility. The period of agricultural certainty – first-fruits and harvest – is thus associated with the king and the political system, for despite the conflicts it contains, from year to year the political system is ordered and stable, beyond the stability of domestic units. However, the uncertainty and wildness of nature may enter into the king's ceremony, though it is the king who personifies these. This happens when, at the climax

of the ceremony, he appears dressed in rushes and animal skins
– a monster or wild thing (*Silo*) – executing a frenzied inspired
dance, since he is not taught it. But even as a nature-spirit, the
king is enticed into society by his allied enemies, the princes,
until he throws away the past year in a last act of aggression, the
casting of a gourd on to the shield of a warrior who will die. Then
he becomes king again, but in tabooed seclusion which marks
his subordination to the political order. The king is the servant
of his subjects. Nature is subdued by the political system, in a
ritual which is timed by the surest of natural phenomena – the
movements of sun and moon.

Professors Fortes and Evans-Pritchard have suggested a more
specifically sociological hypothesis, to explain how social cohesion
in the political ceremony is associated with the new crops.[30]
If the community is to achieve any of the things it values – good
fellowship, children, many cattle, victory, in short, prosperity –
it must have food. This is trite and obvious enough. But it is
perhaps less obvious to point out that communal interests in the
procuring of food may conflict with the interests of particular
individuals. For to obtain food, men need land and hoes, and
cattle; they need wives to cultivate their gardens. Particular
individuals or groups may come into conflict over items of land,
or implements, or cattle, or women. Hence individual interests
in the food that is so essential stand in a sense in opposition to the
community's interests that all its people be prosperous and have
plenty of food. Thus elements of conflict arise over the very food
that is so desired. These conflicts are settled because in holding
and cultivating land, in herding cattle, and in marrying wives,
men are involved not only in technical activities, but also in
actions which have a legal and moral aspect in associating them
with their fellows. They must on the whole fulfil their obligations
and respect the rights of others 'or else the material needs of
existence could no longer be satisfied. Productive labour would
come to a standstill and the society disintegrate.' The greatest
common interest is thus in peace and good order, and the observance of Law. Since the political structure guarantees this order
and peace, which will allow food to be produced, the political
structure becomes associated with food for the community at
large. At the ceremony the new food is opened to all the nation,
though some subjects may steal it. Thus the political order of

interconnected rights and duties is made sacred: and the king who represents that order enters the divine kingship. Perhaps we may now go further, and add that conflicts between individuals and the political order as a whole are demonstrated in the ritual of rebellion. Everyone, including the king himself, is restrained by the order's authority against his individual gratification.[31] Even the king approaches the kingship with care: restraints on the Swazi king are very heavy on the day when he is associated most closely with his people. His personal inadequacy and his liability to desecrate the values of kingship are exhibited in the insults he suffers.

7

In order to make my analysis by contrast, I have suggested that modern political ceremonies may not take this form because our social order itself is questioned. Clearly this contrast only skirts the problem. There are tensions between too many diverse political and other groups in our society to be dramatized simply, and, paradoxically, because of the very fragmentation of our social relationships we do not have as well-developed or as frequent rituals which involve the appearance of persons according to their social roles.[31a] The individual under pressure has some scope for escape by altering his rôle or joining other types of social relationships. Again, our monarch reigns, but does not rule; and though Swazi and Zulu kings perforce acted through, and were constrained by, officials, they ruled as well as reigned. In our society the parliamentary system and local government provide two among many secular mechanisms to express opposition overtly. These secular mechanisms also exist in Bantu society, and it is notable that political rituals of rebellion barely occur among the Lozi of Northern Rhodesia whose governmental organization, unlike that of the South-Eastern Bantu, provides elaborately for the tensions between various components of the state.[32] Nevertheless, there is point to stressing that 'ritual rebellion' can be enjoyed by tradition, as a social blessing, in repetitive social systems, but not in systems where revolution is possible. This emerges clearly in an early French traveller's account of the Zulu first-fruits ceremony. He comments on this ceremony in analysing their so-called despotic government:

It is at the time of the general assembly of warriors (towards December 8th) when the maize ripens, that lively discussion takes place. There are free interrogations which the king must immediately answer, and in a manner which will satisfy the people. I have seen at that time ordinary warriors come leaping out of their ranks, transformed into orators full of spirit, extremely excited, not only returning the fiery glance of [king] Panda, but even denouncing him before everyone, blaming his actions, stigmatizing them as base and cowardly, obliging him to explain, destroying the reasoning in his answers, dissecting them and unmasking their falsehood; then proudly threatening him and ending with a gesture of contempt. I have also seen, after such discussions, the king's party and that of the opposition on the point of hurling themselves on one another. I have seen that the voice of the despot was no longer heeded, and that a revolution could have exploded then and there had a single ambitious man come forward to profit by the indignation of the party opposed to the king. But what surprised me no less, was the order which succeeded the end of this kind of popular tribunal.[33]

We need not be surprised, after our analysis, for clearly no revolutionary leader could come forward at that point. The attack on the king was demanded by tradition; and it naturally culminated in the warriors exhorting the king to lead them to war.

We are left with a number of important problems. Were the rituals effective, as a cathartic purging, only for the period of their performance and shortly afterwards? Or did they animate persistent sentiments to hallow the succeeding wars and great tribal hunts, and the enduring secular institutions of power, which united and maintained the nation? Does the tendency to rebellion require ritual expression if the social structure is to be maintained? Why is the reversal of rôles so important a mechanism in this process? How does the ritual itself keep within bounds the rebellious sentiments which it arouses?[34] Why should some ceremonies not exhibit this rebellious process, and why should ceremonies thus organized not occur in many situations of conflict? Here I suggest that rebellious rituals may perhaps be confined to situations where strong tensions are aroused by conflict between different structural principles, which are not controlled in distinct secular institutions.[35] But the answer to all these problems lies in comparative research, and here we must always follow in Sir James Frazer's footsteps.

Chapter Four

THE MAGIC OF DESPAIR

[INTRODUCTORY NOTE: This essay was broadcast on the Third Programme of the B.B.C. and published in *The Listener* on 29 April 1954. I came to write it in the following way. The Editor of the *Manchester Guardian* asked me to review *African Worlds*, edited by C. D. Forde, and S. F. Nadel's *Nupe Religion*, in 300 words. I asked him if I could have a little more space, since both these books indicated that the reputed Mau Mau oaths, with their high obscenity, were not a return to African pagan religion, as was commonly alleged, but were quite a different kind of phenomenon. He thereupon invited me to write a 1,200 word leader page article on Mau Mau, and to review the books separately. My article produced a strong rejoinder from Sir Philip Mitchell, former Governor of Kenya, and a reply by myself, and by Professor Asa Briggs, as well as other letters. The B.B.C. then asked me to deliver a talk on the subject on the Third Programme.

I would like to refer to some works which stimulated the ideas set out here, and my interpretation of the Mau Mau rites, a description of which I had seen. My attention was first directed to these types of rites by Evans-Pritchard's 'Some Collective Expressions of Obscenity in Africa' (*Journal of the Royal Anthropological Institute*, lix, 1929), and by his analysis of secret societies in his *Witchcraft, Oracles and Magic among the Azande of the Anglo-Egyptian Sudan* (1937). Here, almost casually, as an aside, he penetrated the essence of these movements, in a passage which is often overlooked:

Yet perhaps the associations assist Azande to fight against the pessimism and loss of confidence that their sophisticated manners cannot entirely conceal. In so far as the magic of the associations is not redundant it is directed against the vagaries of European rule. Azande, faced with a power they can neither stand up against or avoid, have found in magic their last defence. New situations demand new magic, and European rule which is responsible for the new situations has opened up roads into neighbouring countries which can supply new magic.

Furthermore, when I speak of a break-down of tradition I do not speak in an evaluatory sense but merely record changes in modes of behaviour. It may be that the associations appear revolutionary only when we think of Zande culture as it has been and that the behaviour which they encourage is in character with other changes going on among Azande in adapting themselves to European rule. I do not wish to pursue such speculations here (at p. 513).

I would like also to mention Dr A. I. Richards's 'A Modern Movement of Witchfinders' (*Africa*, viii, 1935), and Professor Bengt Sundkler's *Bantu Prophets of South Africa* (1948). These are studies in Africa: I knew of course of work on the Ghost Dance and other North American movements by colleagues there.

Finally, around the time when I wrote this broadcast I was discussing with Professor Norman Cohn his account of *The Pursuit of the Millenium* (1957) in the Middle Ages. Later, some of the hastily assembled ideas in this essay were, independently, developed much further by Peter Worsley in *The Trumpet Shall Sound: A Study of 'Cargo' Cults in Melanesia* (1957). Also arising out of this broadcast, Dr Eric Hobsbawn visited us in Manchester to discuss with us why there had been no 'Mau Mau' movement in the history of Europe. After these seminars, he gave some lectures to us which he subsequently published as *Primitive Rebels* (1959). Dr Hobsbawn's work suggested to me that the alleged virulence of Mau Mau oaths arose from the fact that the movement's followers themselves thought that much they were required to do was criminal. Hobsbawn found similar actions only among Carpathian bandits: I am told urban gangs of criminals commit crimes together in similar ways. For a deep understanding of this problem I recommend F. C. Weiskopf's novel *The Firing Squad*, which shows how the Nazis used similar techniques to break down the conscience.

In a broadcast one is strictly confined to 2,700 words: hence I could not refer specifically to Kikuyu religion and rituals. I would note here, therefore, that the custom of 'oathtaking' is very highly developed among the Kikuyu and surrounding tribes.]

Everyone who has studied Africa's problems must be impressed by the Report of the Parliamentary Delegation to Kenya.*

* Report to the Secretary of State for the Colonies by the Parliamentary Delegation to Kenya, July 1954 (Cd. 9081).

It states clearly the political and economic problems which produce unrest among the Kikuyu. But the Members of Parliament confess themselves defeated by Mau Mau itself, its savagery and ritual obscenities. They recommend that 'an inquiry into all the aspects of Mau Mau, psychological and sociological, should be undertaken'. Meanwhile, though the details of Mau Mau rites have not been made public, we know their general character. And even this bare knowledge enables us to speculate about the nature of Mau Mau in the light of other religious and revolutionary movements in Africa. I believe I can show in these other movements, the main drives of Mau Mau. And it seems to me that Mau Mau has been produced by the colonization of Africa, and not by indigenous Africa itself.

'Mau Mau', says the Parliamentary Delegation, 'intentionally and deliberately seeks to lead the Africans of Kenya back to the bush and savagery, not forward into progress'. This is a recurring theme. A member of the delegation in a Sunday newspaper described Mau Mau as 'a bestial "back-to-the-bush" trend'. A great daily newspaper, editorially, goes further: it considers Mau Mau to be the product of 30,000 years (why not 40,000?) of stagnation. Yet there is nothing in African religions akin to the obscenities of Mau Mau. So whatever it is, we cannot simply assume that it is 'a "back-to-the-bush" trend', if by that we are to understand a reversion to African pagan religion and magic.

We now know a good deal about African religions. From the writings of missionaries and administrators, as well as those of anthropologists like myself, one thing is clear. African religions deal with the same problems of human destiny that have been the concern of all religions, in all places and at all times. What is man? Whence does he come and wither does he go? Why should there be good and evil, prosperity and misfortune? How is human society set in the world of nature? What of the relations of men and women, parents and children, magistrates and people? These and other problems have worried all men, no less in Africa than around the Mediterranean and in India and China, where the great universal religions were born. If we look at African religions, and at the answers they give to these problems, we find not darkness but doubts and aspirations akin to our own.

I see these problems as all springing from the question: What is man's destiny, as a member of society, in the universe? But in

African religions it was a small universe. African tribes were small in scale; and they answered the question on a small scale. Beyond their borders lay other tribes, with their own religions. They had, mostly, some idea of a High-God to answer ultimate questions of creation and fate. After creating the world, say many tribes, He withdrew Himself from direct interest in the affairs of men. He is immanent in the world, but no man knows Him now. Indeed the Barotse, a Northern Rhodesian people on the Upper Zambezi, among whom I have worked, say that man's cleverness drove God in fright from the earth. He is now a residue of explanation for how the world came to be what it is, a being who is shrugged away as knowing what no man can know. So that when I asked a Barotse how things were at his home he would reply, 'All were well when I left home this morning; since then – well, God Nyambe knows if there is illness or other misfortune now'. Thus he summed up the chance fate of man, born to sorrow, in this world.

Before the Barotse God fled to Heaven, to avoid man's cleverness and destructiveness, He made Himself wives, and on these wives He begat the various tribes of the region. The Barotse royal family itself is descended from one of God Nyambe's daughters, whom He Himself took to wife. That was, in their reckoning, about eleven generations ago. Thus the Barotse myth of creation gives them recent descent from God. This is a common type of belief, in which a society, as a whole or through its royal rulers, is linked with God. It is characteristic of small-scale societies. Their religions embrace the men of one region only and not of the whole world.

The doctrines of these religions were also defined by the particular structures of the tribes which held them. Africans lacked writing, so they could not work out meticulous and consistent theologies. They had elaborate theologies, but these were developed in social relations, rather than in intellectual speculations. Indeed, because of this setting of theology in social relationships, their religions have a complexity which makes Christianity, Judaism, Islam, and Buddhism seem simple. For a tribal religion covers every kind of social relationship and activity: there is little which is not ritualized. We might expect this in a small-scale society which is dominated by personal relations. Here any activity, such as sowing or harvest, or going on a hunt, involves changes in intimate adjustments, and may be made the subject of ritual. Similarly, the birth of children and their growing up, marriages and deaths, not only affect domestic relations, but also cause widespread disturbances in the tribal social structure. And these changes again may be effected ritually, in ceremonies where all persons affected by the changes appear, and are adjusted to them.

In this situation, the particular rôles of individuals in social life become invested with ceremonial. And in ceremonies, correspondingly, men and women, chiefs and people, appear in terms of their social rôles: they act their relations with each other, either directly or in some special symbolic way, or by inverting their behaviour so that, for example, women behave as men. Some of these ceremonies do indeed involve collective obscenities – lewd songs and dances, sometimes even a relaxation of sexual taboos. This type of ritual is associated with occasions when heavy work or hardship is undertaken, for permitted obscenity within limits seems to be related to the release of stores of energy.

Rituals Containing Theological Dogmas

In brief, then, indigenous African rituals are related to the rôles of their congregations, and to their particular institutions. These rituals contain a set of theological dogmas. And these dogmas are particularistic. But Africa has now been swept into the western world. In both South and Eastern Africa tribesmen go to work for Europeans. Money, cash crops, new skills: all these and more involve them in relationships with other Africans, and with Europeans. The old homogeneity of tribal life has gone. This has struck heavily at tribal religions. More, these small-scale religions cannot be expanded to cover relations with foreigners and strangers, whether they be black or white. Rituals rooted in particular institutions cannot easily cover alien institutions. Most African tribes attend on lines of ancestors: but besides giving general prosperity to their descendants, ancestors are concerned with relations between their descendants. The ancestral-cult has kinship boundaries. It cannot cater for the new multifarious activities in which people deal with strangers. Hence African religions are helpless to aid people challenged by urbanization, by labour migration, by increased competition, by European overlordship.

Thus these religions, which explained man's destiny in the

universe, and which pursued the goals of communal peace, prosperity, and morality, appear to be fragile. They last on in tribal areas: they have no place in European centres. In tribes whose men are away at work – sometimes fifty per cent or more of the able-bodied – the rituals of household, village, and state, can scarcely be performed. Beliefs persist and are carried to labour-centres: but they are isolated and torn out of context.

To meet the threat to their way of life, and to cope with new strains, Africans turned in several directions for supernatural aid. One trend was increasing reliance on another set of their beliefs – those in magic, in oracles, and in witchcraft. Only part of the answer to the problem of man's destiny, and the source of good and evil, fortune and misfortune, was provided by their religion. They also believed that individual misfortunes were due to the evil nature of fellow-men, witches and sorcerers, and they sought to combat these by magic. Professor Evans-Pritchard has explained how these beliefs work.

Briefly, every misfortune has to be accounted for by a 'how' and by a 'why'. If an elephant kills a man by trampling on him, the African sees that he has been killed because elephants are mighty beasts. That is the 'how'. But a series of problems remains: why was this man killed and not another man, by this elephant and not another elephant, on this hunt and not another hunt? Science cannot answer problems of this kind. We say: chance, fate, providence, divine will. All are metaphysical answers. The African says it is due to witchcraft. The belief in witchcraft which explains the particularity of phenomena thus does not contradict science: indeed, it embraces science. For witches do their ill-deeds by using elephants to crush, snakes to poison, overturned canoes to drown, diseases to kill, their victims. And witches do not kill haphazardly. They attack those they envy and hate. So the existence of misfortune is ascribed to the social vices of men – the lack of charity and love. Hence when a man suffers a misfortune, he seeks for the witch among his enemies. He uses magic to combat the witch, and to ensure personal success in advance.

Fears of Witchcraft

These beliefs in witchcraft and magic, and their associated actions, are not firmly tied to particular sets of relationships, as religious ritual is. They can be applied to all new relationships in which men are involved with strangers, and even with whites; and they can be turned into old relationships, from which they were excluded in the past, as these begin to break up. Throughout Africa, while ancient religious rituals have faded, fears of witchcraft have burgeoned and magic has blossomed. Struggles for increasingly scarce land, competition for jobs and houses in the towns, conflicts due to cultural disintegration, fights for power between old and new leaders – all these have loosed greed, envy, hatred, spite, in unrestrained relationships. Fears and accusations of witchcraft multiply in response, and medicine and fetish-cults multiply to meet those fears.

One result has been the development of anti-witchcraft movements. Both in South and in Central Africa there have emerged men who moved through the country with new medicines to cleanse the people of their witchcraft: many people, aware of their vicious feelings, admitted these and asked to be cleansed. The philosophy of these movements has been that if Africans cease to hate and envy each other their present social ills will pass. But, on the whole, magic against witchcraft has burgeoned in individual isolation.

Another movement has been the emergence of nativistic cults – religious movements of return to old rituals. But these have a different value in the new situation: they stand not for native culture in itself but for native culture as a refuge from modern stress. They have been more common in North America and Oceania than in Africa, for some Red Indian and South Sea Island societies have crumbled or been destroyed, as African tribes have not.

Meanwhile, egalitarian Islam has offered spiritual consolation to many Africans; and the spiritual message of Christianity has been important. But in South and Central and East Africa, Christianity has come up against the colour bar. There are many practising Christian Africans: but throughout these regions there has been a proliferation of separatist Christian sects, sects led by Africans, for Africans, against white domination. Some are modelled on the sects of missionaries: others draw both on Christianity and on indigenous belief. Many are revivalistic, and believe in a Heaven where the colour bar is reversed, and the white skin is a signal for exclusion. These churches are based on the Old Testament and the coming of a Messiah: they cleanse from sin and witchcraft, and

they heal the sick. Some are rackets. But all are political movements. In South Africa where almost all trade-union and political
association among Africans is restricted, they are almost the only
forms of organization allowed.

Bullets into Water

This, then, is the general scene in which I see Mau Mau. For
many years Africa has been a turmoil of religious movements and
magical practices. These have to be set in a continent where men
are always on the move between rural homes and white centres of
employment, separated for long periods from wives and children,
crowded in slums, seeing their land reduced and eroded, their
culture decaying. They live under an alien overlordship which is
often unintelligible to them. All too frequently when they have
attempted to form political and industrial unions these have been
proscribed and their leaders arrested. The military strength of
their rulers is dominating. Sporadically rebellions occur: magic is
then called on to turn bullets into water, as in the Zulu Bambada
Rebellion of 1906.

Our Parliamentary Delegation describes Kenya in terms of the
colour bar, the slums of Nairobi, wages fixed on the assumption
that the man's family lives on the land, and that land deteriorating,
the flow of migrants separated from kin, the gulf between Government and people, lack of social security, the difficulties of labour
organization. The delegation does not mention the separatist sects
which are common in Kenya, nor the efflorescence of magic and
witchcraft. All these conditions seem likely to have produced
Mau Mau; at least it is not a product of pagan Africa. Why it
should have emerged among the Kikuyu I cannot say, since we
know too little. But we do know that the Kikuyu had no indigenous chiefs, and since the government-appointed chiefs have been
frequently attacked, there is clearly some connection with internecine struggle for power among a people close to a big town,
short of land, without native leaders of a united people. Beyond
this, all the evidence indicates that to some extent Mau Mau is a
nihilistic movement of desperation – kill and be killed. Its adherents, to quote a Czech doctor on whom the Parliamentary Delegation relies, 'murder but not for the sake of furthering a cause, they
just kill on being instructed to kill. . . . Death for them means
only deliverance'. Its savagery is not specifically African: all-too-

recent history shows that European nations with a long tradition of Christianity can be savage in this way, too. From what we know of the rituals, we can see two strains. One is the use of magic, to counter overwhelming force, and of Kikuyu-type oaths. But these oaths are now based on fantasies of what sorcerers and secret societies in other parts of Africa are reputed to do. And the result is not a reversion to pagan rituals, even what we call obscene rituals. For the second strain is a regression to instinctual desires which we know are universal. These oaths use, as all secret oaths must, a few limited themes: blood, sex, excreta, bestiality, the threat to murder near kin.

The release of nihilistic courage to revolt releases instinctual urges which break the conscience, already weakened since Kikuyu controls now operate with difficulty. A cycle is set up as the oath-takers break taboos on sex, and menstrual blood, and so forth, and gain fresh energy. They are bound together, in shame and guilt, through the ranks of a disunited, shifting people. Mau Mau is dominantly a movement of despair, and uses a magic of despair.

This is, of course, a hypothesis. We know enough of Kikuyu religion to say Mau Mau is not pagan: what we know of other events in Africa suggests the line on which we have to interpret Mau Mau. And it is important to note that not all Kikuyu have regressed thus: this does not mean they do not resent the conditions which I suggest have bred Mau Mau. The Parliamentary Delegation's proposals bravely admit these conditions and show the way we can remedy them. If my hypothesis is correct, improvement of these conditions will prevent other Kikuyu from succumbing, and cure those who have succumbed.

Chapter Five

THE VILLAGE HEADMAN IN BRITISH CENTRAL AFRICA*

1. *Introduction:* MAX GLUCKMAN

THE RHODES-LIVINGSTONE INSTITUTE is attempting a comparative study of the tribes of British Central Africa and of the processes of change affecting their lives today. Social anthropologists have been sent to tribes selected both for the variety of forms in their indigenous social organization and for the different ways in which they have been absorbed in the modern world-system. Though we, of the Institute's staff, are spread over thousands of square miles, and have had very different trainings, we have tried to collect our data on comparable bases and to study similar problems. This short symposium, which opens what we have come to consider a crucial problem, is the first-fruits of our collaboration.[1]

Many district officers have described the village headman as the invaluable non-commissioned officer of native administration. Yet despite various references in earlier literature to his important political, legal, and ritual responsibility for his dependants, there has not yet been an adequate appreciation of his key position in the social structure.

Many tribes of different cultures live in the region now known as British Central Africa (Northern and Southern Rhodesia and Nyasaland). East African peoples have entered between the Great Lakes and there has been a steady stream of migration from what are now the Belgian Congo and Angola. In the nineteenth century three groups of Southern Bantu, halted by the Europeans on the Great Fish River, marauded back into the region which they had earlier traversed southwards: the Ndebele, the Ngoni, and the Sotho Kololo who temporarily conquered the Lozi masters of

---

* Reprinted from *Africa*, xix (1949): the three papers by Mitchell, Barnes and myself were read at a joint meeting of the Royal Anthropological Institute and the International African Institute on 4 May 1948.

Barotseland. Except for a few Bushmen all the peoples are Bantu-speaking, but their social systems are very varied. The Tonga of Mazabuka have a stateless polity which lacks even the framework of a segmentary lineage structure, such as is found among many West and East African peoples. Their political communities are ritually linked in ephemeral bonds to rain-shrines which themselves are short-lived.[2] The Ila relatives of the Tonga live in large villages which are in a constant state of feud with one another. There are large substantially homogeneous states such as that of the Bemba, and kingdoms like the Lozi and Ngoni which embrace members of many tribes. Types of kinship grouping are equally varied. The Bemba and most of the Congo tribes are matrilineal and uxorilocal, as are the Yao who came from East Africa. The Ila-Tonga, of whose ancestral home we know nothing, are matrilineal but dominantly virilocal. The north-eastern peoples (Inamwanga, Mambwe) are patrilineal and virilocal, including the Nyakyusa and Ngonde with their unusual age-village system. Also patrilineal and virilocal are the Shona, as were the southern invaders: Ndebele, Ngoni, and Kololo. The Lozi have a patrilineal bias, but among them descent, inheritance, and residence go in all lines. These tribes live in a great variety of environments and their modes of production, and the economic and physical settings of their settlements, vary correspondingly. Many of them are slash-and-burn shifting cultivators, who are constantly moving their villages in pursuit of virgin or regenerated woodland. There are fishing-peoples by the lakes and in the swamps. The Ila inhabit the cultivable margins of a vast flood plain into which they drive their herds to temporary camps; the Lozi, who live in a similar plain but escape from the flood-waters to temporary homes on the margins, have a complicated system of gardening, fishing, and pasturing.

One social group occurs in all the tribes, whatever their environment and whatever their other forms of social organization. This is the village – a discrete group of people who reside in usually adjacent huts, who recognize allegiance to a headman, and who have a corporate identity against other similar groups. It is significant that the root of the word 'village' is common to practically all Bantu languages.

Most of the inhabitants of any village in any tribe are related to the headman and to one another. Some may be related to the headman indirectly through other members of the village. A few strangers are found in some villages and in the past there were domestic slaves who were ultimately absorbed as relatives and who were generally treated as such. The village is thus a corporate group of relatives. In any Bantu tribe cognatic kinship and affinity spread widely over the land, interlinking individuals with each other in an infinitely complicated and intricate web of relationships. This web of kinship is peculiar to, and unique for, every individual, except twins of the same sex. Even for these twins it diverges when they marry. Therefore the actual kinship relationships between people are ephemeral, though the kinship system itself is not. In most tribes one or another set of kinship links forms the basis of groups which persist through time, in that the groups endure while they lose old members through death and departures and absorb new members by birth and adoption. Groups of this kind often are formed on a frame of unilateral descent, giving the lineage which is typical of the Southern Bantu, North-East Africa, most West African peoples, the Arabs, and so on. Among these peoples segments of kin-groups are the nuclei of local groups such as villages, wards, and districts. The corporate-kinship and territorial systems tend to coincide, and village headmen hold office by genealogical position in a segmentary system. The lineage, defined in this way, is not general for Central Africa, and where it does occur it is shallow in depth and unites only small numbers of people. But whether or not there are these 'lineages', we do find corporate groups of kindred, the inhabitants of the villages. They are formed crucially by common allegiance to the headman. The kinship links between the headman and his followers may vary from tribe to tribe, or within a tribe, and within a single village there may be different kinds of kinsmen, but the headman is always regarded as a senior kinsman. Save in royal villages belonging to the chief, he obtains his position by right of inheritance within a kinship system, be it by patriliny, matriliny, or by choice from either of these lines. With the headmanship of the village he inherits wealth, such as cattle or slaves or land, which he has to administer in the interests of his villagers. Where land is limited he is frequently responsible for allocating it. He is consulted in matters of marriage and of work. He may have ritual duties to perform on behalf of the villagers.

The village is a kinship and domestic organization in which

subsistence peasants make their living and spend most of their time, and where it is proper for a man to die. Since it is formed by common allegiance to the headman, he occupies a crucial position in the frame of domestic and kinship relations. In many Central African tribes villages may consist of a number of alien groups held together by their common, if variant, attachment to the headman. This will be made clear in Mitchell's analysis of the Yao village. The Yao are spreading steadily into unworked land. They live in villages composed of a number of matrilineal kin-groups of little depth and of differing origin. One set of these kin-groups is descended from the wives of headmen who alone marry virilocally, the other set from the sisters of headmen. We believe this to be the internal constitution of a number of our other matrilineal peoples. The Lozi[3] build their villages on small islands in the vast flood-plain of the Upper Zambezi. These villages therefore have histories of hundreds of years, though the limited size of the islands and of the gardens and fishing-sites attached to them has prevented any village population from becoming very numerous. There is a constant flow of kindred out of and into each village, in an ever-changing pattern, for the Lozi inherit in all their lines of ancestry. But at any one moment each village is a corporate group of kinsmen, united under the dominance of their headman. The Tonga village is made up of a very varied set of kindred, joined under a headman.[4] In the Nyakyusa age-village, composed of a number of contemporaries, the election of the headman is of fundamental importance.[5]

Internally the village has a kinship constitution; it is also a political unit. Indeed, we regard it as the smallest group which may be thus described. Until recently its political importance has been enhanced by Government rules using villages as units of administration and usually compelling all Africans to live in villages of defined minimum sizes. We judge from early travellers' reports that the village-group has always been characteristic of, and important in, the region. In organized kingdoms the headman was held responsible for his followers to the chief, and their allegiance to the chief in most relations was expressed through their village membership. The headman also represented their interests against other villages. Usually he held a somewhat unorganized court to settle disputes within the village, or joined with the headman of some other village when two of their followers were disputing. Among the strongly organized Lozi it is considered best that a quarrel within a village should be settled by the headman, and not come to the capital. I have frequently heard councillors stressing this to litigants and exhorting headmen on how to govern wisely and impartially. The headman in these kingdoms thus stands at the bottom of the political organization and is an essential part of it. In the stateless tribes, as the centre of village unity, he has equal political importance.

The headman's crucial position in the frame of political relations is not a mere administrative one. Politically he symbolizes the corporate identity of the village and where it forms part of an organized state he should attend its members in disputes at the capital. All the tribes of the region attach very high value to 'the big village', and the village is identified with the headman. Often it takes his name which is inherited. New villages crystallize about leaders who become the headmen, and are not amorphous groups; when people move between villages they go to join a headman. The desire to attain headmanship and its adherents is a dominant ambition throughout. In addition, the ordinary person considers it desirable to belong to as big a village as he can. The maintaining of a village's harmony and numbers are themes that are constantly praised, and it is the headman's onerous task to try to achieve this. His people express through him their desire for political importance, which is rated by a headman's following and his position in the prestige system. Meanwhile heads of subordinate sections themselves wish to become headmen. The villages are constantly riven by witchcraft charges, which are a reflex of tensions between and within their component groups. The headman is particularly susceptible to the charge of using witchcraft, and believes himself most liable to attack by witches. Dr Smith and Captain Dale in their classic study quoted the Ila definition 'chieftainship is serfdom'; and the burdens and uneasiness of authority, from chief to headman, are stressed in all our tribes. The Lozi Paramount Chief and the Ngoni village headman both describe their appointment in the words, 'you have killed me'. Barnes' analysis will elaborate this theme.

For lack of space, we cannot here describe in detail the external relationships of villages to one another. In brief, we see the political systems of these peoples as being rooted in the self-assertion of villages, the smallest corporate units, against one another.

Among the Ngoni, for example, people sit at beer-drinks by villages, and villagers help one another in fights. Village herdboys pit their bulls against one another. Village-loyalty, despite internal divisions, is strong against other villages, and tensions inside the group are balanced against external pressures. In the past, people lived in villages, they say, for protection against enemies. These were not only external foes – foreign tribes, slavers, wild animals – but also sorcerers and the spirits of the bush. This indicates that though the economic and political setting of the village may vary between tribes, it is also, *sui generis*, a basic element of social structure.

The hypothesis on which we are basing our future work is that the delicacy of the headman's position arises from conflicting principles. First, it arises from his position within the village group as such, even though the ties and obligations involved vary from tribe to tribe. But the main source of the ambivalence of his situation is that he is the personality in whom the domestic-kinship and the political systems intersect. A very simple illustration is that if a man goes to settle in a distant kinsman's village, he enters into a group with whose members he has personal and specific ties of kinship. He also becomes a subject of the headman in a specific sense. The headman is the senior kinsman in a group of kinsmen interrelated in various ways, but who have corporate bonds in their common allegiance to him. These bonds are political in kingdoms since the chief recognizes them; in stateless tribes, they are the main political bonds. Thus a headman is entangled in the web of kinship links and yet has power of another kind, either from the chief or as an autonomous political leader, in relation to the same set of people. The sanctions on him are dual: the diffuse moral sanctions of kinship, and the organized and legal sanctions supported by political authority.

On the other hand, there is a general tendency to speak of political allegiance in kinship terms. Africans say that 'the chief is father of his people' and speak of the kingdom as 'the chief's village'. There appears to us to be a fundamental extension of links from the village to the kingdom as such, and we consider that the headman's position is the key to understanding the relation of kinship links and political bonds in these tribes.

We suggest then that we need a far more intensive analysis than has yet been made of the headman's structural rôle, both in his personal and in his dual corporate links. He interlocks two distinct systems of social relations and therefore the attitudes of his followers to him are fundamentally ambivalent. He symbolizes their common corporate values and yet he is caught personally in their internal struggles. The chief stands largely outside the struggles of the groups and persons he unites; the headman is closely involved in every matter over which he should preside impartially. Therefore it appears to us that the ritual he undergoes is likely to reflect in its symbolism hostility as much as unity.

The difficulties of the headman's position are enormously aggravated in the modern political system. In the past he and his followers, with their neighbours and the chief, held a common set of values. They do not accept the values of the dominant modern authorities today: those of the British administration. Yet the headman is a key official, if usually unpaid, in that administration. For example, he has to report suspicious deaths and illnesses and strangers, and he has to see that his villagers keep the village clean, hoe paths, use latrines, follow agricultural and veterinary regulations, pay tax, etc. He is no more ready than they are to accept these as good, but he tries to enforce the rules for he is liable to be punished if he does not, by fining, imprisonment, and ultimately deposition. As he applies these unwelcome and unaccepted rules, his position becomes subject to still greater strains.

2. *The Yao of Southern Nyasaland:* J. C. MITCHELL

The Yao people were notorious at the end of last century because of their reputation as slavers. Livingstone had noted their close association with the Arabs in this trade and much of the effort of the early administrators of Nyasaland was directed to suppressing the slaving activities of the Yao. While the slave trade has been fairly well studied, the associated but different phenomenon of domestic slavery has not been nearly so thoroughly investigated. It seems that domestic slavery was an important part of the Yao social structure in those days, before the coming of the white man abolished at one stroke this and many other social institutions. But, though the institution of domestic slavery ceased to exist, the system of values upon which it was built still survives and still affects the social structure of the modern Yao. We might summarize this system of values by saying that the status of a man depends on the number of people over whom he exercises certain rights and for whom, in turn, he is responsible. In the past, a man could increase his status in the community by acquiring slaves. This he did by buying them with calico obtained through the slave trade, or with ivory, beeswax, tobacco, and other natural products; by taking them in compensation for the death of a relative; or simply by kidnapping them. Slaves were often taken as spouses by the members of the group over which the man exercised his command, or by the man himself as wives, and thus the group was further enlarged by natural increase. Though these slaves and slave-children had fairly well-defined rights, they were not free to leave the command of their owner, and the group was from that point of view a stable one. The leader's command over his matrilineal and other relatives, however, was not so absolute and it is with this aspect of the social structure that I am here concerned. This system of values still persists and forms the basis for evaluating the status of men in the Yao community. The high status of a village headman is usually expressed in such terms as: 'He is a big man – he has many people', or 'he has many huts'. The village headman himself and the men under him are motivated by the same system of values so that in any village at any time there is a balance between the desire of certain members of that village to break away and establish units with their own dependants, and the desire of the headman to retain those people under his charge.

The tensions that exist in this situation are well recognized by the Yao and they always express them explicitly during the ceremonial succession to village headmanship. The difficulties of his position are brought home to the neophyte village-headman in speeches made by old and experienced men. On one such occasion I heard a man say, 'Some men who marry into a village are bad and can split a village like this one by telling lies to the headman, saying that his sisters are talking behind his back and are insulting him. When a headman hears all this he might break his village by ill-treating his relatives, thus causing himself to be left all alone.' In this way the headman's responsibility for maintaining harmonious relations between the members of the village and himself is emphasized. His failure to do so results in what they call a break in the village – the departure of some of the members to live elsewhere – which is a severe blow to the status of the headman. In fact, he is dependent on his dependants for status, and the Yao are quick to point this out to neophyte headmen saying, 'A tree cannot grow without branches.'

We can better understand the situation if we consider the social structure of the Yao village a little more closely. The Yao are a matrilineal people and are dominantly uxorilocal. They live in small groups of huts scattered fairly evenly over the country and from a few hundred yards to possibly a mile or so apart. Such clusters may contain as few as five or as many as sixty or more huts, occupied by between 20 and 200 people.

These people are almost always kinsfolk, and in the smaller villages they are usually all either matrilineal descendants of a common ancestress or their spouses. In the larger groups there is a more complex situation which I shall analyse below. In the simpler groups there may be no male matrilineal descendant in the village and the leadership of the group is taken over by a senior female descendant of the founder of the village. Usually, however, if the group is large, one of the male matrilineal descendants lives virilocally in the village and assumes leadership.

The relationship between a male matrilineal descendant and the female matrilineal descendants who are in his charge is signified by the word '*mbumba*'. The word particularly refers to the relationship between a man and his sisters and I have therefore translated it as 'sorority-group'. It includes a man's full sisters, matrilineal female collaterals (whom he calls sisters), their female children, and the female children of those female children, and so on. It is usually used in the sense of 'somebody's sorority-group'. A man belonging to the descent-group of the sorority-group may refer to these women as 'our sorority-group'. The man who is in charge of the sorority-group is referred to as the *asyene mbumba*. This could be translated as 'owner of the sorority-group' but because of the property associations with the word 'owner' in our language, I have instead translated this as 'warden of the sorority-group' which expresses more accurately the relationship between a man and his female relatives. Even in those groups where there is a female in charge of the village and no male matrilineal descendant is resident in the group, there is usually some one man, possibly married in some other village, who is warden of the sorority-group. The warden of a sorority-group has certain precise duties to perform on behalf of his charges.

First, he is concerned with the good relations between members of the sorority-group and with other such groups. He has to settle most of the domestic quarrels that take place between members of the sorority-groups. Second, and this is considered to be a most important function, he is the person who is the marriage-surety for the marriages of the members of the group. Briefly this means that he must be approached before a marriage can be legally contracted by any member of his charge, he or his representative is present at the ceremony which formally announces the marriage, and he is responsible for the behaviour of his female relative in that marriage. Third, he is immediately concerned with the physical welfare and health of his sorority-group. He must track down the sorcerers causing their illnesses and supply the medicine to heal them. He has to arrange for the ritual purification of mourners after the death of one of the sorority-group's members. Fourth, he must be present in the court-house if one of his charges is involved in a case and he is usually looked to for the money for the fine. I have known a case not to begin because the warden of the sorority-group was not present. Frequently if the husbands of the female members in his charge default, he has to provide the hut-tax money.

Usually the warden of the sorority-group is the eldest brother of a group of adult full sisters. The younger brothers of the group of sisters, while concerned with their welfare, do not stand in this particular responsible position. They refer to the sorority-group as 'our sorority-group'. The elder brother refers to the sorority-group, be it noted, as 'my sorority-group', and this sets him over and against his younger brothers. The position that the warden holds, however, is not rigidly fixed, for a younger brother may assume control of the sorority-group if for some reason he is dissatisfied with the way in which affairs are being conducted, and is able so to assert himself.

If we recall that the status in a man in a Yao community is determined by the number of dependants that he can command, it is easy to see that relationships between an elder brother and his younger brother are distinctive. The elder brother is responsible for the actions of his younger brother in much the same way as he is for one of his sorority-group, and the younger brothers have a great emotional attachment to their older brothers. Yet at the same time the elder brother stands in the way of the younger brother in his striving for status, in that while the elder brother is warden of the sorority-group the younger brother cannot be, and therefore cannot have dependants and status. It is not surprising to find that accusations of sorcery are frequently made between brothers and the result often is that the younger brother takes the sorority group away from his 'sorcerer' brother to some other place and sets up a new village with it. Therefore one possible source of instability in the Yao village lies in the operation of the kinship system of values which reckons status by adherents.

I have thus far been describing the simpler types of village. In the larger groups it is common for the warden of the sorority-group to live in the village where his sorority-group is. Then he usually brings one (or sometimes more) of his wives to the village, where she lives virilocally. The daughters that are born to her do not return to the sorority-group from which the headman's wife came but marry and set up households near their mother in the village of their father. Thus there develops in time a second sorority-group in the village, alongside the first sorority-group, and related to it through the headman. At this point we may say that the man's position has changed from that of headman of a village containing a single sorority-group, to the more complicated and less secure one of village headman over a more heterogenous group, in which his jurisdiction over one part of the village arises from his position as the warden of a sorority-group, and that which he exercises over the other sorority-group derives partly from his position as a non-matrilineal relative and partly from his own personal qualities. The warden of the second sorority-group is the headman's own son and it is he who takes over all the functions proper to that position, but the successor to the headmanship is a man's sister's son, usually, though not invariably, the first-born son of the eldest sister. Each village headman in turn brings his wife to live in his village and each headman's wife in turn tends to set up a fresh group which is of a different lineage affiliation from that of the headman. In addition to this the warden of the sorority-group formed from the first headman's children tends in due course to live virilocally and the children of his wife set up yet another foreign group in the village. Hence, theoretically, with each generation the number of opposed groups in a village doubles itself, and in a few generations, were this to continue, the position would become extremely complex. In fact a village of long standing is seen to be composed of a central lineage group to which the headman belongs, and a series of other lineage groups related to the headman's lineage group through one or other of the past and present headmen of that village. Such groups of different lineage make-up are usually mutually opposed and are held together only by the combined influences of a weak patrilineal connexion with the headman's lineage and the personality of the present headman.

This situation is clearly an uneasy one for the headman. His wife is looked upon as a stranger and is often made to feel it. The headman's sorority-group often expresses its hostility and jealousy towards her. The children of the two groups are on no easier terms. They call each other 'cross-cousin' (*asiwani*) and are expected to marry one another. At the same time the hostility between them is formulated in joking relationships. This critical situation of the headman is made clear to him on the day of his succession. One headman was told: 'As you have got wives, do not listen to what they say. They may be lying. Sometimes they will quarrel with your sisters and say that your sisters have been insulting you. This is false. When you hear these reports you may be unfair to your sisters and the people will say that you have broken your village through listening to nonsense.' Thus when conflicts arise between members of a village the headman is in a peculiar position and it is difficult for him to remain impartial. In such a situation the tendency is to call in an outsider to try to settle the differences. Sometimes these differences are patched up and the village continues as a unit. But, particularly after the death of the first village headman, the tendency is for one of the groups to move away to a completeley new area, there to set up a unit of its own.

I quote an actual case to illustrate this procedure:

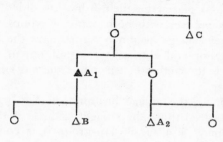

In 1946 village A had about 30 huts in it. A certain man B was the son of the previous headman called A1 and hence mother's brother's son or cross-cousin of the present headman called A2. B had two wives living virilocally and while B was serving in the Army he had a letter from one of his sisters (i.e. his mother's brother's daughter or cross-cousin to the headman) to say that A2 was sleeping with B's wives. When B returned he started making inquiries from his wives and he eventually secured a confession from them. B then went to a man called C, who stood in the relationship of mother's brother to the original A1 and complained about the behaviour of the village headman. C also instituted inquiries and ascertained that it was true. C then approached a local headman of some standing (whom I shall call D) and asked him to arbitrate in the case. D pronounced A2 guilty and awarded compensation of £6 10s. to B. B, however, refused to take the money, and said that he wished to leave the village. D observed that he had every right to do this and that A2 had no right to complain 'since he had broken the village himself'. B took his sorority-group, who occupied about twenty of the thirty huts, to a place about thirty miles away and set up a village of his own. The sorority-group of the village headman A2 remained behind in the old village.

This case illustrates the points that I have made. It shows how the two groups in this village stand opposed to each other in that B's sister wrote to tell him of A2's conduct. Also when the village did break up it did so along certain very clear lines of genealogical relationship. Second, it illustrates the operation of the desire for dependants in that B refused what by Yao standards is a very large sum of money for compensation and preferred to move off and establish a village of his own. This attitude is also shown by the arbitrator who takes the point of view that regrettable as it is, the village must in the circumstances split, and while he appreciates the headman's feelings he makes it clear that the headman has no one to blame but himself. Third, it is interesting to note that this split took place after the death of the old village headman when the personal ties with both opposed groups were severed. Though the new village headman A2 assumes the kinship terms of his predecessor and also calls the children of A1 'children' yet in fact he is their cross-cousin while the old village headman was their father.

The position of the village headman in Yao social structure may be summarized thus: the village headman is the leader of a group which may be a simple kin-group or a composite group of two or more opposed matrilineages linked to each other through himself or one of his predecessors whom he represents to them. The numerical size of the village determines the status of the headman, but the size that it can reach is limited by an immanent instability in the kinship structure which is expressed, in terms of their status system, first, in the competition of brothers for the wardenship of the sorority-group, and second, in the competition between the headman and the wardens of the patrilineally linked sorority-groups, who wish to set up villages of their own.

The Yao see villages as units and this is clearly shown at the initiation ceremonies of boys, when the initiates are kept in grass-sheds, each partition of which refers to a particular village. In the same way a person is identified as belonging to a particular village known by the name of the village headman. Thus a man might say: 'I come from Kumpumbe's village.'

Village headmen themselves are graded in importance and there are certain marks of rank which distinguish the more important headmen. We have already examined one of the most obvious ways in which the village headman's importance is judged, that is, by the number of people in his village. In addition there are other ways in which village headmen may be distinguished both from the common people and from less important headmen. Thus, for example, some of the more important village headmen have the right to conduct initiation ceremonies, this right being granted to them by the man who is in a way the most important village headman of all – the Chief. The right to hold a boys' initiation ceremony (*lupanda*) is of more importance than the right to hold a girls' initiation ceremony (*ciputu*). Yet another mark of rank is the right to wear a plain crimson band around the forehead (*mlangali*), this right also being granted by the chief.

The Administration has recognized the more important village headmen and has entrusted to them certain duties. By no means all the people called 'village headmen' in this paper are recognized as such by the Administration, but I do not know of any person who has the right to wear a red band and is not also an Administrative village headman.

The status system has apparently been taken over from pre-European days, but it is uncertain to what extent these important village headmen had powers. Some today have all the marks of rank that the chief has, i.e., they hold both boys' and girls' initiation ceremonies, are entitled to the special greeting accorded to important village headmen (*subahe*), wear a red band, have the right to be buried in the village and not in the common cemeteries, and to have their bodies prepared for interment by people of similar rank. It appears that such people exercised a certain amount of power, by reason of their personal qualities, over less powerful neighbours, and some were able in the past to demonstrate their autonomy by moving off to establish petty chiefdoms of their own.

Nowadays the Administrative village headmen have certain statutory duties to perform towards other minor groups actually independent but considered, for the purposes of the Administration, to belong to the village. The relative importance of the headman is still the deciding factor in such questions as determining who is to be called in to arbitrate in a case. Thus, though for Administrative purposes a small village may be considered to be a part of a larger Administrative village under an Administrative village headman, yet when a case for arbitration occurs within that smaller village, some other person than the Administrative village headman may be called in as arbitrator.

Laws promulgated by the Administration are conveyed through the chief to the Administrative village headman and in this way a heirarchy of power is being introduced. The small village headman now sees the Administrative village headman as a representative of the chief and the Administration. The Administrative village headman in turn sees the chief in this light. But in matters directly affecting the Administration, the small village headman also sees the Administrative village headman as his own representative *vis-à-vis* the chief and the Administration.

In general the village is by far the most important corporate body in the social organization of the Yao, not only as a significant primary group but also as an element in the political sphere. The position of the village headman therefore is of cardinal importance and merits further study.

3. *The Fort Jameson Ngoni*: J. A. BARNES

The Fort Jameson Ngoni live in the Eastern Province of Northern Rhodesia under Chief Mpezeni, and number about 60,000 people. Their villages range in size from half a dozen up to about 120 huts, corresponding to a population range of about 15 to 300. The distance from one village to the next may be as little as ten yards or as much as a mile and a half. Every ten years or so, when the garden-land round the village is exhausted, the villagers move to some new site where fresh gardens can be made and new huts built.

Most of the villages are commoner villages with headmen who succeed patrilineally. It is rare to find anyone in a village who is not related to the headman in one way or another as a kinsman or an affine, and a considerable portion of the inhabitants are his close kin. Marriage residence may, however, be either virilocal or uxorilocal, and intra-village marriages also occur, so that these ties of relationship to the headman are of many different kinds. This diversity is increased by the custom of sending children away from their parents after weaning to live in another village with one of their grandparents, whose village they come to regard as their own. The headman is usually succeeded on his death by his eldest son by his chief wife. If the heir is a minor a brother of the former headman may act as regent, and may be able to secure succession to the headmanship for his own heirs. Alternatively, the legitimate heir may be unwilling to succeed, or universally unpopular, or, more frequently, away at work in Southern Rhodesia, and so may be passed over. A son may be called back from his grandparents' village to take up the headmanship of his father's village.

The headman is responsible to the chief and the Administration for the well-being of the diverse collection of relatives living in his village. He receives notice of tribal meetings, provides labour for public works, and is responsible for informing the chief of any incidents of importance that may occur in the village. Litigants from the village get the headman to testify to their good character, and his approval is theoretically required before anyone may move out of or into the village except in connexion with marriage. He arranges hospitality for strangers and should take the initiative in moving the site of the village when necessary. He is responsible for trying to deal with quarrels in the village, but he would in these days be regarded as exceeding his powers if he awarded any monetary damages. There is not the same feeling that the headman ought to settle all quarrels before they reach the court that is reported in other areas. For a serious quarrel to be discussed in the village without calling in the headman is regarded as challenging his authority.

In return for these services the headman is accorded a certain amount of deference by the Administration and the chief, and he receives gifts, principally in the form of beer. He does not appear to have the same ritual duties as have been described for Bemba headmen.[6] He is assisted by his deputy and his lieutenants. The deputy is usually a patrilineal kinsman of the same generation. Each successive headman can choose his own deputy, so that the post is not a hereditary one. The lieutenants occupy hereditary posts which were usually created by the founder of the village for the most trusted of his captured followers.

I propose to discuss some of the tensions that exist within a village with a structure such as I have outlined. They are well brought out in a ceremony for installing a new headman's deputy that I attended in July 1947, in a village called Tsong'oto.[7] The headman, Wilson of the Tembo clan, had succeeded in 1926, but had not appointed a deputy of his own as his father's deputy was still alive. There was no obligation on him to adopt this course, but as it happened the man eventually appointed as Wilson's deputy was the son of Wilson's father's deputy, and it would have put him in a rather invidious position had he been appointed while his father was alive, particularly in a medium-sized village like Tsong'oto, containing perhaps 100 people. The father's deputy died about 1936, and nothing was done before the outbreak of war in 1939. Then the deputy-elect, Kondwelani, joined the army and did not return to the village until 1946. In 1947 the adolescent boys of the village decided among themselves that it would be pleasant to hold the ceremony of formal induction of the deputy. Such a ceremony would call for much dancing and beer-drinking and all the adolescent girls of the neighbourhood would come into the village. This project was referred to their elders and the organization of the ceremony was undertaken. Eight women brewed beer.

Prior to the ceremony I had been told that only two people outside the village would be formally invited to attend. One was Kambokonje, the headman of an adjacent village from which Tsong'oto had hived off in about 1880. The father's father of headman Wilson was the first person called Tsong'oto, and was a lieutenant of a former headman of Kambokonje's village. It was thought that Kambokonje might invite the chief of the county to attend the ceremony. The other person to be invited by the village was the deputy's mother's elder brother. It was thought that he might invite his paternal half-brother.

The ceremony was announced for a Saturday, but on the Friday night one of the drum-skins split, and in addition the beer failed to come to a head. It was postponed a day to give time for a new skin to be prepared and to give the beer more chance to mature. By 10.30 on Sunday morning about 200 people, men and women, had arrived in the village. They gathered on the verandahs near the deputy's hut and Wilson put down a reed mat under a tree in the middle of the assembly. The local chief arrived, people came back to the village from church, and without further delay three women came and sat down on the mat with three men sitting down behind them, all facing the deputy's hut. The men were the deputy and two of his brothers, and the three women were their wives. The headman sat down on the verandah of the hut next to the deputy's hut, while the chief was given a chair at one side of the circle of onlookers. The headman walked into the centre of the gathering and made the opening speech:

'You are many people that have come here to see what is happening here, and I know many of you have come with lies to tell other people when you get back to your homes. I am pleased to see many important people coming to see what is happening here. Everyone knows that I must speak the truth.'

Here the mother of the headman stepped forward and placed a new cloth over the heads of the three women. Her son continued:

We are proud of seeing this woman. Excuse me, you important people here, among the Chewa tribe, and among the Ngoni it is the same thing that is happening here; among the Chewa it is the custom to throw beads on the ground. Now here everybody can help these people sitting on the mat by giving them money or anything that can be offered to them.

He sat down and his place was taken by a younger brother of the deputy, who merely said that he was the first to give, put a coin into a plate that had been placed by the headman on the edge of the mat, and sat down again. An old man followed him who said:

The deputy must fear the real headman. The people in this village are all related. You must leave your knobkerry on the floor. Though you

163

find us wrong, still you must forgive us. See what your elder brother does. There are people who are going away. There are people who are talking this and that. We have grown up as men because we have learnt to respect people. We say *dade* [elder sister] and we respect our mother's mother. Do not curse people. Look at your elder brother. . . . There are your people who will tell you, you will be grown up as from to-day. You must become a man.

He was followed by a man from another village whose child had married into the headman's family:

We are all pleased, you Tembo people, to come here because of the new deputy. These are our words. You, my father, ought to know who Tsong'oto is. What Tsong'oto speaks and what you speak must be the same. There are people who will spoil words for you and say that you are a better man than Tsong'oto. If Wilson is wrong, you must discuss the matter with him. The headman does not drink beer, so you must be the eyes of the headman [Wilson was a member of the Dutch Reformed Church whose members do not attend beer parties]. You children of the parents-in-law of our child, do not listen to other people. Tomorrow people will come and say, 'Do you know what Tsong'oto people are saying?' Wilson was the headman when the village was at a former site and we have heard nothing bad of him. He has never fought. He is just a man like anyone else. But now we have no more words. You would do well to remember Kambokonje, he is the owner. Today we have sat you on the mat. You have two mothers and you must fear them. [Turning to the women on the mat] Others see you. When you are given a thing, you must say that you have been given a thing. Beer brewed merely for sale is not a good thing. Beer is best when all people are of good heart. Look after the people of Tembo here. The chief is always a woman not a man. [Turning now to the headman] . . . You are the elder, you are the chicken who has laid the eggs. Look after the eggs well. If the deputy's brother tells lies just ask him about it. If you ask people, they will stop telling lies. All these people are your children. You people who are living in the village, the headman is your father and your mother, but beware, the headman also looks after his own interests. Hatch the eggs well.

He put some money in the plate and sat down.

He was followed by a woman, a classificatory mother of the headman, who burst into tears, crying, 'You have won nothing.' She knelt down in front of the mat and continued to weep. Another woman, the daughter of the headman of another village, got up and said:

Always when you come here you curse me. You don't give me any beer. Stop cursing me from today: you always curse me. Why curse a fellow woman? It would be good to curse if there were a divorce, but don't curse me who drinks in your house.

The kneeling woman then started to speak, 'I am a woman. If I stop helping you, what will you say? Answer me, Tembo' [addressing the headman].

Headman: 'Everyone must listen to what she says.' She went on:

You hear from my son, are you deaf? There is now a separation. He is now a big person. People will put troubles in the family. You must tell me. You must talk in the gardens and not take the troubles to our home. They must not ask in Kambokonje village what it is we have done in this village. You often brew beer and you don't give the beer to people. You do the same for her son. You must not do it in your house, you must cook porridge, you must throw away your bad habits from today.

Here there were shouts from the onlookers, 'They won't throw away their bad habits. They won't do it.'

About a dozen speakers, men and women, followed in succession, each proclaiming how ungrateful, miserly, and deceitful were the deputy and his wife and how they must now change their ways. Throughout this harangue the six people on the mat remained completely impassive, their heads bowed slightly, the women with the cloth draped over their heads. Another woman from time to time went up to them and wiped the sweat from their faces with a cloth. After several people had spoken, the chief sent the councillor, with whom he had arrived, out into the middle to make a speech:

You are grown today and you ought to be a good younger brother to your elder brother. Ask him when you have troubles. Don't be misled by other people in the village who will say what a bad brother he is to you. You are today two in your village. You must not carry on these bad things. There are many people here, it is good to look after them.

After a few more speeches and after a number of people had come up to contribute money without making speeches, the headman got up:

We must now stop. Everyone is now well instructed. There are well-respected persons here, but if they offend my laws I will not respect them. You killed me in 1926 and it is now 1947. That was 22 years ago. I thought I was alone. God made someone to come and help me. We should therefore thank God. I am just reading words.

He put his Bible on to the ground and started to read from it the passage from St Matthew's Gospel, 'Ye have heard that it hath been said, an eye for an eye and a tooth for a tooth, But I say unto you resist not evil. . . .'

After finishing the chapter, he expounded it in rather simpler language, ending up:

I know very well there are enemies, but they (who keep Christ's laws) do not fear them. I do not say, you can go away to Southern Rhodesia. In Southern Rhodesia, you will only encounter the same troubles. I have no more words. Thank you for all your words. I am an Nsenga, and in Nsenga we say. . . .

Here he broke into a song in which he was joined by the crowd and at the end said, 'Today you will say that Wilson is a bad man.' He then called on the people to pray. A prayer was said by a preacher from another village and, with this, the instructional phase of the ceremony may be said to have ended.

The headman announced that there was beer, and called on the people to sit together by villages to drink it. Some old women danced round the village, calling at the huts of the three principal participants in the ceremony, Wilson, the deputy, and the deputy's brother. Then the crowd broke up and the younger people went off to dance on their own.

We have in this ceremony, I think, a fairly clear exposition of the attitude adopted towards positions of power and responsibility and of the rôle of the different social personalities that interact within the village social structure. Perhaps we can best begin our analysis by considering the part played by the chief.

His invitation to attend the ceremony came not directly from Tsong'oto but from Kambokonje, in accordance with the traditional chain of responsibility from commoner through regional governor and royal lieutenant to the chief. This was the main principle by which civil action was organized before the European conquest. The chief was referred to from time to time by such phrases as 'the important person who is here', and respect for the chief was included in the virtues enumerated by the headman. The headman referred to himself as Nsenga, thus, by implication, associating himself with his people who, like him, are not Ngoni in the same way as the chief is Ngoni. At the same time it is the chief who is the unifying personality, whose rule of law unites the very diverse ethnic elements in Ngoni society. A ceremony such as this is a public ratification of a decision made previously within a smaller group. The presence of the chief sets the seal on the ratification and reduces the likelihood of the validity of the appointment of the deputy being questioned at a later date. But if he had not come the ceremony would have gone on without him. The crucial action is the prior intimation to the superior that the event will take place.

The importance of the village as a social group is reflected in the request of the headman that people should drink by villages and also in some of the other speeches. As one woman said:

This is the village of Tsong'oto; it came from here a long time ago. There are lies here old and young. But you cannot break this village. Just recently it came to this site. It just captured you like a chicken. Now you say that you are the people who built this village. You cry now.

The village is an entity persisting through time; it does not belong to any one generation, but includes successive generations within itself. At the same time it is only by the actions of its members, and in particular by their avoidance of quarrels, that the village manages to survive intact.

The tension between two branches of one family is emphasized throughout the speeches. The deputy in this instance was the headman's father's paternal half-brother's son, and was some fifteen years his junior in age. Many of the speeches dwelt on the inevitability of conflict between the two, on the fact that other people would try to play one off against the other and how these attempts must be defeated. The deputy and his brothers were isolated spatially on the reed mat from the generality of the village and from the headman himself.

The importance of the matrilineal links in this patrilineally biased society is indicated by the fact that a special invitation to attend the ceremony was issued to the deputy's mother's brother. I was told beforehand that the mother's brother would say 'You have killed my son' when he made his speech, since his sister's son would now be second in the village to the headman; people might therefore not like him and would try to kill him. Although he did not actually say this, at least we may conclude that his rôle is socially regarded in the light of the expected statement. This striking metaphor 'You have killed my son', the headman's 'You killed me in 1926', and the remark made by another speaker, 'This our child you have killed for us. We thought he was big enough, but you have killed him', are indicative of the attitude of Ngoni towards positions of power. On the one hand the child must respect his elders; villagers must respect their headman; the people must respect their chief. At the same time if a man is a good man, he ought to be rewarded with office; society is not static, and in the days of peace Mpezeni was continually raising up people of humble origin and giving them followers. And yet to be given such a post is to expose oneself to all the dangers that are associated with high office. It is the rich man who has many troubles, the poor man who lives in peace. Therefore to be rewarded by being selected for a post is to be killed; it is to call down on oneself the envy and jealousy of those who were not selected, and who will attempt to kill one, not only directly by poisons and other medicines, but also by troubles, which break a man's spirit and divide his people so that they flee from him and he is left isolated, his position and his office gone. Thus runs the argument.

In normal everyday life the hostility of the commonalty towards the holders of office does not often find overt expression, although headmen and chiefs are not averse from mentioning openly the hostility that they realize the people feel towards them. In this ceremony, however, there is ample opportunity for the expression of violent hostility on the part of the common people. As we have seen, the commonest idioms in which this is phrased refer to the failure to provide beer and to telling lies. 'I hear from other people that you are all liars. You must stop. . . . You come to follow the customs of people here. Now you tell lies here . . .' and 'You often brew and do not give beer to the people'. 'Beer brewed merely for sale is not a good thing.' 'You were a very bad mother. In future you will be very bad. Always if a woman sits on the mat she is a very bad woman in future. . . .' Such accusations, which in this case were, as far as I could ascertain, unfounded, would have led in the ordinary course of events to a quarrel and a court case. But in this ceremony we have a socially sanctioned occasion at which they can be made with impunity. The recipients of these insults sit passively on the mat, their eyes fixed on the ground. Even while they are being abused, they are being rewarded, since no one makes a speech without putting some contribution into the plate. There are no doubt elements of great psychological importance in this situation, but we are here concerned with the sociological significance of the picture. The people, all of them related in one way or another to the headman, by their attendance at the ceremony give their approval to the appointment of this man to a post in which he will be set over and against them and in which he must become, from one point of view, their enemy.

Ngoni women, in most public situations, do not make speeches and indeed often say nothing at all. At the same time they exercise a very great influence in public affairs. In this ceremony, where they do speak, the tension between the sexes receives explicit recognition. A man said in his speech, 'Always there is something wrong with the women. The men are all right. Women are back-biters; after a thing, they tell it all wrong. It is not because of people that we are here, it is because of women.' And another, 'The chief is always a woman, not a man.' The position of the deputy's wife is formally recognized by placing her on the mat with her husband and she is harangued by the speakers as much as the deputy himself. The emphasis on hospitality in the role of an important person reacts on the part played by his wife as the brewer of beer and controller of the supplies of food. Without a co-operative wife no man can be hospitable. The respect paid to a person's senior female relatives is cited as a disciplinary factor in the headman's speech: 'We say *dade* and fear our mothers' mother' – *dade* being a special term of respect used by a man in speaking of or to an elder sister.

Such ceremonies as these occur infrequently, although there are certain features, such as the formal instruction of a person whose status has recently changed, which are found in marriage and funeral ceremonies. From the tribal point of view the post of headman's deputy is not a very important one, nor is it recognized in any way by the Administration. Not every village headman, indeed, has a deputy. The presence of a large crowd cannot be explained merely in terms of beer, as on a Sunday there is, at that time of the year, always plenty of beer to be found. It was known beforehand that the beer had not matured properly on the appointed day so that it was doubtful whether it would be good to drink on the Sunday; most of it was in fact unpleasantly sour. The dance probably attracted many of the younger people but it was ignored by the older participants in the ceremony and their presence must be attributed to their interest in the ceremony as such. They came because of their relationship, genealogical and geographical, to the headman of Tsong'oto and his deputy, to ensure that correct instruction was given to the new deputy, and to demonstrate by their presence their support of, and their hostility towards, the office and its holder.

Chapter Six

CHIEF AND NATIVE COMMISSIONER IN MODERN ZULULAND*

BETWEEN 1887–8 the British Government finally took over the rule of Zululand, despite Dinuzulu's armed opposition. In a short time Government rule was confirmed.[2] Today it is a vital part of Zulu life: of ten matters I heard discussed one day in a chief's council seven were directly concerned with Government. Fifty years of close contact with Europeans have radically changed Zulu life along the lines known all over South Africa.[3] The military organization has been broken and peace established. The adoption of the plough has put agricultural labour on to the men, and they go out to work for Europeans in Durban, Johannesburg, and elsewhere. The development of new activities and needs, the work of various Government departments, missions, schools, stores, all daily affect the life of the modern Zulu. Communication has become easier, though pressure on the land is greater. Money is a common standard of value. The ancestral cult and much old ceremonial have fallen into disuse.

Zululand is divided into a number of magisterial districts, which are divided into tribes under chiefs,[4] who are granted a limited judicial authority and who are required to assist the Government in many administrative matters.[5] Within a district the magistrate is the superior political and judicial officer. He is the representative of Government. His court applies European law and is a court of first instance and of appeal from chiefs in cases between 'Natives' decided according to Zulu law. He co-operates with other Government departments, and with the chiefs and their *indunas*.

---

* This essay is section VII of my essay on 'The Kingdom of the Zulu of South Africa' in *African Political Systems*. The other eight sections are not reproduced here, since they are easily accessible. On the argument of this section, see further my *Analysis of a Social Situation in Modern Zululand*, Rhodes-Livingstone Paper 28 (1958: first published 1940 and 1942).

This, according to statute, is the political system: the chiefs are servants of Government under the magistrate, whom they are bound to obey. In Zulu life the magistrate and the chief occupy different, and in many ways opposed positions.

The modern Zulu political system is ultimately dominated by the force of Government, represented in the district by the police. They are few in number, for the area and population they control, but behind them lies the overwhelming military power of the Europeans. The magistrate is backed by this power and he is vested with all the authority of the white upper class in the South African community. In the development of new activities which has marked the change in Zulu life, Government has played a leading role. It has established peace, encouraged men to go to work for Europeans, supported schools, started health, veterinary, and agricultural services. The magistrate, therefore, not only applies Government regulations, but he is also the chief head of the organization which is bringing new enterprise and some adaptation to new conditions to the Zulu.[6] He has to do many things which the chief cannot do for lack of power, organization, and knowledge. People go to the magistracy with questions and troubles. Thus the magistracy has come to stand for many of the new values and beliefs which today affect Zulu behaviour.

However, while the Zulu acknowledge and use the magistracy, their attitude to Government is mainly hostile and suspicious. They blame it for the new conflicts in their community; they point to laws which they consider oppressive;[7] they regard measures which Government intends in their interests as being designed to take from them their land and cattle, and cite in argument the encroaching of whites on Zululand in the past and what they regard as a series of broken promises to them. Moreover, many of these measures conflict with their pleasures, beliefs, and mode of life, as, for example, the forbidding of hemp-smoking and of sorcery trials, and the dipping of cattle and control of cattle movements. Therefore while Government requires the chiefs to support its measures, the people expect their chiefs to oppose them. And, indeed, the chiefs are usually opposed to them. This position was clearly emphasized in 1938, when a chief who opposed the building of cattle paddocks to prevent soil-erosion was praised by his people, but condemned by officials; a chief who asked for a cattle paddock was praised by officials, but condemned by his people. They complained against him to the Zulu king. For the people look to their native leaders to examine Government projects and 'stand up for the people' against them.

The imposition of white rule and the development of new activities have radically curtailed and altered the chief's powers. He is subordinate to Government rule; he cannot compel, though he levies, labour service; he still owns the land, but it is less and less subject to Government control; he has lost his relatively enormous wealth and often uses what he has in his own, and not his subjects', interests; he is surpassed in the new knowledge by many of his people. The men now have less time to devote to their chief's interests. A chief may try to enforce old forms of allegiance which some subjects will not render and this leads to conflict between them. If he tries to exploit or oppress a man, the latter can turn to the magistrate who will protect him. This last important point needs no elaboration, though it may be noted that as far back as the civil wars the different factions tried to persuade the British Government that they were in the right and should be helped. The chief can compel only that allegiance which Government, in its desire to rule through the chiefs, will make the people render, though his disapproval is a serious penalty in public life. Nevertheless, the chief still occupies a vital position in the people's life. Not only does he lead them in their opposition to Government, but he also has for them a value the magistrate cannot have. The magistrate cannot cross the barrier between white and black. He talks with his people and discusses their troubles, but his social life is with other Europeans in the district. The chief's social life is with his people. Though he is their superior, he is equal with them as against the whites and 'feels together' with them. 'He has the same skin as we have. When our hearts feel pain, his heart feels pain. What we find good, he finds good.' A white man cannot do this, cannot represent them. The Zulu are ignorant of European history and it can have no value for them: the chiefs, and especially the king, symbolize Zulu traditions and values. They appreciate with their people the value of cattle as ends in themselves and of customs like bride-wealth which are decried by Europeans. The chief is related to many of them by kinship ties and any man may become so related by marriage; the social and endogamous barrier between whites and blacks cannot be satisfactorily crossed. The Zulu acknowledge their chiefs' position largely through conservatism and partly because Government recognizes it. But a chief is usually chief by inheritance: 'he has the blood and the prestige of chieftainship and they extend to his relatives; the magistrate has only the prestige of his office.' By this contrast Zulu express the chief's position as it exists independently of Government's acknowledgement and rooted in the values and habits of the people. Chiefs and members of the royal family are greeted with traditional modes of respect. Their family history is retailed. Their capitals are centres of social life. They are given loyalty and tribute.

I have outlined the opposed positions of chief and magistrate: the balance between them is the dominant characteristic of the political system. However, it shifts from situation to situation in Zulu life. A certain minimum of allegiance to both magistrate and chief is legally enforced by Government; the influence of each may vary above that minimum with their characters and relations to each other, or according to the matter considered. A sympathetic magistrate who understands the Zulu will draw them to him, especially from a chief who is unsatisfactory; a harsh magistrate keeps people away from him and they go more to their chiefs. Even more the balance shifts for different individuals in different situations. A man who considers the chief to be biased against him, favours the magistrate as impartial; but for him the chief is the source of justice when the magistrate enforces an unwelcome law. The people rally to the chief when they oppose measures such as the reduction of bride-wealth. If the chief tries to force labour from people, they compare him unfavourably with the magistrate who pays for the labour he employs. Though in many situations it cannot be done, the Zulu constantly compare Zulu officials and European officers and switch their allegiance according to what is to their own advantage or by what values they are being guided on different occasions.

It has been necessary for this analysis to emphasize the opposition between chief and magistrate. It is strong, and appears in the jealousy each often has of the other's power. But in routine administration the system functions fairly well. Chiefs and *indunas* actively assist in the administration of law and the carrying out of certain activities. The magistrates, keen on their work and anxious to see their districts progress, may as individuals win the trust of their people, though it is never complete and the fundamental attitude to Government remains unchanged. They represent their people to Government, and the administration, in developing the Native reserves, seems to be coming into conflict with Parliament in so far as Parliament represents white interests. But though in general the system works, the opposition between the two sets of authorities becomes patent over major issues. Then ultimately the superior power of Government can force a measure through unless it depends on the willing co-operation of people and chief. The Zulu now have little hope of resisting Government rule and sullenly accept Government decisions. In the chiefs' councils, they vent their opposition in talk.

In evaluating this reaction to modern political institutions it is necessary to distinguish between two groups of Zulu, the pagan and the Christian (or schooled). Any schooled Zulu is in general much readier to accept European innovations than are the pagans. However, the majority of Christians have the same attitude as the pagans, though their complaints against Government and whites may be differently formulated. Some better educated Christians measure the chief's value by the materialistic standard of the practical work done by Government and hold that the chiefs are reactionaries opposing progress and they favour a system like the Transkeian Bunga. They are possibly moved by desire for power themselves. In general it may be said that most schooled Zulu regard the magistracy with more favour than do pagans, but among the best educated Zulu, who come out most strongly against the colour bar, there is a tendency to a violent reaction to their own people and culture and values away from the Europeans. Nevertheless, it is through the Christians that the Europeans introduce most new ideas into Zulu life. This is causing hostility between pagans and Christians and creating, on the basis of differences in education, adaptability, enterprise, and values, a new opposition in the nation. Aside from these Christians, there are the pagans who attend on whites, seeking some advantage and trying to profit from the political situation: thus Zulu unity against the whites is weakened. The people tend not to see a conflict in their own actions, though they feel and suffer under it, but often they criticize other Zulu for their allegiance to the whites, saying that they are selling their people to the white man.

Though all Zulu tend to be united against the Europeans, old tribal loyalties and oppositions are still at work and faction fights frequently occur. Tribes are often hostile to one another, but they are again beginning to support the Zulu king. He is recognized legally only as the head of a small tribe in Nongoma district, though Government recognizes his superior status and through him speaks to, and hears from, the Zulu people. He has been used on several occasions to settle disputes in other tribes and always gets precedence over other chiefs. The present Regent is Government's nominee to the Union Native Representative Council. Government thus recognizes the continued existence of the Zulu nation. The strength of Zulu nationalism is growing after a period of weakness. The head of the royal house is again the king (*inkosi*); other chiefs are *abantwana* (princes) or *abanumzana* (big people). He exercises influence, aside from what Government allows him, in other tribes. Nearly all the tribes of Zululand and Natal and some in the Transvaal acknowledge him as their king, though many of them were never ruled by the kings and fought in various wars for the whites against them. The king's present power is partly due to the fact that he symbolizes the great tradition of the Zulu kings, which gives the Zulu their greatness as against other peoples, such as the Swazi. Bantu national loyalties, pride, and antagonisms are still strong despite a growing sense of black unity. The king's power is also part of the reaction against white domination, for the Zulu feel that he has the ear of Government and therefore power to help them in their present difficulties, and that he has the courage and strength to oppose Government. Nevertheless, under Government each chief is independent. Jealousy and desire for power still divide the chiefs, but only the Mandlakazi and Qwabe chiefs are jealous of the king, though he could not get all the tribes to adopt his nominee to represent the Natal Natives in the Union Senate; but other chiefs find that, as representatives of the king, their position among their people is stronger than it is as independent Government chiefs. As such, their people suspect them of being afraid to criticize Government. The allegiance they give the king varies from constant consultation to recognition when he travels. All Zulu crowd to see him when they can and heap gifts on him.

Within a tribe there remains the division into sections under brothers of the chief or *indunas* which sometimes leads to fighting. The chief must rule according to tradition or the tribe will support his brothers and weaken his court, though the magistrate is, as pointed out, the strongest sanction on misrule. If a chief truckles to Government, his subjects may turn from him to a more obdurate brother, or sometimes if the chiefs say they approve of a measure, the people may accept it. The chief has to pick his way between satisfying Government and his people and has to control political officers over whom he has only slight material sanction, though, since these officials and the councils of the people are not legally constituted by Government, he may disregard them.

I am unable, for lack of space, to examine the way in which the political system functions in modern Zulu social and economic life; or the effect on the political situation of the division of the white colour-group into Afrikaans-speakers and English-speakers, and other divisions within it. Briefly, it should be noted that the white group itself has contradictory values in approaching the Zulu; though many Europeans are influenced by both sets of values, the missionaries, various other Europeans, and administrators, educationalists, and people in similar positions give more active expression to the Christian and liberal values. Many of these Europeans are on very friendly terms with Zulu. They fight for Zulu interests and the Zulu recognize this to some extent, though they still regard them as whites and therefore suspect. In economic life the ties between Europeans and Zulu are strong. This may be seen in the traders who have to compete for Zulu customers and in the various labour employers competing with each other for the limited supply of labour. They attempt to get the goodwill of chiefs in their enterprises and at the Rand mines members of the royal family are employed to control Zulu workers as well as to attract them there. Meanwhile, the recognition accorded by these labour employers and traders, and also by missionaries, to the chiefs adds to their powers in the present situation, even while the labour flow and Christianity are weakening in other ways the tribal organization.

Chapter Seven

THE REASONABLE MAN IN BAROTSE LAW*

1. *The Case of the Violent Councillor*

I COME FROM A FAMILY OF LAWYERS, and through my childhood I constantly heard my father and his colleagues discussing their cases at the family-table. Later I intended to go to the South African Bar, and besides reading Law at the University I worked in my father's office in Johannesburg and attended on him in court. Therefore when, diverted by a desire for the exotic, I became an anthrolopogist and began to study African social life, I hoped I might make some contribution on the problems of African law. But I found that, though the setting of this law might be exotic, its problems were those which are common to all systems of jurisprudence. I can still recall vividly how I was

* This essay consists of four talks delivered on the Third Programme of the B.B.C. in August 1954. They abstract a part of the argument of my book, *The Judicial Process among the Barotse*, published in 1955; I reduced certain important parts of the argument there set out in 367 pages, to 11,000 words. The talks were successful: indeed, they got an appreciation index equivalent to that of the star comedy feature on the Light Programme, 'Take It From Here' – I mean an appreciation index as Third Programme talks. When I told an American friend this, he replied: 'You have reached the top now. All that is left is a long, slow, coast downhill.' Higher praise still came from a B.B.C. producer who told an anthropological colleague that the talks 'were almost good enough for the Home Programme.' When I heard the late Sir Arthur Grimble broadcast his *Pattern of Islands*, I realized how right she was: mine were not good enough for the Home. Still, they were sufficiently good for the General Overseas Service to get me to produce a version yet further reduced, to 1,350 words, I hope to end with the word 'Om'. The talks were printed in the *Journal of African Administration*, (vii, 1955, and viii, 1956).

While my own book was in press, I read a newly published book, *It's Your Law*, by Mr Charles P. Curtis of Boston. Mr Curtis argues about American legal terminology in much the way that I argue about Barotse legal terminology. But he put in five words, as a sub-title to a section, what I had striven to say through many pages. Legal terms, he said, had 'a precise degree of imprecision'.

sitting in my deckchair one day listening to a trial in a Barotse Court, when I recognized an old friend. He is inscribed in huge letters on the blank page opposite my notebook's record of the process of cross-examination: 'Hullo, the reasonable man!'

This was not the first Barotse trial I had attended, and in an earlier piece of research in Zululand I had also listened to cases. So I share with many colleagues a long blindness to the existence of this basic figure of jurisprudence in African law. Indeed, it was the facts of the case, rather than my own perception, which made me aware of his existence in Barotse law. But once I had observed him, I was able to reconsider all the cases I had heard as exhibitions of his dominant rôle in the judicial process. I came to appreciate that he was the means by which the judges applied the fixed rules of general law and morality to the varied circumstances of Barotse life. Above all, he was the means by which they adjusted these fixed rules to cope with the great changes which the Barotse's life is undergoing as they are absorbed in the modern world.

This is the general problem I am going to talk about. Obviously, it is a problem which is fundamental to our own jurisprudence, where the reasonable man is an equally important figure. The phrases, 'reasonable man', 'reasonable behaviour', 'reasonable care', 'reasonable precautions', and the like, crop up in every judgment and every chapter of a textbook of law. Indeed, in the very first of his *Misleading Cases at Common Law*, Sir Alan Herbert – in a case in which the judges hold that there is no such thing as a reasonable woman in English law – comes to the following conclusion:

There has never been a problem, however difficult, which His Majesty's judges have not in the end been able to resolve by asking themselves the simple question, 'Was this or was it not the conduct of a reasonable man?', and leaving that question to be answered by the jury.

It seems to me that in this misleading case Sir Alan puts the reasonable man into his proper position, at the centre of the law. The reasonable man occupies this central position because he is the means by which abstract legal rules are focused on to the varied circumstances of life. In textbooks of law he is cut up according to the technical divisions of jurisprudence – he comes in under many separate heads, such as reasonable care and guilty beyond reasonable doubt. In this process of dissection he loses his integrated character. And it is this integrated character which interests me as an anthropologist. I am going to exhibit his dominance in Barotse lawsuits, and to suggest that this exhibition may help to solve certain long-standing controversies in our own jurisprudence. For as Barotse judges define the reasonable man, they bring into their definitions many facets of Barotse life which are not ostensibly part of the law. These facets include a variety of social and personal prejudices. I believe the same process can be detected in the decisions of our own judges and juries.

Let me describe the exotic setting in which I first met this familiar figure. From its source in the Belgian Congo, the Zambezi flows southwards towards the Kalahari Desert, before it bends east towards the Indian Ocean. About half-way down its north to south course the river has carved out a great plain in the woodlands which cover North-Western Rhodesia. This plain is 120 miles long and about thirty-five miles wide, and it is the homeland of the tribe who rule over the vast region marked as Barotseland on maps. Each year the summer rains flood the plain, so that it becomes a great lake. The Barotse therefore build their villages on mounds in the plain, which are islands in the flood-season; though as snakes and rodents and insects seek sanctuary in the villages, life in the flood is so uncomfortable that the Barotse move for these months to dwell in other villages on the margins of the plain. From their plain-villages the Barotse work rich pockets of alluvial soil, pasture their cattle, and trap fish in many ways. These villages, on the only building land available, are of strategic importance in Barotse life. Rights to work land and to fish in certain trap-sites and pools depend on membership of a village.

The Barotse have a Paramount Chief who has two capitals, one in the heart of the plain, the other at the margin, to which he moves for the flood-season. The chief rules through an elaborately organized council, which is a court of law, a cabinet, a parliament, a civil service, an ecclesiastical chapter, and, in the old days, was a military headquarters. Now war is a thing of the past, for under a treaty signed in 1900 the Barotse accepted British protection. Under the Treaty the Barotse Chief's rights to punish his subjects were defined by British law, but his council still tries civil and some criminal cases. It does so by old procedures. The plaintiff states his case in full detail to the numerous judges, and the defendant replies. The judges themselves cross-examine the parties and witnesses, and when they are satisfied that they have heard all the evidence, give judgment. There are no lawyers to assist the parties, and their rôle is played by the judges. The chief himself does not listen to lawsuits, but the judgments are referred to him in his Palace for the final verdict.

It was at Lialui, the flood-season capital, that I recognized the reasonable man during a trial which I call 'The Case of the Violent Councillor'. Most Barotse villages are inhabited by a grouping of kinsfolk, but some are attached to members of the royal family and are inhabited by several families, all of which are ruled by a councillor. A quarrel had broken out in the village which was destined to be the burial-village of the then reigning chief. Hot words had passed between the son of the councillor and a young villager. The villager had gone to the councillor's house to complain about the son's behaviour, and he alleged that he was attacked there by three of the councillor's children who flung him to the ground. The councillor seized his wrist and dragged him along the ground, with the three youngsters clinging to his waist. He screamed: 'The councillor is breaking me, the councillor is breaking me.' His wife came in and accused the councillor of fighting: this is a heinous offence for a councillor, since a councillor is not a policeman, and must never take violent action. The councillor released him and got one of the stamping-poles with which the women pound grain. It was taken away by another man. The councillor seized a whip which was also taken away. The plaintiff was then released by the councillor's children and carried away, fainting. He sued the councillor and children in a subordinate court which fined the councillor £1, of which it said ten shillings were to go to the plaintiff, and ten shillings as a fine to the Barotse Treasury. The plaintiff said he would appeal for the latter ten shillings to the court at the capital, and persisted in this appeal even when he was offered fifteen shillings, with five shillings only to the Treasury.

This was the story which the plaintiff told the appeal court where I was listening in, since Barotse appeal courts hear all the evidence anew. He had independent witnesses for most of the incidents. But the councillor's defence was as follows. He said that the plaintiff had come to his house spoiling for a fight with

his son. His children had attacked the plaintiff who was thrown
to the ground. He had seized the plaintiff's arm in an attempt to
raise him and stop the fight. Then he had taken the stamping-pole
to put it out of the way in case someone seized it as a weapon.
Finally he had taken the whip to frighten the fighters into their
senses, but had not intended to use it.

The serious aspect of this case was that the councillor had
taken violent action – had fought. Barotse gave me several precedents in which councillors, who are supposed to be restrained,
grave, controlled, and so forth, had been discharged for taking
action against wrongdoers with their own hands. The violent
councillor was afraid that this would happen to him, and he therefore cast his story so that his witnessed actions would appear
to conform to Barotse ideas of right conduct – so that he would
appear to have acted reasonably. It seems probable that he was
lying, but it is very important to notice that he lied in such a way
that he accepted the rules for rightdoing. In almost every case
which I heard in Barotseland litigants and witnesses, whether
they lied or were mistaken, worked with the same moral and legal
rules as the judges did. This is the mark of a homogeneous
society; and it alone allows a satisfactory process of law. If the
litigants have rules of rightdoing different from those of the
judges, the judges can punish them, but not convict them.

Since the violent councillor accepted the standard rules of
how a councillor should behave, he lied in terms of these rules, and
this enabled the judges to attack him. A prince asked him: 'When
the plaintiff came to your house, why did you not tell him to
sit down, and then summon your children, so that you could
enquire into the dispute between them?' The councillor hedged
and replied, 'They are binding me with lies'. The head of the
court pressed him: 'Why did you not make them sit down so that
you could judge between them?' The councillor did not reply.
The head of the court, who is noted for his gentleness but was
enraged by the offence, went on angrily: 'You should have seated
the plaintiff, called your son, and summoned all the men of the
village to hear their quarrel.' The councillor said, 'I did not do
this.' The head of the court commented: 'This is councillorship
– this is ruling!' The councillor made an attempt to defend himself: 'It was night, I could not.' The head of the court pursued
his point:

If an affair comes here to the capital at night to me, I go to the prime minister, I call the senior councillors. If it is a thief, we put him in gaol for the District Commissioner. Also, you say you tried to raise the plaintiff, that you did not drag him along the ground. What manner of arbitrating in a fight is this, to seize the one who is on the ground, who is being overwhelmed, not to seize those who are fighting him?

Here the judges have set up two standards by which they can break the councillor's ingenious defence of his witnessed actions. First, he did not behave as a reasonable man would do in intervening in a fight; second, he behaved quite unlike a reasonable councillor, acting by the customs of a good councillor, in handling the quarrel when it was brought to him. It was at this point that I realized how the Barotse had elaborated the concept of the reasonable man.

The court was aware that the councillor feared discharge, but did not mind paying a fine for his children's assault. This is implicit in the next question put to him, though it seems also to stem only from the concept of a reasonable man. For the court knew the councillor did not want it to become aware of his offence. A prince challenged him: 'You deny that you were at fault. Why then when the subordinate court penalized you £1, did you not appeal?' The councillor replied: 'If a man is penalized, what can he do?' The prince insisted: 'He can appeal.' The councillor hedged: 'I would have appealed if the plaintiff had not done so.' The prince crushed him: 'But you did not protest in the lower court. This boy complained that the court was taking ten shillings of his money for the Treasury, you did not protest that you should pay nothing. . . . Your fault was that you, a councillor, entered into a fight.'

With this question the bias of the trial shifted from the assault to whether the defendant was fit to be a councillor. Another judge asked him: 'Why when the plaintiff's wife cried, "The councillor is fighting", did you release him, if you were trying to raise him? You knew you were wrong, as a councillor, to fight.' And another prince concluded the cross-examination: 'You say you came with the whip to frighten them. Is it your custom to threaten with a whip?' The councillor was caught in a cleft stick, because only a policeman and not a councillor should threaten with violent action. He had to answer, 'No'. The prince asked: 'Did you shout as you came with the whip, to show that you wanted to beat them, but did not mean to beat them?' Here the councillor perforce answered, 'Yes'. The prince concluded: 'Then why has not one witness of all who heard the plaintiff cry, "The councillor is breaking me", said that he heard you shout?'

All the judges held he was guilty. Some wished to raise the payment, but the final judgment held that he should pay £1 and it should all go to the plaintiff. He and his children were warned that if they did not behave properly he would be discharged from his post and they might be expelled from the chief's village.

There are many implications in this brilliant cross-examination. I can discuss only a few. First, we see that an African court decides on the facts of a lawsuit by listening to and sifting evidence, and weighing it by cogency and corroboration, just as an English court does. The judges also insisted on direct as against hearsay evidence: a witness was told, 'What you heard with your ears, what you saw with your eyes, tell us. Hearing and seeing the quarrel are good. Do not tell us everything you have been told about the fight.' This has always been the procedure of Barotse courts: ordeals and magical oracles were only resorted to in accusations of sorcery, which cannot be demonstrated by ordinary evidence, and in criminal cases where the verdict on the evidence was, 'almost certainly guilty, but not proven.'

But the truth is arrived at mainly by contrasting the behaviour of the parties, as witnesses report it and as the parties themselves describe it, against the standards of how a reasonable man would behave. Both the parties and the judges erect common standards of reasonable behaviour, and this makes possible judicial cross-examination. But the standards in this case are twofold. First there is the standard of a generally reasonable man – a man who arbitrates in a fight by helping the person who is overwhelmed and intervening with the attackers, i.e. a reasonable peacemaker; a man who appeals against an unjust conviction, i.e. a reasonable innocent man. Second, there is the standard of a reasonable councillor, who when people are quarrelling makes them sit down and tell their stories so that he can judge between them, who summons the public to assist in this process, who is firm and authoritative but not violent, who is impartial and not biased in favour of his own children. After this case gave me the clue, I found this two-fold character present in every lawsuit – the generally reasonable person, and what I call 'the reasonable incumbent of a particular social position', be it councillor, husband or wife, father or son. And as these characters were held up as standards before litigants, as when the head of the court described how he handled an affair coming to him at night, I saw how important the reasonable man is during that part of a lawsuit when the raw facts given in evidence are assessed, and become facts-in-law for the purpose of judgment. This process is barely handled in orthodox legal studies. But it is here, in defining the reasonable standards which are the yardstick in cross-examination, that many things creep into the law which are not part of its rules. No Barotse law says that an innocent man must appeal against conviction: but, with other circumstances, if he does not, he is held guilty. No law says a councillor must summon and seat people who quarrel: but if he does not, with other facts, he may be convicted of bias. I suggest that an analysis of trials in English courts would show that there too all sorts or presumptions, customs, standards and ideas about how persons of different types should behave, enter into cross-examination and influence the process of litigation. They enter through the definition of the reasonable man, because 'reasonable' is a flexible concept which can cover many different things and ways of behaviour. This is its strength for it enables rules of wide moral validity to be accommodated to quite new situations. The duty of 'reasonable care', formulated in ancient Roman times, can cope with the accidents of the machine-age. In Barotseland, a traveller recorded in 1896 a case involving 'the reasonable councillor'; this character can be re-defined by the judges to meet the conditions of modern life.

2. *The Case of the Eloping Wife*

Our textbooks of law take as their units of analysis a series of abstract concepts like right and duty, marriage, property, care and negligence, guilt, contract, crime; and they analyse legal rules grouped under these concepts. The anthropologist's units of investigation are social positions – such as husband and wife, owner, thief, councillor, king and so forth. These social positions are linked together by rights which the incumbents of the positions can claim and by duties they should fulfill. The anthropologist studies how rights are claimed and duties fulfilled, and how breaches of their rules are enforced in relation to all the social positions in a community. So that he regards the same facts from a viewpoint which differs from that of the lawyer.

Now every one of these social positions carries with it certain ideals – a councillor is grave and impartial, a king is brave and just, there are the perfect husband and the perfect wife. Human frailty, alas, acting in the vicissitudes of life, is such that few people can live up to the ideals of the positions they occupy. But fortunately the law, both in England and in Barotseland, only demands that we attain these ideals up to a reasonable standard, so that most of us, despite our deserts, escape whipping. Therefore, trials often reduce to the question, was the defendant a reasonable councillor? a reasonable husband? or wife? or father? Even before that stage of the trial is reached, the judges in their cross-examination begin to assess litigants' behaviour against these standards. And because as an anthropologist I am dominantly interested in social positions, I came to concentrate in my study of Barotse law on the problem of the reasonable incumbent of a position, and to pull legal rules together about this problem. I began also to look anew, in these terms, at problems of English jurisprudence.

Every individual occupies several positions in society – as father, workman, citizen, and so forth. In Barotseland, because commercial life is little developed in a small-scale community, people act in all their capacities with the same lot of their fellows. Hence in any trial all of a person's actions, in his several rôles, are considered by the judges in assessing the evidence against him. Let me illustrate this with a trial which I call 'The Case of the Eloping Wife'.

A Barotse woman married a foreign immigrant. They had a quarrel and the wife left home. Shortly afterwards her husband visited a nearby white township where he found his wife living with another man. He reported this to his wife's father, and sued the abductor for damages. The abductor and the woman pleaded in defence first, that the husband had divorced his wife by driving her away, and secondly that when the abductor went to the woman's father, the father demanded 30s. as marriage payment. Therefore, they argued, if the husband had not divorced his wife and he had a case for damages, it lay against the father who had married off his daughter before she'd been divorced from her husband. In the course of their statements the two defendants abused the husband as a foreigner.

It quickly became clear that the husband had a claim for damages against someone, since his wife could not prove that he had sent her away (as a man is entitled to do), nor had she obtained a divorce in court (which a woman must do). But was he to be recompensed for the loss of his wife by her abductor or by her father? The father admitted he had taken 30s. from the abductor, but he said he took the money as a fine for the abduction, and not as a marriage-payment to validate the new marriage.

The court satisfied itself that the father was telling the truth by the following cross-examination. Under questioning by the court, the woman said that after the quarrel she left her husband and stayed for two days in her father's home, from which he was absent, for two days. On the third day she married the defendant. As she put it, 'I thought I would take my husband to court to get a divorce, then this man came to marry me and I saw time was passing, so I married him.' The judges burst into laughter and exclaimed: 'Time was passing, to wait two days!' That is, the judges have an idea of 'reasonable time' which reasonable people ought to take over certain social actions, and this involves that they conform with various customs and rules. Similarly, the abductor was forced to admit that the first night he slept with the woman they were fornicating, because it was only on the next day that he made payment to the woman's father. Again, this was not a reasonable and customary order of actions in time. The father argued that he could not have taken the money as a marriage-payment, since, in his words: 'How can you come to ask for a girl in marriage when you come from the bed on which you have slept with her?'

On this evidence the court had no hesitation in making the abductor pay the damages. The judges argued as follows: No father would accept marriage-payment for his daughter from a man who came to him from a bed shared with his daughter. That is, no reasonable father would do this. But they rebuked the father for taking the 30s. as a fine on abduction, since his daughter was stolen not as an unmarried ward of his, but as a married ward of her husband. The father must return the money to the abductor to give to the husband. Please note that this argument involves a judicial presumption about how fathers – reasonable fathers – behave. Secondly, no good woman, or reasonable woman, would in three days move from one marriage to another. And, as they showed the woman in another piece of cross-examination, no

187

good woman goes by herself to her husband *before* arrangements are made with her father. She should be escorted to the husband's hut by a party of her friends and his. So too no reasonable would-be son-in-law would approach his sweetheart's father to seek her in marriage *after* sleeping with her. The time periods involved here were patently unreasonable: in some cases they involve complex calculations of gestation for women and cows, or the cycle of growing crops. Thirdly, the two defendants were bad citizens, not *reasonable* citizens: they had not waited for a court to adjudicate on the woman's quarrel with her husband, and they had abused the husband because he was a foreigner. On this the senior judge, in a speech which reminded me of Shylock's, said:

About his being a foreigner. All the different tribes – they are all people under our one great king. . . . There is no such thing as a foreigner. We are one thing, with two eyes and two ears, and our children marry them. They feel hunger like us and ask us for land which we give to them.

Over all, in every one of their positions, the defendants had behaved unreasonably: the woman as wife, daughter, woman, and citizen: the man, as son-in-law, husband, and citizen. Hence their stories could be totally discredited. Thus there are implicit in the judges' views of the evidence a series of presumptions: that fathers will not take marriage-payments from seducers of their daughters; that reasonable and good daughters consult their fathers before marriage; that reasonable citizens seek the protection of the court and don't abuse foreign immigrants. These presumptions about how reasonable people behave flow into judgment but are not always formulated. They arise from the judges' views of morality, and of custom, and from their personal experience in society. Nor are all the presumptions rules of law. But they control the vital process of forming judgment on evidence. Some presumptions about witnesses' demeanour influence the value judges attach to the evidence of different people. By these presumptions about 'reasonable behaviour' the judges perform their vital task of assessing circumstantial evidence, which is what produces chanciness in litigation. Now the judges can state any presumption of this kind with the *ex cathedra* authority of a legal rule, since it can be absorbed in the meaning of 'reasonable behaviour'. I do not mean to suggest that the judgments are entirely subjective, since there is continuous social control of the presumptions, and an accepted logic in the way judges have to expound their decisions: the logic of how reasonable fathers act, with its implied science of psychology, the logic that reasonable women seek divorce in courts, that reasonable women wait a reasonable time before remarrying, that reasonable suitors consult their sweetheart's parents and marry them usually with ceremonies.

But the presumptions can vary, and can be based on mistaken ideas, or rumours, or even personal prejudices. This is not a process confined to African judges. A learned but naïve South African judge is reputed to have once refused to grant a divorce although a detective proved the wife had spent an afternoon in a hotel with a man. The judge stated baldly that he did not believe people had sexual relations in the daylight: hence the alleged lovers would not have committed adultery even if they spent an afternoon in a bedroom.

Similar personal prejudices are exhibited in another Barotse case. A husband returned home from a visit to find his wife absent, and their children crying hungrily, unfed, and not sent back to school. He fed them. When his wife returned home she said she had been hoeing in her garden. This happened again the next day, and the wife made the same excuse. On the third day, when his wife was again late, the husband went to the garden and failed to find his wife. He therefore challenged her excuse and she admitted she had been lying in the bush with the defendant, a young teacher. The teacher denied the charge, and said when the husband sued him that the woman was using him to conceal her true lover. He alleged that she had a grudge against him because he had refused to acept her invitation, conveyed to him by letter, to become her lover. He asked the judges if a woman would thus admit who was her lover, just on her husband's challenge. The first judge accepted this argument on the grounds (which may or may not be true – I don't know) that a girl at her puberty ceremony is taught by the older women to conceal her true lover. This judge had a man's prejudice about women, whom – like all Barotse men – he holds responsible for all sexual lapses; hence this would be for him the behaviour of a reasonable woman – but not an upright woman. But the second judge smashed this argument: 'I've been caught that way myself!' He had committed adultery and been exposed in this way. Hence his personal experience overcame the belief held by men about how women act. Some judges held that the evidence was not strong enough to convict; but most considered that if the teacher was innocent he would, like a reasonable man, have shown the women's letter tempting him to adultery, to her kinsmen, or to her husband immediately the husband returned. He would have done this especially as the woman had a bad reputation. Moreover, while the husband was away, he had sat at her hut and accepted food from her; and since there is a presumption in Barotseland that unrelated men and women do not have platonic relations, only a lover of the woman would act in this way. Hence, reasonably, he was guilty.

This last case suggests that the Barotse have a picture not only of reasonable and customary right ways of behaving, but also a picture of the reasonable wrongdoer – the reasonable thief, adulterer, slanderer, and so forth. By this paradox, – the reasonable wrongdoer – I sum up the fact that wrongdoers in any society also behave in customary ways which are socially stereotyped – there are the criminal slouch as against the scholarly stoop, the spiv's clothes and hairstyle, the whole manner of loitering with intent to commit a criminal action. When there is only circumstantial evidence, these sorts of actions build up before the judges till they conclude that, as in the Case of the Eloping Wife, the total picture is that of a reasonable wrongdoer – as we say, a person guilty beyond reasonable doubt. And I have heard cases which indicate that these customary ways of doing wrong in fact influence adulterers and thieves, so that they give themselves away in circumstances in which they could have acted so as to cover up their misdeeds.

Barotse judges have no police or detectives, no expertize of fingerprinting, no lawyers, to help them in collecting and sifting evidence. Therefore they have to depend almost entirely on their cross-examination of evidence to arrive at the truth. And for these reasons they must rely on testing the creditibility of a story told by any person against the flexible standards of reasonable behaviour for the incumbent of the social position involved. This is largely true of our own courts, though our lawyers and not our judges conduct the cross-examination. But this point is not always appreciated in the academic view of law. Nor do all lawyers see how these flexible standards enable the raw facts of a case to be fitted into the fixed and abstract rules of law. When I once lectured on this theme to an audience of Scottish lawyers, one of them protested on behalf of the poor Barotse that they should be so subjected to the control of the vague, ill-defined, litigation-breeding reasonable man. He asked if a code of the reasonable man could not be promulgated each year to protect them. This view fails to see the value of the concept. Many rules of law in Barotseland are necessarily general principles such as, 'a councillor must not be partial', or 'a husband must care well for his wife'. Beyond these are more general principles like, anyone who injures another shall make recompense. This principle exists in all systems of law. But in litigation these general rules have to cover a great variety of actual situations in life. They can only do so if the general moral ideas involved can be brought to bear on the particularities of a perhaps unique situation. This is the function of reasonble standards, and, despite aberrations of particular judges as in the cases of adultery I have just narrated, the standards are defined by the objective tests of traditional and developing customs and morals. For these general rules of law last through the life of a society despite great social changes. The development of 'reasonableness' for such positions as the reasonable husband, the reasonable wife, the reasonable landlord and tenant and king and subject, enables the law to cope with all changes. Without this the law would ossify.

This is well illustrated by a Barotse divorce suit – 'The Case of the Prudish Wife'. Here the wife sued for divorce on several grounds. First she complained that when she was ill her husband did not treat her at his home, as required by law, but took her to her parents. The husband replied that he obtained to treat her a medicine which had to be inserted in cuts on her body; but he could not give her the medicine himself as she would not let him see her naked (astonishment in court). Then drums had to be beaten for her treatment and this could not be done in his village which was inhabited by converts to Jehovah's Witnesses who do not allow drumming. So he took her to her mother. The judges held that in the circumstances of the wife's unique prudery, and in the new situation created by the coming of the Jehovah's Witnesses Christian sect, a reasonable husband could only take her to her mother. She claimed divorce secondly because her husband before going to work at a distant place took from her some blankets, which he then used with a new wife – thus breaking the law which forbids a Barotse to confuse his relations with two wives. The court found that her husband had given her eight blankets (a new form of goods), that this was wealth by the standards of Barotse poverty, and that he could therefore *reasonably* take back two blankets for himself on a new type of journey – and then use them with a new wife. He was a reasonable husband and her plea for divorce was rejected. Thus in fact many cases are decisions about whether a person has been a reasonable husband, or other incumbent of a particular social position.

In this way Barotse judges are constantly re-defining the scope of 'reasonable' standards for spouses, kinsfolk, lords and underlings, so as to handle new conditions of life. Judicial decision supplements legislation. Through the 'reasonable standards' they maintain their traditional laws and traditional morals, and yet cope with the effects of the introduction of Christianity and schools, labour for whites and money and trade-goods, new skills, changes in every aspect of Barotse life. Hence it seems to me that it is in the study of the reasonable man, in every society, that anthropologists and lawyers can meet. In him social principles and prejudices, customs and habits, group interests and individual experiences, are absorbed, to relate the fixed rules of law to the changing variety of life. But the law aims at justice, and the idea of a reasonable man implies an upright man. I shall next describe what the Barotse think about the upright man.

3. *The Case of the 'Dog-in-the-Manger' Headman*

Generally, Barotse law demands from people only reasonable exercise of rights, and correspondingly only reasonable fulfilment of duties. This is all the judges will enforce. But in practice Barotse judges tend to erect higher standards – those of the upright man, or woman – the upright husband, wife, lord or underling. In this way they bring into the trial the ultimate standards of Barotse ethics, which lie beyond those of the law. The law demands right and reasonable action: morality asks for right and generous action. A man should not insist on the letter of his rights, and he should be prodigal in meeting his obligations.

This does not mean that the judges can enforce these very high ethical standards, but only that they set upright behaviour as the goal of all good men and women. They can only *order* men to meet the demands of the law. For example, under Barotse law a man can divorce his wife by sending her home to her parents. If he does this, the court will compel him to give her half of the crops she planted in his land, and also half of the goods in their house – dresses, pots, blankets and so forth. A woman must sue in court for a divorce and has to establish that her husband has not been a reasonable husband. If she gets her divorce, she obtains half the crops grown by *her* labour, but on *his* land. However, as she rejects the marriage, she also rejects all the goods which his earnings have bought for her own needs and for her domestic tasks. I once heard a case tried in which the woman thus established her claim to be divorced. Listen to the senior judge's decision: 'The woman is freed, and she will take home with her half of the crops which she planted. There has been so much ill-feeling in this case that we will send a judge to see that it is fairly done'. Turning to the husband he went on: 'Now what else, my kinsman, will you give her of the goods of the marriage to take with her?'

The husband objected: 'I will give her nothing; she has infected me with disease, and bound me here with lies'. The judge admonished him:

Come, my kinsman, you cannot do this. When you married her, taking her from her parents, you all rejoiced together. You hoped that you would have a strong marriage, with children to bind you together. It has not worked out thus, but you cannot send a woman home to her parents, naked like a dog. We beg you, give her a blanket and a dress and some plates.

But the husband persisted in his meanness: 'I will give her nothing, not even a shawl.'

The judge had to resign himself to this: 'Very well; we have power to make you divide the crops, and we will send someone to see this is done. But we have not power to make you behave like an upright man. Go.'

Later that day the husband craved permission to speak again to the court. He said he had been reflecting on the judge's words, and saw that he was wrong. He would give his wife a dress, a shawl, a blanket, a hoe, a pot and a plate.

The judge approved: 'We thank you, my child. This is behaving like a decent upright man.' And he called on the other judges to salute this generosity.

This case shows that the law limits the extent to which judges can enforce morality. Judges on occasion, in Barotseland as in England, cannot enforce upright behaviour, and may even have to find for the person who has behaved wrongfully by moral standards, but who is supported by the law. The judges find for the wrongdoer in the interests of certainty of law: our maxim states, 'Hard cases make bad law.' The Barotse say, 'It is hard, but it is the law.' Sometimes an English judge feels compelled to say something after this form to a wrongful litigant: 'Fortunately for you this is a court of law, and not a court of justice or morals.' And he then proceeds to upbraid in round terms the litigant who is successful in law but morally in the wrong. Conversely, a judge may openly state his reluctance to convict a person who is legally a wrongdoer, but morally justified. I do not believe that these situations arise because a court is only a forum of law, and not a source of justice and morality. I myself consider that these situations demonstrate that courts of law are in fact courts of morality: for the judge uses his high office publicly to state what morality demands and to upbraid the person who has departed from it and kept within the law, or to justify the person who is trapped by a technical law or driven by altruistic motives to commit an offence. This is certainly the way in which Barotse regard their judges and their courts.

Let me quote another divorce case to emphasize the point. The Barotse believe that it is natural to help one's blood relatives, and that the true test of the upright man is how he behaves to his relatives-in-law. In this case the wife made various allegations about her husband's neglect of herself and her relatives, but the court accepted his evidence, backed by her own parents, that he had behaved more than punctiliously. The senior judge rejected the pleas for divorce thus:

You, woman, have astonished us by your suit. You thought you would shame your husband before the country, which we represent. But you have instead brought honour to him, for we have never heard of so good a son-in-law. Your father told us the overcoat he wears is a present from your husband; see how your husband sits himself in a ragged jacket. He is not a rich man, but when he brought an overcoat for his father, he brought one for your father; when he brought a dress for his mother, he brought one for your mother. He gave shawls to your unmarried sisters, and he built granaries for them and moved their crops on the flood, not in the dugout of your village, but in his own dugout. And so forth. You have not disgraced your husband here before the judges of the land, but you have brought fame to him, for none of us is as good a son-in-law as he. You, my son, we admire what you have done, and we thank you. Do not cease to behave thus because your wife has brought you to court; continue to look after your relatives-in-law as you have done in the past. We thank you.

He then instructed his fellow-judges, and all in court, to join him in saluting the husband.

I mention these two cases because they show the judges upholding, to a mean husband and to a generous husband, the ideal of the man who is upright beyond the demands of reasonable standards. Their standards are similar in cases of property-holding and of contract, but to describe these would involve me in the intricacies of the Barotse environmental situation. Marital relations are familiar to us from our own life – they are the same the whole world over. But these cases did not catch the judges between the law and morality. Here is a case – 'The Case of the Dog-in-the-Manger Headman' – which did this. It led to divergent judgments.

The Barotse dwell in higher pieces of land in the great Zambezi flood-plain which is their habitat. From these islands – as they are during the flood – the Barotse cultivate pockets of alluvial soil and use sites for fish-traps. I was told again and again that in Barotse law a man has to dwell in a village if he wishes to work any of the resources which belong to the village. If he leaves the village, he loses his rights in its land. This land is vested in the title of the village-headman.

A certain village-headman, named Mahalihali, was very quarrelsome, and his bad temper drove many people out of the village. He personally expelled one of his daughters whom he accused of sorcery. Eventually he died and his son inherited his position, and took his title as Mahalihali the Second. He found himself with a village, but few villagers. His nephew, son of the sister expelled from the village, was using some of its trap-sites in a fish-dam, but was living with his widowed mother in her mother's village. Another sister of the new headman had married into a nearby village and her sons were using a fish-dam which her father had let her have. The new headman brought a suit that his sisters and their sons must stop using the fish-dams unless they moved into his village. The judges satisfied themselves that the one sister, accused of sorcery, had been badly wronged when she was driven out of the village. Since then she and her son, and the married sister married nearby and her sons – that is, all the defendants – had behaved with proper respect to the headman. Hence arose the judges' dilemma. The law, I repeat, is clear: if you do not live in my village, you lose your rights in its land. By this rule the headman was upheld in his claim that the others join his village or cease to use its fish-dams. But the defendants had not done him any wrong, and the headman was behaving unjustly – like the dog-in-the-manger in our fable. How did the judges solve this dilemma.

In Barotse courts when the judges come to give their decision, the most junior judge speaks first, and then his seniors in turn, until the head of the court gives judgment. This is the binding decision, even if it contradicts the verdicts of all other judges, though it is referred to the king in his palace for confirmation. Well, the first three judges felt themselves bound by the basic premiss of their land-tenure law: the dog-in-the-manger headman was entitled to expel his sisters and their sons from the dams unless they moved into his village. *But* they all stressed that he ought not to treat his relatives in this niggardly way since there was more land than his villagers could use; being rich, he ought to help his relatives. Nevertheless, the dams were his. The next set of judges were reluctant to apply the letter of the law in favour of the dog-in-the-manger headman, against people who, in their words, had 'done nothing wrong'. Many judges told the headman, 'If they had done wrong, you would have a case.' Most judges therefore contented themselves with stating the moral issue, that he ought to let his relatives fish. One said the fish-dams had passed out of his control, though this was upsetting the basic law of Barotse land-holding. But the senior judge sitting in court returned to this basic law: the dams were the headman Mahalihali's. But, the judge added, he ought to let his kin fish them. As it happens, the head of the court was busy on administrative business elsewhere. Next day he came to deliver his decision on the basis of reports of evidence and judgments made to him by other judges. He found the headman still insisting on his rights to take the dams unless the others moved to join him, as laid down in the last decision. So the head of the court found a brilliant solution to the judicial dilemma. The dams clearly belonged to the title Mahali-

hali; but if the present incumbent of that title was not upright –
generous to his kin who did not live with him – the court would
discharge him from his headmanship and appoint a more generous
successor.

What happened here was that the judge achieved a just and
equitable solution by stressing a new kind of sanction. He invoked
the administrative powers of the court to discharge unsatisfactory
headmen, in order to compel a headman to be generous in exer-
cising his rights. In this way, the judge enforced the standards
of the upright headman in favour of the defendants who had
done no wrong, while he maintained the basic law of land tenure.
For the fish-dams remained vested in the headman's title.

This case shows strikingly that Barotse courts are dominated by
ideas of justice and equity. These ideas influence their total
evaluation of evidence; and on occasion spur them to apply
particular equities, as against the dog-in-the-manger headman.
The Barotse believe that justice in this sense is self-evident to
all men, and they call their principles within this justice, laws of
God, or laws of humankind. That is, the Barotse have a clear idea
of natural justice, which they constantly apply. They apply
natural justice, of course, within particular economic and social
conditions: for they have set ideas on the relations of men and
women, lords and underlings, and so forth. But it is natural
justice. And natural justice involves for them, as for us, certain
ultimate principles of law, as that a man who injures another
shall make recompense; no man should be judge in his own suit;
a judge should not come to a decision before hearing both sides;
a man should be generous and not mean. These and other moral
rules they share with us; and the rules are axiomatic, they cannot
be demonstrated. An example of such a rule is equivalent to the
Roman Law maxim, *volenti non fit injuria*: a man who willingly
exposes himself to injury, cannot sue for damages if he is then
injured. The Barotse maxim is, 'If you are invited to a meal and a
fish-bone sticks in your throat, you cannot sue your host.' Under
this rule (which they say is patently fair), they will not allow damages to a man who is injured in a fishing-party when men enter a
pool at the dry season, and blindly hurl bundles of spears to get
catfish buried in the mud. Nor will they allow damages to a man
injured on a hunt. Nor did they allow damages to a woman who
became pregnant, or contracted venereal disease, in illicit inter-

course – though they have now, by statute, imposed penalties on the man who infects a woman thus.

These general moral rules, and a host of particular rules defining Barotse personal relations, property-holding, contracts, and so forth, constitute the total body of Barotse law. Besides moral rules, the body of law embraces customary ways and relations, statutes of their king and of the British Government, judicial precedents. Their law includes the ordered regularities of the environment, of organic life, and of human psychology – what we call scientific laws. The judges draw on all these sources to make their decisions. But the different rules of this body of law are not entirely dependent on one another. And the judges therefore can achieve justice by applying different rules in different situations, according to how they see the moral deserts of the parties. In contrast to the case of the dog-in-the-manger headman, I heard several cases in which the judges insisted on the rule that if a man leaves a village, he loses his rights to land in it; but these were cases where the underlings were in the wrong. Where it was the dog-in-the-manger headman who was in the wrong, the judges did not want to support him. Some judges felt compelled to do so, against their view of the moral merits of the case, in order to meet the demand for certainty of law. Others tried to vary the law to meet those moral merits. The final decision seized on a different rule – the power of the court to discharge unsatisfactory headmen – to achieve justice, while maintaining the law of land-tenure itself.

This decision illustrates one important way in which judicial discretion can operate in the interests of justice. The body of Barotse law consists of a large number of different kinds of rules. These rules may be consistent with one another, but they do not depend on one another. There is no essential logical interdependence between the rule that a man loses his rights in land belonging to a village if he leaves the village, and the rule that the court can discharge an unsatisfactory headman. The judges can often, as in this case, decide to apply one rule rather than another, out of the whole body of law, to achieve justice. In doing so, they – so to speak – *manipulate* the independence of the rules. This gives great scope to intelligent judicial discretion.

But the judges' main power to manipulate legal rules during a trial arises from the nature of the words which compose the rules.

A law such as that if a man leaves a village he loses his rights in its land is a general statement: in particular disputes the judges have to apply it to very different circumstances. Do these actions amount to 'leaving' the village? In the case of the dog-in-the-manger headman, for instance, one woman did not 'leave' village; on the contrary, she was driven out of it. If a simple word like 'leaves' requires this kind of interpretation the problem becomes more complex and uncertain with the abstract ideas of law. But there is an inherent uncertainty of this kind in all legal words, which enables them to cover a great variety of actual events. And application of these uncertain concepts to actual events is the major part of the judges' task. In the case I have been describing, what is an 'unsatisfactory' headman? He is, by prevailing standards, not a 'reasonable' headman. We are back with the 'reasonable' man; and I have already shown that this valuable uncertainty is a prime characteristic of 'the reasonable man'.

4. *The Case of the Unfaithful Councillor*

The divorce rate in Barotseland is very high. Men can divorce their wives simply by sending them home; women have to go to a Barotse court and establish a case for their release from marriage. They can do so successfully on many grounds. In fact a woman has only to show that her husband has not behaved as a reasonable husband to her in order to obtain a divorce.

What then, for the Barotse, is a reasonable husband? He is one who cares properly for his wife, sleeps with her adequately so that she has children, does not discriminate between her and his other wives, and does not drive her out of his home. These are old rules of Barotse law which date from the days before the British protectorate was established. And Barotse life has altered considerably since those days. Women who previously wore one skin-skirt and had a skin-rug, now want dresses, petticoats, shawls and blankets. They need kerosene lamps, iron pots, plates and cups and cutlery, and many other of the goods of our civilization. Some men can earn the money to purchase these things by selling fish, cattle or crops; but most Barotse men have to go out for long periods to earn wages at distant European settlements. And it is therefore in a radically different situation that Barotse judges now apply their ancient rules about the duties of husbands and the rights of wives. The judges have continually to decide what amount of goods a husband must nowadays give his wife if he is to be a reasonable husband. To do this they interpret what is the meaning of 'care for a wife' by reasonable modern standards.

One element in the modern situation produces a radical conflict to prevent a husband fulfilling two of his conjugal duties. He has to buy European goods for his wife, and to do this he must go away to work: then he cannot sleep with her and be a companion to her. The Barotse have therefore by legislation fixed a maximum period for which a husband can be away. If a husband is away for longer than this period his wife is entitled to a divorce. And while he is away, he must send goods or money to her. These statutes aim to bring the nation's men home and to maintain contented marriages. But a difficult legal problem arose even out of the apparently simple judicial task of deciding whether a husband has been absent for the set period. A woman brought suit for divorce on grounds that her husband had been away for longer than the period allowed: his kinsmen opposed the suit, pleading that he had sent her money, blankets, and so forth. The court held, 'This woman did not marry a blanket', and granted the divorce. Within a few days the husband arrived: he had been on the journey home when the divorce was granted. His wife wished to return to him, but her father demanded a new marriage-payment for what, under the court's decision for divorce, was a new marriage. The court held that had it known the husband was on his way home, it would not have granted a divorce. The court thus interpreted 'return home' to mean 'leave place of employment', because the purpose of the statute is to maintain marriages. The judges thus upheld what they believed to be good morals and public policy.

This case seems simple enough, but it illustrates a crucial task which Barotse judges have to perform if they are to help their people adjust to the new situation in which they are living. The judges have constantly to reinterpret their definitions of what are reasonable husbands and wives, reasonable councillors and headmen, and so forth. This process of defining how a reasonable incumbent of some social position should behave, lies at the core of the way in which judges nowadays define what is reasonable companionship of husband and wife, in terms of modern conditions. These new conditions and the standards they contain according to modern public opinion, are brought into the law through the elasticity of the concept 'reasonableness'. And meanwhile the basic law remains unchanged from the very different past – a husband must be a reasonable husband.

Here is a case in a different kind of relationship to illustrate the elasticity of legal concepts, and to show how this elasticity enables the law to cope with new situations. I call it 'The Case of the Unfaithful Councillor'. Some villages in the Barotse plain on the Upper Zambezi belong to members of the royal family. These princes and princesses may not actually reside in their villages, which they leave in charge of a headman. Under Barotse law a man holds land first by being a citizen; and he is entitled to keep that land as long as he is a faithful subject of the king. Secondly, he must be a member of a village, and he must be a faithful underling of the owner of the village, respectful and helpful. In 1945 a certain princess had as headman of one of her villages a councillor holding the title Indiye. She sued to have him dismissed from the title, and from its rights in village and land, on the grounds that he did not work for her. He pleaded in defence that he worked as overseer of a barge carrying goods down the 300 miles of the Zambezi from Barotseland to Livingstone. He had no time to work for her or attend on her. The court held that this plea indeed absolved him, since men nowadays earn their living by working for Europeans, and not for their Barotse overlords. But he did not go to say farewell to the princess before he started on a journey, or to greet her when he returned. This he could easily do. Hence, he did not respect the princess, and was not faithful to her, and so he merited dismissal from her village. The court thus defined 'faithful' – and incidentally a reasonably faithful councillor – to accommodate modern conditions. But the law remains that a man must be faithful to his overlord.

These judicial problems are common to all countries. Judges have to apply certain well-known rules to the great variety of circumstances which occur in social life, and which may well be changing, as they are in modern Barotseland. Judges must maintain the law, in the sense of abiding by its rules, and yet they must serve justice in every case if possible. I am suggesting that they do so by manipulating the uncertainty which resides in all words when these are applied to the facts of life. Is this 'two years' absence? Is this 'caring for a wife'? Is this 'fidelity to an overlord'?

The judges make these definitions in terms of 'reasonableness' for a particular kind of reasonable man – husband or councillor or citizen or son. And because 'reasonableness' itself is flexible, they can adapt a persisting body of legal rules to quite new conditions and standards. Therefore the law remains certain, since Barotse judges state their decisions in terms of old well-established rules. But my examples show that judicial decisions, and hence litigation, are often uncertain.

So that when judges are interpreting words by applying them to external facts, they do so by the flexible test of 'reasonableness'. This allows them great play, and it means that they can introduce into their decisions a whole variety of social presumptions, and indeed of prejudices personal to them, or peculiar to the group they represent. But on the whole the standard of 'reasonableness' is drawn from the Barotse community as a whole – Barotse public opinion, and customs, and standards. And all these change as Barotse life changes, and the law develops to accommodate new facts. In short, changing Barotse life itself controls the way in which Barotse judges reinterpret legal concepts.

Barotse judges have had to reinterpret sharply the implications of many of their legal concepts to meet this abruptly changed situation. Hence we can see clearly in their judicial process a problem which is present in our own. Let me illustrate this. Section 154 of our Public Health Act of 1936 lays down that a rag-and-bone merchant shall not give children under 14 'any article whatsoever'. In 1952 a rag-and-bone merchant gave a child a goldfish, and a stipendiary magistrate held that the goldfish was not 'an article' in the meaning of this section. About a year later a bench of justices held that a live chick was an article for purposes of the statute, and another bench held again that a goldfish was *not* an article. This last case went on appeal to a court of three judges who dismissed the appeal and upheld the view that a goldfish is not an article – though it was said that if the goldfish were in a bowl, that bowl would be an article. The word 'article' was here being defined for purposes of a statute which aimed to prevent the spread of disease: under another statute, 'article' might cover goldfish; and the court followed the rule that where a penalty is imposed, it applies the narrow interpretation in favour of the accused. As the judges put it, 'Would anyone in common parlance talk about a goldfish as an article? I do not think they would. . . . I think that it is a straining of language to say a gold-fish is an article.'

I do not believe there is any way in which we can establish by objective evidence, so to speak, that a chicken or a goldfish is or is not an article. But I have already said that the process of decision is not entirely subjective. In English law the process is controlled by written rules, judicial precedents, and textbooks of law. But something else is left – the question which is so often framed, 'Would a reasonable man call a goldfish an article?' This passes the uncertainty to, what is a reasonable man? And here I have suggested that defining the reasonable man – which is indirectly defining an 'article' – may give room for judges to introduce not only social ideas, but also individual prejudices, into their decisions. I take the goldfish case as an entirely hypothetical example – I feel safer that way. I can imagine a judge who feels that there is too much statutory interference in our lives interpreting the word 'article' as narrowly as possible; while a judge who favours benevolent government control would interpret it widely. This is a possibility only; and I use it just to illustrate that the uncertainty which resides in all words, allows judges to manipulate the words in the interests of what they believe to be justice. In doing so, they accommodate into their decisions changes in public opinion and in morals.

It is obvious that this flexibility of words is a great source of strength in judicial logic. Without it, judges could not apply the general rules of law to actual disputes. Despite this, many academic lawyers have attacked it as a source of uncertainty in law, and have therefore regarded it as a weakness. Even judges have done so. But judges are more aware of the value of this characteristic of words. This is clearly exhibited in the words of Lord Chief Justice Coleridge: 'The Attorney-General has asked us where we are to draw the line. The answer is that it is not necessary to draw it at any precise point. It is enough for us to say that the present case is on the right side of any reasonable line that could be drawn.' This judicial statement seems to me to sum up admirably the judicial value of uncertainty in reference of legal terms. Every case is in a sense unique. How is a unique case to be settled? It may have to be covered by legal rules which are stated in very abstract terms, such as that any man who injures another shall make recompense. Even if the rule contains as specific a term as 'article', some judicial decision on the application of the terms to the facts of the situation must be made. What test can there be except that of 'reasonableness'?

But 'reasonableness' itself has a great deal of uncertainty. The line may be drawn differently by different judges. More importantly, it will be drawn differently by judges in new centuries, in accordance with new standards and problems and with advancing knowledge. There may be aberrant decisions: most societies have foolish, ignorant, and perhaps even unjust, judges. But generally the judges will be influenced by changing public opinion in their community, or at least that section of the community from which they are drawn.

Imprecision is thus an inherent attribute of legal concepts. Yet a few years ago a Professor of Jurisprudence complained that, 'Philosophy stands out as a striking example of the flatulencies that may gather round the unacknowledged puns of language. On the whole, lawyers have appreciated the danger, and have been at pains to construct and preserve a moderately precise technical language. Oddly enough, it is least precise in its most fundamental parts. We use the word "right" in some half-dozen different senses and often pass insensibly from one to the other, of course with disastrous results upon our reasoning.' Thus the jurist. As an anthropologist I would suggest that the results may have been disastrous for the reasoning of formal logic; but they may well have resulted, in judicial logic, in a number of very just decisions. Judicial logic has rules of its own: by formal logic alone a judge could not fit the raw facts of evidence into legal categories. Nor could he get justice. For example, this word 'right' that has some half-dozen meanings. I heard Barotse judges in many cases listen to evidence on a whole series of actions by the litigants: then come to the conclusion that, say, defendant had done 'right'. From this they made a jump to saying he was in the 'right', therefore that he had 'a right' to the piece of land in dispute. Then they manipulated the rules of law to defend that right. Here are three different meanings of 'right' – Barotse also have one word for all three, and this word also means 'duty'. So they can make a 'right' into a 'duty'. It is, formally, bad logic: but it may be brilliant judicial logic.

I think myself that it is not at all odd that lawyers' language should be least precise in its most fundamental parts – terms like law, right and duty, crime and injury, property, and so forth. For clearly these are the words which have to serve the most manifold functions in a legal system. They have to cover the greatest number of types of legal situations, and within each type, the greatest variety of actual situations. Hence I would expect them to have the greatest imprecision; and therefore to be capable of the greatest judicial manipulation.

Since Barotse law is unwritten I was made vividly aware of how important is this judicial manipulation. It convinced me that while it is obviously necessary for jurists to dispute this manipulation, they might also accept imprecision as an attribute – and clearly a valuable attribute – of legal concepts. Once one makes this acceptance, one can begin to study how and why judges operate the imprecision of their verbal apparatus. And there are different kinds of imprecision. The Barotse word *swanelo* covers 'right' and 'duty', and as a 'right' or 'duty' it refers to many different kinds of actions and claims. Most fundamental concepts – like 'law' and 'injury' and 'property' – have this kind of imprecision. Other concepts are elastic in that they can be stretched to cover different kinds of action – and frequently they form pairs which can only be defined in terms of one another, such as 'guilt' and 'innocence', or 'negligence' and 'due care'. They form two poles at each end of an elastic line along which litigants' behaviour can be measured. But it is a reasonably elastic line. Barotse judges listen to the evidence, stretch the elastic concepts to decide which man is 'guilty' and which is 'innocent', and then cover these decisions by applying to them the concepts of right and duty which can refer to many things.

In doing this the judges have to make words like 'guilt', or 'negligence', or 'right', cover a great variety of facts. Therefore I call the concepts 'absorbent', for they absorb into their abstract categories the raw material of life. And they have another important attribute. A survey of the law of all societies shows that they have the same fundamental conceptions – law itself, right, duty, property, guilt, innocence – and, in addition, these conceptions are built into similar principles. But they operate in quite different social conditions. Therefore I call them 'permeable' – they are permeated by their social background. A husband must everywhere be reasonable: but the demands on a reasonable husband vary from country to country and at different periods in the same country.

Acceptance of this inherent imprecision of words immediately disposes of certain long-standing controversies in jurisprudence. What is 'law'? Many volumes have been written proffering various definitions. But 'law', which has to cover every kind of regularity in social and physical and organic life, the whole process of social control, and so forth, cannot be restricted within a single definition. The *Concise Oxford Dictionary* gives thirteen definitions: obviously then for every definition advanced by one scholar, another definition can be advanced by another scholar. This breeds only fruitless controversy. The Barotse word *mulao*, which can be translated – reasonably translated – as 'law', means a body of rules accepted by the community as binding, a particular decision of a court, the existence of courts, a personal habit, the regularities of the natural world and of human physiology and psychology and so forth. It is all regularity and order, and all control. Hence it has to be accepted as having many definitions.

At the moment, in particular, controversy rages between orthodox jurists who hold that law is certain, and a so-called sceptical or realist school of American lawyers, who hold that law is uncertain. If we examine their arguments, it is obvious that they are talking about law in two different kinds of senses. Those who insist on law's certainty are examining law in the sense of a body of rules, which judges use and in terms of which they state their decisions. The sceptical lawyers who consider the certainty of law to be a myth are speaking of judges' decisions, and guesses as to future probable decisions. Only those who know nothing of litigation can doubt that law in this sense is uncertain and chancy. But law in this sense – going to law – is litigation. And it results in adjudication. Law in the orthodox sense is a known code of moral principles and legal rules many of which have endured for centuries and are known in most countries – in Ancient Rome, in France and England, and in Barotseland. The body of rules is fairly certain; judges' decisions, in terms of those rules, on various disputes may be uncertain. But the decisions are given in those rules. They can be given thus because the rules are composed of flexible concepts which can be permeated by changing social presumptions and which can absorb the variety of life itself. The 'certainty' of law depends on the 'uncertainty' of its basic concepts. I have punned on the word 'certainty': but I hope this does not negate the value of my paradox.

Chapter Eight

MALINOWSKI'S 'FUNCTIONAL'
ANALYSIS OF SOCIAL CHANGE*

1. *Introduction*

THERE CAN BE no single right analysis of social change. The data
are so complex and our tools as yet so crude that we must expect to
work with various hypotheses and many types of abstractions.
Some will be better instruments of analysis than others, and we

---

* B. Malinowski, *The Dynamics of Culture Change, An Inquiry into Race Relations in Africa*, edited with an introduction by Phyllis M. Kaberry, Yale University Press, 1946, xiv + 171 pp., index.

The two following essays reviewing theoretical statements by the late Bronislaw Malinowski were published in *African Studies* (March 1947) and *Africa*
(April 1947) while I was Director of the Rhodes-Livingstone Institute, and
subsequently reprinted as a Rhodes-Livingstone Paper.

I have not altered the essays, save in detail, because the two points that I wish
to stress in answer to comments I have received, are best emphasized in an
introductory note. First, I had hoped that I had made clear that I regard Malinowski as one of the most significant figures in the social anthropology of this
century. My essays are critical reviews of two statements of his theoretical
principles, which I consider are very inadequate. A full assessment of his work
would require an analysis of his own reports on the Trobriand Islanders; of his
influence on social anthropologists in Europe, America, and the Dominions;
and of the development of anthropological fieldwork and theory during the last
forty years. The advance which social anthropology has made during that period
is remarkable, though it shows most clearly in the difference between reports on
particular peoples written at different stages during the four decades. To that
advance Malinowski made a vital contribution.

Second, I hope my remarks in the first essay pleading for more comparative
work will not be interpreted, as they have been by two colleagues, as a denial
of the fundamental value of fieldwork both for training and for supplying the
foundation for theoretical argument. I state explicitly here that I consider
every social anthropologist should preferably study at least two social systems.

The third essay was broadcast on the Third Programme of the B.B.C. in
January 1959 as reflections on the book *Man and Culture* (1957: edited by R.
Firth) in which twelve of Malinowski's pupils assess his work and influence. I
have paid further tribute in my paper on 'the case-method' in Transactions of
the Fourth International Congress of Sociology at Stresa, 1959 (*The Sociological
Review*, N.S. ix, 1961).

must hope that we shall be able to subsume several of these in more comprehensive and consistent bodies of ordered knowledge. I immediately distrust such works as this latest polemic of the late Professor Malinowski's which is written in the strident terms of the one-and-only orthodoxy.

The book is a posthumous compilation of published essays and unpublished notes. Naturally this prevents its being a polished work, but it does not explain away the book's weaknesses. Each published essay shows that Malinowski failed to work out clearly the structure of his own thesis. He is muddled about his basic philosophical and moral assumptions, and his reasoning is illogical and internally inconsistent. He attacks those who do not belong to his elect by distorting what they have said, and then he unconsciously puts forward their views to demolish someone else. Had Malinowski been an isolated student, this book could have passed unnoticed. But it is published with all the weight that has come rightly to attach to Malinowski's reputation, and the acceptance of the editorship by Dr Kaberry shows that Malinowski was the leader of a school of thought. Therefore I have struggled to analyse his book in order to assess what it contributes to our discipline.

I should prefer to begin this analysis by setting out Malinowski's strength, rather than his weakness, but his whole tone is so polemical that I must first clear away the smoke-screen with which he clouds his argument. Therefore I shall discuss his approach to the historical analysis of culture contact (I prefer 'social change'), his conception of the field-situation, his abstractions, and the 'practical anthropology' which he bases on his thesis.

2. *Malinowski's Approach to the Historical Analysis of Social Change*

Malinowski neither analyses logically what historical studies contribute to our understanding of social change, nor does he refer to the works of any leading historian. Instead, he puts forward the views of two of his own pupils who studied African tribes. In demolishing these, he claims that he has disposed of historical interpretation, even though he admits that social change is an historical process. Thus he cites (p. 20) Hunter as setting the task of anthropology to be 'as far as possible to distinguish elements borrowed from European culture from those which were a part of Pondo culture before the coming of the Europeans'. He shows easily that this is an inadequate definition, and that many complexes in Africa cannot be handled thus.[1] Second, he takes up Mair for arguing that, in Malinowski's words (p. 27): 'The discovery of maladjustments requires as a starting-point a reconstruction of the working of these institutions in precontact times.' He objects to the assumption that old times were good, and new times are 'pathological'. But what I, as a social anthropologist, protest against is the summary dismissal of historical analysis in these two doctrines. For without expressing any judgment on the intrinsic merit of these anthropologists, I can say that it is absurd to give as 'typical historians' two Africanists, and not to refer to the work of people such as Mommsen, Gibbon, Halévy, Weber, Maine, Maitland, Marx, the Webbs, Tawney, the Hammonds, Power, Toynbee, Trevelyan, and many others who have made major contributions to the understanding of historical processes in social life. Not even those sociological historians who have concentrated on Africa, such as Macmillan, Marais, and de Kiewiet are mentioned.

In general Malinowski is completely confused about what history is. He fails to distinguish the understanding of a culture, derived from knowledge of its history and the analysis of historical processes, from the significance which their history, as they know it, has for the bearers of a culture. Malinowski may be right in stating that the former cannibalism of a tribe is in fact irrelevant to its modern nutrition. He is not justified in arguing from this, and similar examples, that there is no value in historical study.

The first basic point he does not appreciate is that every event is the product of a unique history through which, we assume, there has operated a variety of scientific laws. Therefore in order to know why an event is as it is, and not something else, we must know its history. Even in a physicist's laboratory experiment, the bringing together of selected events and the control of external conditions constitute a particular history which enables the experimenter to test only those interdependencies he wishes to determine. An essential section in the report of any experiment is the description of its set-up, i.e. of its history. The need for historical knowledge is as urgent in the humanistic disciplines, which study events whose histories are more complicated and more particular, and which are subject to more numerous and more varied laws. For we observe that individuals and their material goods, their groupings and relationships, persist through changes; and it is the study of their interdependencies which is our field. To analyse these we must study them over a period of time, and the analysis of change therefore involves historical study within a period set by the problem. If we neglect this we get a distorted view. For example, in discussing African warfare Malinowski states (pp. 84–5): 'European occupation . . . has obliterated the old tribal hostilities.' The facts we have show that these old tribal hostilities are by no means obliterated, but are largely denied military expression. In addition, previously hostile tribes may unite against the Europeans. Any historian would have expected this.

Furthermore, without an historical study we cannot understand the drives which lie beneath the changes in the relationships of personalities and groups. In a typically naïve statement, Malinowski criticizes the study of archives:

> The paper programme is never the actuality of contact. We have only to look at the Transkei where the original purpose [of the Glen Grey Acts] was the transformation of the Natives into moderately prosperous small farmers, working their land under a system of individual land tenure, yet as a body still in need of employment, to see that such policies are never realized (p. 114).

Obviously, their failure, if universal, poses an historical problem. A similar problem is dealt with at length in Tawney's *Religion and the Rise of Capitalism*. Malinowski himself shows elsewhere that the Glen Grey Acts failed because of the demand for African labour and the reaction of the Africans in terms of their valuation of land – which itself is an historical analysis. It is certain that the Glen Grey Acts had important effects.

In this particular example Malinowski's obsession against history leads him to a shattering egocentricity. At p. 117 he says of the failure of South African Native land policy:

> All these conclusions provide us with a moral [!] lesson, but it is still wisdom after the event. Had our tripartite scheme for the study of culture contact [discussed below] been applied during the earlier periods, it would have provided invaluable material for the framing of such policies as the Glen Grey Acts, the Land Acts of 1913, and so on.

It might have provided material, but would it, as the context implies, have altered the land policy in South Africa? A government unmoved by the sufferings of thousands of people is not likely to be moved by the pretty chart of an anthropologist. Knowledge alone cannot make a moral policy; it can as easily serve an immoral one.

I examine now Malinowski's conception of what history is. He argues that the anthropologist is concerned not with 'history dead and buried, but with tradition alive and at work'. The distinction is valid, for psychically people are moved by what they believe their history to be and not by what it was. English schoolboys know the names of Poictiers, Crecy, and Agincourt: how many know the names of the French victories? Yet the French victories kept France independent of England and so affected English history and England. Therefore from another point of view people are affected by what their history actually was: i.e. by history dead and buried. The whole of Britain's history gives her a place in the world which affects her present structure. The Thirty Years War by its material results affected German life for many generations. The Zulu conquest of Natal created relationships with other tribes which still operate, unknown to the people.

This distinction, in itself useful, certainly does not reject historical study which aims to understand processes of change. No one would dispute that 'fictitious' reconstruction is bad, and all reconstruction is difficult. But the work of historians of Europe shows how much can be done; Eileen Power put flesh and blood on medieval people. The anthropologist who is working to a smaller time-depth can use similar material, not only of Native informants, but also from official records, books of travellers and missionaries, etc. These may not always be accurate reports of Native culture, but their descriptions are by actors in the contemporary scene. Obviously their accounts will not be as good or as comprehensive as those of modern field-workers, but they are often illuminating. The extent to which this reconstruction can be made obviously depends on the records available.

Reconstruction has two purposes. First, it gives one essential part of our understanding of the present – of why things are as they are. Second, it provides data for the analysis of social processes, both in static and in changing societies. There is no difference in essence between processes of change observed today, and those observed in the past, or reconstructed if data are available.

Knowledge of processes that have occurred in the past adds to our range of comparative generalization. This is obvious enough, but Malinowski pays it only lip-service. It is true that he grants (at pp. 33–4) some value to historical studies of Greek city-states, etc., and he claims that he himself introduced the biographical study of kinship, and historical technique. Nevertheless, his obscurantist bias against history is patent, for example, in his chiding of Mair: 'A shaking off completely of the historical obsession' (p. 136, n. 60.).

Similar processes may occur at different times and in different societies. For example, some field-workers have noticed that the evangelical drive among Africans has passed from most established churches such as the Anglicans, Presbyterians, Catholics, etc., to sects such as the Seventh Day Adventists and Salvation Army, above all to Jehovah's Witnesses and separatist African churches. These convert pagans and adherents of the 'established churches'. This suggests comparison with the types of sects joined by the working-class of England in the early nineteenth century, as discussed by the Hammonds and Halévy, and with the flocking of Russians after the 1917 Revolution to the evangelical churches which had been restricted by the Tsarist régime as well as with one of Max Weber's most important generalizations. In making such a comparison we should have to look at the processes at work, and not only at the complex and incommensurable realities. Moreover, this poses a field-problem in historical terms: the compilation from mission records of the numbers of adherents of the various sects over a period.

Malinowski himself is constantly driven to formulate similar problems in historical terms. Thus he has a section called 'the lines of tribal renegation [!] and integral rebuff' (p. 158), in which he discusses how Africans, after a first responsive acceptance of some European influences, are rebuffed by the colour bar and turn back to their own culture. The movement is expressed in separatist churches, renewed loyalty to tribal authorities, and a return to Native customs, rituals, and art with heightened value. This is sound enough – and it is historical.

Malinowski's theoretical denial of the value of historical reconstruction is thus contradicted by his constant use of it, wherever he makes a good analysis. We see here not only the necessity to study history in order to observe processes of social change, but also the need to record historical developments in order to understand the latent drives in existing organization, as well as its present form. Historians over centuries have been aware of this, and have tried to formulate general processes. On the whole they have resigned themselves to analysing the unique relationships in their material. It is clear that if we are to formulate processes of change in general terms, we must abstract them from each historical reality. There can be no comparison of the overladen complexity of real events. The problem that remains is: can we compare the processes of change in a variety of societies?

3. *Malinowski's Conception of the Field of Study*

Malinowski introduces his conception of the field of study by attacking the view which regards the Africans of today as an integral part of the modern world. To do this, he distorts the arguments supporting this view. Then, with the inconsistency. which we found in his use of history, he adopts it in many of his own analyses. I shall briefly demonstrate this and indicate that his concepts make it inevitable.

The view that Malinowski attacks is assumed in the studies of historians (e.g. Macmillan), economists (e.g. Frankel), and psychologists (e.g. Macrone). He attacks it as put forward by Fortes and Schapera. I have already exposed his distortions[2] but have here to repeat the argument, because Dr Kaberry, in editing this book, similarly distorts what I wrote.

Malinowski writes:

It is now generally agreed upon that Europeans form an integral part of any contact situation. . . . But I think it is pushing a legitimate commonplace too far when it is suggested [by Schapera] that 'the missionary, administrator, trader and labour recruiter must be regarded as factors in the tribal life in the same way as are the chief and the magician'. . . . Yet another writer [Fortes] has claimed that 'Contact agents can be treated as integrally part of the community'.

Malinowski attacks:

Unfortunately, this type of simplification is not advisable. The treatment of the complex situations of change as one 'well-integrated whole', the 'one-entry' approach as we might call it, ignores the whole dynamism of the process. . . . The concept of a well-integrated community would, indeed, ignore such facts as the colour bar, the permanent rift which divides the two partners in change and keeps them apart in church and factory, in matters of mine labour and political influence. (pp. 14 ff.)

I need not quote more extensively. 'Integral' becomes 'well-integrated whole', and then a 'well-integrated community' meaning 'harmonious'. Similarly, Schapera's statement that white personalities have to be studied *in the same way* as black, is perverted by reading the words *in the same way* as if they referred to the social position of the personalities, and not to a field-technique. Then obviously the missionary is not socially equivalent to the magician. Again, where Schapera speaks of using white informants on matters which they know about, Malinowski says 'we should [then] have only a slight numerical addition to our informants': as if an administrator cannot give valuable data on the matters which Africans bring to his office.

Dr Kaberry uses the same technique to dismiss my argument.

Dr Gluckman . . . states: 'We see that the dominant form of the structure is the existence *within a single community* [Kaberry's italics] of two co-operating colour groups which are differentiated by a large number of criteria so as to stand opposed and even hostile to one another.' Dr Gluckman admits the existence of a colour bar; unfortunately, he does not define the term community. If, however, we take it to mean a territorial group which participates in a common culture, it is difficult to see how it can be applied to the African contact situation, in view of the profound differences of language and culture between the groups involved. (p. 14, n. 3.)

If, indeed, one defines *community* as an ethnic group recognizing common values – or as a group of people who believe the earth is flat – or as anything I clearly did not imply it to mean, then I wrote nonsense. It is unfortunate, perhaps, that I used the word *community*: it was the best term I could find to express the fact that there is a large field of interdependence in which individuals of the two colour groups have standardized norms of behaviour to each other. But it is unfair to give to a word a meaning other than the one I intended, and then to make it the basis for a rejection of my whole analysis. The unfairness is made manifest in the words: 'Dr Gluckman *admits* [my italics] the existence of a colour bar'; whereas in fact my analysis of the situation dealt wholly with the colour bar, the opposition of colour groups, and the differences in culture.

We can thus reject Malinowski's initial denial of the existence of a single social body, to use a neutral word, of whites and blacks. Nevertheless, Malinowski might still be justified in rejecting the concept as a tool of analysis. Let us examine his own position. He says that the missionary 'cannot "be regarded in the same way as the magician". . . . The missionary would not be true to his vocation if he ever agreed to act on the principle that Christianity is as "any other form of cult" [Schapera said Christianity has to be studied in the same way as any other form of cult] . . . his brief is to regard all other forms of religion as misguided. . . . Far from leaving other cults side by side in juxtaposition with the message of the Gospels, the missionary is actively engaged in superseding them.' He contrasts similarly administrator and chief. He states that it would be difficult to regard the 'settler and his African neighbour as brethren of a large family' (p. 17) – and who has said they are?

Nor can industrial enterprise be regarded as part of a tribal unit. It would be a strange African tribe which would embrace the gold mines of the Rand with their gigantic plant; the stock exchange of Johannesburg, and the banking system stretching from Cape to Cairo. The communication systems, railroads and planes . . . all this is part of culture contact. But the concept of an extended African tribe, into which this could be squeezed in order to produce a unified tribal horizon, falls to the ground as soon as it is stated. (pp. 16–17.)

No one has said that the Rand mines, etc., were within the embrace of an African tribe or could be 'squeezed' into 'a unified tribal horizon'. We state that the Rand mines and the African tribe which supplies their labour are both parts of a single social field; that the administrator who represents a government in London ruling over settlers and Africans, and the chief who rules over only a tribe whose members are in constant relationships with settlers and with government, are both parts of a single political body. For example, the son of a Zulu councillor was selected by the Zulu paramount to work for him, a signal honour for the father. The youth ran away home. His father upbraided the youth for spoiling his name with the paramount. The youth retorted that the chief paid him nothing – look at his clothes; the Native Commissioner was better than the chief, since he paid those he employed. Afraid of his father's wrath and desirous of money, the youth ran away to a sugar-cane plantation – it might well have been the Rand mines. He could only flee from the paramount because the latter's writ of compulsion was limited by government. Here we have a right of the chief to call for labour which honours a father, the son desiring money and asserting a 'preference' for the administrator because he pays, the development of a family conflict, and the solution of the conflict by flight to an enterprise of European capital. I quote this simple example to make explicit our conception of tribal group and Rand mines, of administrator and chief, as parts of a single social field. Indeed, Malinowski himself constantly has to use the conception, though he explicitly denies it.

Divination and witchcraft found in a town yard are not mere replicas of the genuine African institution. The performance I saw in Johannesburg was African divination, but it was applied to a case of witchcraft turning around the competitions and jealousies of mine employment; the fee was paid in English money, and the verdict was given in terms which no tribesman would understand. (p. 22.)

But his denial of the existence of this single social body involves him in difficulties of which he is not aware. This emerges, for example, when he discusses 'the problems of Native diet in their economic setting'. He states (p. 102) that 'the method of study here, of course, would be based on field work among the whites who control Native nutrition, including the research workers in biology, medicine and social conditions'. He goes on (p. 109) to point out that though mine-labourers are well fed, the diet of their women and children at home suffers because the men are away and are not producing food. Cash wages 'on broad and sociological lines' should compensate for this. Presumably, the diet of the women and children in the reserves has to be studied by the biochemist, who is himself studied by the sociologist. The biochemist thus becomes a factor in the tribal horizon though the administrator is not. The facts force Malinowski to analyse in terms of a social frame in which all personalities and groups, black and white, are in theory mutually interdependent.

Malinowski's inconsistency is not chance: it arises from the weakness of his theoretical framework. Briefly, in general wherever blacks and whites co-operate he classifies the phenomena as 'processes of social contact and change'; wherever they conflict he regards them as distinct and 'not integrated'. I am aware that examples from his writings can be cited against this statement, but these are the fruits of his inconsistency. Thus at p. 65 he says:

> Whenever effective co-operation occurs, a new form of social organization is engendered: a Native Christian congregation under the supervision and guidance of a white clergy; a mine or a factory where African labour works under the direction of a white staff; a bush school where African children are taught by European teachers; an organized system of Native administration under European control. Thus, what results from impact is not a higgledy-piggledy assortment of traits, but new institutions, organized on a definite charter, run by a mixed personnel, related to European plans, ideas, and needs, and at times satisfying certain African interests.

But he cannot admit 'conflict' into his frame of integrated institutions—that is, conflict as an inherent attribute of social organization, though in practice he uses it. He cannot see that the Rand mines are a field of conflict as well as a field of co-operation in which Africans, for the money they desire, assist the Europeans to mine gold. Nor can he see that the separatist sects, which significantly he pigeon-holes not as 'processes of social contact and change' but in a special column, as 'new forces of spontaneous African reintegration or reaction', are an aspect of the colour bar plus 'the Native Christian congregation under . . . white clergy'. Theoretically, he regards the parties to conflicts as not 'integral' factors in the same field and excludes them from the region of culture contact.

4. *Malinowski's Practical Anthropology*

Before I go on to clarify the above points in the realm of analysis, I have to interpolate a section on Malinowski's 'practical anthropology'. This is reduced to absurdity by his failure to appreciate the significance of conflict. He writes (p. 160):

> I am simply pointing out some of the forces which, wisely controlled, may ensure a normal and stable development but when mismanaged may lead to dangerous consequences. . . . It is clear that wise colonial statesmanship in matters administrative, educational, economic, and religious will do well to assess the potentialities and dangers implied in the relation between things promised and things given. For the disproportion between the hopes raised and the advantages promised to the African when he is induced to cross the line of tribalism and the

realization which he receives at the barrier of racial discrimination is the main problem to be considered.

I suggest that first and foremost it would be well to unify, co-ordinate, and harmonize various policies. . . . Whenever Europeans plan the settlement of large portions of any colony, segregation and colour bar become inevitable. This ought to be remembered by the enthusiastic minority of good will, who may involuntarily raise high hopes through such doctrines as the Brotherhood of Man, the Gospel of Labour, and the possibilities of assimilation through education, dress, manners, and morals. If, from the outset, it were possible to make quite clear in preaching the gospel of civilization that no full identity can ever be reached; that what are being given to the Africans are new conditions of existence, better adapted to their needs but always in harmony with European requirements, the smaller would be the chances of a strong reaction and the formation of new, potentially dangerous nationalisms.

But this admonition to the minority of goodwill is not all that the anthropologist has to say. He has also to address a few words to that majority of European interests who naturally are not directly concerned with the welfare of the Natives. Big enterprise, organized trade, and most of the administrative agents act primarily under European imperatives. Through their influence the measure of fulfillment is often made inadequate to the promise of the enthusiastic minority.

The anthropologist must therefore also insist that a substantially increased measure of real and tangible benefits is necessary, in the interests not only of the African but also of the white community. In the long run, African and European interests converge because stable and effective rule by a minority can only be founded on the real satisfaction, prosperity, and welfare of the Native subjects.

I do not here refer to the moral judgments implicit in this passage. Africans are likely to say that one who merely consigns them to a slightly more attractive compound is an unwanted advocate; and I for one reject him as advocate of the anthropologists. Here I am interested in the lack of appreciation of the dynamism within the European interests. Here is not even recognition of hard facts. I cannot imagine that a churchman like the late Archdeacon Owen would compromise to the extent of preaching citizenship Grade B and its duties to his beloved people. It is not mere accident that Christianity and Islam – which Malinowski does not mention, though it is gaining at the expense of Christianity in East Africa and is powerful in West Africa – preach brotherhood. What of the Communist Party? Is that to be banned? And all liberal and progressive writings? And is the news of the Eastern people's demand for independence to be kept from the African?

The argument must be taken seriously, since Malinowski bases on this a concept of the 'common factor' which he raises to the dignity of treatment in a separate essay: 'Whenever there is a common measure between the intentions of European impact and the existing needs of the African society, change can lead to new thriving forms of cultural co-operation . . . the absence of a common factor leads to conflict' (p. 70).

Politically, in the preceding passage Malinowski's compromise on the common factor appears to me as the anthropologist crawling on his knees to beg some white groups for a few more crumbs for the Africans, and then asking the missionary to preach a religion that will be an opiate. Sociologically, it shows two weaknesses. It is a mechanical balancing of policies and group-differences, an unawareness of a situation in which not only does the Anglican Synod protest against the colour bar, but also white entrepreneurs of secondary industries demand stabilization, advance of skill, and increase of purchasing power, in opposition to the migrant labour policy of the mine owners, whose interests stem from the conditions of the extractive industries. This unawareness flows from Malinowski's refusal to see conflict as a mode of integrating groups and to recognize that hostility between groups is a form of social balance. This is not so dangerous in the study of static communities and Malinowski, in his Trobriand analyses on sex and repression and on crime and custom, has stimulated the study of conflict. It is most dangerous when studying a changing society, especially when there are inducements for the anthropologist to tone down 'conflict'.

The second weakness arises from the refusal to regard modern Africa as an 'integral' territorial section of the modern world, and hence the refusal to recognize that though we may isolate for study a reserve, a slum yard, a mine compound, or even a mine, we must allow for the effects of extraneous forces.

This section points to another weakness implicit in Malinowski's scheme. Whenever he tries to frame analytical problems, he poses practical problems in the most naïve terms. He begins the book with a statement that there is no difference between theoretical and applied research. He cannot, with his concepts, do otherwise, for, as we shall see, they bind him to the description

of unique realities. I have cited two examples already, his conclusions on nutrition in its economic setting and on the conflict
between what the African is promised and what he will get. He
says (p. 55) that to change an African to a civilized Christian and
European citizen 'requires above all substance': economic security,
full social status, and freedom. This may be true, but he should
be posing analytical problems: what categories of Africans are
converted at various periods, how does this affect their behaviour
and their relationships with their kin, their chief, and with whites,
and so on. Similarly, he states (pp. 113 ff.) that the land problem
is reducible to 'one which is very simple: whether there is or is
not enough land? Hence it is primarily a technical problem.' The
simplicity of this statement is breath-taking, but it accords with
the sociological unawareness with which he advised missionaries
not to preach Christianity, and thought that his three-column
charts would have changed South African land policy.

5. *Malinowski's Conception of Culture Contact*

I have tried to clear the way for an appraisal of Malinowski's own
theoretical framework. After describing certain impressions of
modern Africa, he continues (p. 64):

> The African world of contact and change consists of three distinct
> orders of cultural reality: the African, the Western, and that of transi-
> tion. Each of these orders is subject to a specific determinism of its
> own. . . . At the same time, all three orders or phrases are related to or
> dependent on each other. The impact and initiative come from the
> organized forces of Western civilization. They are directed onto the
> largely passive tribal resources which respond to contact with adapta-
> tion or conflict. This process of reaction, positive or negative – the
> interaction between black and white, between Western culture and
> tribalism – covers the field of contact and change. Between the two
> boundaries of colour bar on the one side and the dead weight of tribal
> conservatism on the other there lies the no-man's-land of change.
> This is not a narrow strip but really embraces most of what is going on
> in Africa. As yet it is but partly accomplished; adaptation is imperfect
> and piecemeal; conflict is open or concealed; and at times also there is
> fruitful co-operation or else disorganization and decay.

Later I shall examine the threefold research scheme he bases on
this. Here I analyse the theoretical implications.

Malinowski has to see modern Africa in these three distinct

phases. He is concerned with culture, 'the whole body of implements, the charters of its social groups, human ideas, beliefs and
customs' (p. 42). Then when whites landed in Natal, how was
their culture in contact with Zulu culture? And how today can
Zulu culture be said to be in contact with the culture of London?
Malinowski logically argues that wherever whites and blacks co-
operate, we are presented with a 'third cultural reality, the zone of
contact and change, subject to its own determinism'. It is a
tertium quid, not explicable by either of the flanking white or
black cultures.

Let us examine the application of the framework to a particular
set of phenomena. Malinowski describes (p. 23) the establishing
of a mine in Africa:

Once the new industrial venture is organized, we have a complicated
European enterprise, essentially dependent on African labour and resources, a phenomenon which can no more be dissected into bits
African and European. It cannot be understood either as a whole, or
yet in any of its component parts, in terms of European or African
prototypes. There is no European prototype for colour-bar legislation
or practice; for recruiting on reserves; for the method of unemploy-
ment insurance by throwing back superfluous labour onto the tribal
areas in times of slump. . . . What really takes place is an interplay of
specific contact forces: race prejudice, political and economic imperial-
ism, the demand for segregation, the safeguarding of a European
standard of living, and the African reaction to all this. . . .
African labour differs from European labour legally, economically,
and socially. At the same time this labour cannot be related in any way
to African tribal economics. The scale of payments, criminal sanctions
for contracts, pass laws and diet problems which occur in South Africa
cannot be understood in terms of the European or of the African parent
cultures.

Malinowski must adopt this point of view for in fact the real
differences are as marked as he describes: here is European culture, here is African culture, and here is 'the *tertium quid* of contact'. He remains bogged in description of the separate phases.
This prevents his observing certain significant similarities, which
are present in the patent differences he describes.

1. The mine is organized for work on the same principles as a
gold mine anywhere: manager, foreman, labourers, etc. It is
irrelevant if the unskilled labour is European, African, Malayan,

or Chinese. Similarly, from some points of view it is irrelevant that southern Africans do not become capitalists while Chinese and Indians do, though this produces important variant results.

2. The beginnings of industrialization in every country have been marked by migratory labour, since the demand for labour in towns must draw on the rural population. For this purpose, it is irrelevant whether the labourer is brought by the Native Recruiting Corporation from an African village to the Rand, or by a blackbirder from a Polynesian island to Queensland, or from a Russian *mir* to the Don mines, or from Ireland to Birkenhead. The enclosing of land in England, like the taking of African land, drove men to the towns. Here again local factors produce variant effects. In South Africa, the Zulu with their limited wants and sufficient land wished to move for a short while only to earn money: this met the needs of gold-mining. But Zulu have become urbanized as the Irish remained in Birkenhead.

3. Conditions in Africa allow superfluous labour to be thrown back on the reserves in periods of slump. Millions of Americans returned similarly from the towns to the rural areas. And from the viewpoint of capitalist enterprise, this resembles the throwing of superfluous English labour on the dole, or superfluous American labour into public works. The differences are significant, but beneath them a similar process may be seen.

4. The colour bar in Africa has its parallel in Europe in the struggle by trade unions of skilled workers against dilution of labour. British men opposed the entry of women into industry in fear lest they should lower men's standards of living; men teachers resent the employment of married women; British workers hated the undercutting Irish, and Californians the undercutting Okies. One aspect of the colour bar in Africa – of course, by no means the only aspect – is that it marks the struggle of entrenched workers against dilution.

5. There is no parallel in modern Europe to the pass-laws. European workers are bound by economic necessity: so are urbanized Africans; so are African migrant labourers. But the last have a little choice between remaining in the reserves and going to the labour centres – hence the recruiting which Malinowski cites as 'new'. It is not a fully effective choice, for in many reserves, even if Africans can grow their food, they cannot get money for their clothes and taxes. W. M. Macmillan has stressed the similarity

between the restictive legislation on Africans and many of the poor-laws of Elizabeth's reign. Tsarist Russia had 'cards of identity' and it would be profitable to compare the way in which the police handled the relevant laws, with what happens in the 'similar' situation in Africa. Passes and penal sanctions tend to bind the African to a particular master, as apprentices and slaves were bound in European history.

6. A variant of migrant labour from the reserves in South Africa is migrant labour of African labour tenants bound to work six months in a year for the farmer on whose land they live. Statute has been piled on statute to keep these tenants bound to their farmers. All are unsuccessful, for they operate against the dominant movement from country to town. Similar legislation has also occurred in the history of Europe.

This short analysis makes it clear that by concentrating on the particular cultural reality we cannot see the comparable aspects. If we treat the mine and the tribe as parts of a single field, we see that within all the areas where it operates capitalist enterprise produces similar results, i.e. it has an autonomy of its own, in Europe, America, Asia, Australia, and Africa. What actually occurs in each area is affected by local variations, and the variant aspects also have to be studied. Africans now tend to leave paganism and the established churches for the 'curious' and separatist sects: so did British workers in the early nineteenth century. Some of the African separatist sects include belief in witchcraft; the British sects did not. In similar situations similar processes operate, but each has its variants.

Malinowski considers the urban areas of Africa to be 'a new cultural reality with its own determinisms'. It is impossible, in Malinowski's terms, to set lines for studying so-called tribalized and detribalized Africans. In his framework these categories of people live in different 'cultural realities'. It is obvious that even though they may be the same people their behaviour is situational so that from some points of view they can be treated as different individuals. This cannot give us a full analysis of their behaviour. If we conceive the tribal and urban areas to be one social field, we say that as soon as an African moves from a reserve to an urban area he is 'detribalized' in the sense that he comes under white authority without his chief, he works in different ways, he associates with different types of individuals, etc. But he is still tribalized, for of course he does not cease to be influenced by tribal culture. To understand his behaviour we must study: how far does he act under urban and industrial influences, common to all urban areas throughout the world? e.g. in forming civic leagues, trade unions, etc. How far is his behaviour determined by poverty, lack of skill, and other characteristics which he shares with workers elsewhere in capitalist countries? How far does urbanization under segregation in Africa (but not peculiar to Africa) control his actions, and his separate civic status under different laws? What are the effects of his contacts with the white group? And how far do his tribal culture and his allegiance to his tribe still affect his behaviour?

Thus we see that Malinowski's conception of the field in terms of culture leads him to the stultifying scheme of three separate cultural phases, each distinct, each unlike the others. This is correct, if we look at the actual realities: the Africans' barracks at the Rand mines and an Alaskan gold-mining village are not the same. But, as we have seen, it is incorrect to deduce from this, as Malinowski does, that one cannot dissect these real phenomena to show that they share some characteristics, just as a whale and a sheep are both mammals in some respects. Malinowski argues that they are so unlike that each of them must be separately described.

6. Malinowski's 'Institutions' in Culture Contact

Malinowski's conception of culture contact as occurring between 'institutions', organized systems of human activities, shows the same weaknesses. His unit of culture is the 'institution' –

A group of people united for the pursuit of a simple or complex activity; always in possession of a material endowment and a technical outfit; organized on a definite legal or customary charter, linguistically formulated in myth, legend, rule, and maxim; and trained and prepared for carrying out its task (pp. 49–50).

The institutions are related to basic human psychological and physiological needs and he specifically denies (at p. 42) that sociology can be kept apart from the study of these. Culture conditions the individuals to amalgamate nature and nurture. To feed and enjoy sex, to be warm and protected, are needs that animals satisfy directly, but human beings only in co-operation conditioned by the whole external and transcendent apparatus of culture, including the symbols of language and ritual. He establishes a hierarchy of instrumental imperatives to satisfy these needs and other needs derived from them, from the conditioning to a manner of sexual intercourse to the diathesis established by religion or magic. Each institution – economic, political, etc. – relates to a need.

When he proceeds to study culture contact, he logically concludes:

All sociologically relevant impact and interaction is organized, that is, it occurs as between institutions. The real agencies of contact are organized bodies of human beings working for a definite purpose; handling appropriate apparatus of material culture; and subject to a charter of laws, rules and principles (p. 65.).

This is sound. But since his theory is formulated on the basis of needs, he follows this with the statement that each western institution 'has to direct its impact primarily upon its indigenous counterpart. . . . The missionary has to supplant the Native forms of belief and worship', the entrepreneur to use appropriate African labour and resources, the government to work with the Native chieftainship' (p. 65). He bases his practical anthropology on the thesis that

the concept of common measure or common factor is the direct corollary of our principle that human institutions are commensurable across the dividing line of culture; but that in each of these they fulfill the same function under a different type of determinism. One kind of institution can be replaced by another which fulfils a similar function (p. 52.). . . . The African family and type of marriage are equivalents of European marriage and the family, etc. (p. 70).

Clearly we can compare European and African marriage and even say they satisfy similar needs, but I cannot see that this applies save to a limited extent to the analysis of culture change with its complicated strands of interaction. Certainly it does not justify Malinowski's statement that 'commensurable institutions' act *primarily* on one another across the division of culture. Not even Malinowski can maintain this in his analyses. For example, he shows that missionary work affects chieftainship, sex morality, economic life, etc. Conversion itself cannot be studied only as the supplanting of one set of religious beliefs by another; it has to be analysed in a complex social situation. Not all Zulu are converted because they feel that Christianity is a better religion than the ancestor-cult. It does not, for all Zulu respond better to 'the human psychology of thwarted hope, of fears and anxieties', or provide a stronger affirmation of human immorality (pp. 47–8). More women than men become Christians, more younger sons than elder sons, more unimportant than important people: there are here wide ranges of structural problems. These can be studied, but not the satisfaction of needs which are in fact assumed from the beginning of the analysis.

Malinowski would have accepted the above formulations. I am here opposing his concept of 'the primacy of commensurable interaction' which can be discarded as useless. It indicates the analytical sterility of the approach from needs, which even becomes misleading when Malinowski expresses it explicitly and makes it the compass of his search for 'the common factor in culture change' (pp. 64 ff.). The Zulu migrant labourer goes to the mines to earn money to feed and clothe his family: that is one reason why the mine owner develops the mine. Is this a common factor, because both satisfy in the mine their basic needs? It is the centre of their interdependence, and also the centre of their conflicts. The situation is too complex for this reduction. The processes by which the Zulu is induced to want more goods, is driven to work by tax and shortage of land, develops pride in his experiences in 'white country', etc., require a survey of wide social fields, not a reiteration of basic needs.

Malinowski here, as in his more general theoretical writings, concentrates on the relation of institutions to needs and otherwise leaves his analysis of institutions on a descriptive plane without attempting to dissect them into smaller units susceptible of comparative analysis. The institutions, except in the general terms in which they satisfy needs, remain overloaded with reality: we must recount personnel, material apparatus, charter, norms. Since 'the so-called elements or "traits" of a culture do not form a medley . . . but are always integrated into well-defined units', he implies that it is wrong to break up these units and abstracts parts or aspects of them for analysis. But to generalize we must isolate certain aspects of a situation or institution; real situations and institutions are too complicated for comparative analysis. Four results flow from this.

The first is that his analysis of culture hardly moves from the descriptive plane of the individual and unique. As a technique for getting comprehensive data it is magnificent and that is Malinowski's great contribution to the methods of sociology. It may well prove that this is the most that sociology can do: to produce accurate, detailed, and comprehensive descriptions of cultures in all their complicated interdependence. But this explains why Malinowski poses no comparative problems. I conned the book meticulously but found not one attempt to abstract change from its complicated real context.

Second, his concept of institutions as 'well-integrated units' breaks down in the field of social change. It is probably the dominance of this concept which led him to pervert Fortes and Schapera's 'integral' into 'well-integrated' and then to reject this. It prevents him from fitting in the idea of conflict at all, and stultifies his handling of history. His 'theory' of institutions still provides a chart for field-work: it is useless for analyses of social change. Nowhere does he describe change in any but vague and glib general terms, tied always to a particular and unique reality. In so far as his charts on specific problems have value, it is a descriptive value only.

Third, Malinowski makes no clear analysis of what he means when he says that 'impact occurs between institutions'. It is obvious enough that when an administrator deals with a chief, each represents a set of human institutions, in the sense that they are not simply people, but are social personalities in specific relationship with each other, and with specific interests and values, etc. In this sense also their positions become centres of new 'institutions'. But it is necessary to break up this concept into smaller units if we are to make further analysis.

Fourth, Malinowski frequently repeats that in the social changes that occur when culturally heterogeneous groups are brought into contact, goods and customs do not pass from one group to another, and are not accepted, in isolation. I illustrate this patent fact with an example from my own data. The plough does not just drop into Zulu hands. In the past, most agricultural work was done by the women. Cattle were taboo to women, but cattle had to draw the plough. After initial resistance to the plough, men, freed from their life at the king's military barracks, began to plough; the ritual taboo on the handling of cattle by women and the emphasis on cattle-handling as men's work dominated the rule that garden-work was appropriate to women. We assume that this altered the property relations of men and women: the relative importance of crops worked by men increased and though wives retained their own fields, they did not work these themselves, but their husbands or sons ploughed parts. However, villages got smaller, boys went to school, and youths to work for whites. A man might find himself short of help in ploughing, since the Zulu have one man at the plough and one driving the oxen. This happened particularly to Christians who built on their own and were anxious to send all their children to school. They allowed their wives to drive but not to handle the cattle or the plough. Government enforces dipping. If a man is ill and there is no other help, a wife or daughter will drive the cattle to the dip. There other men, to keep her from their cattle, might drive her herd through the dip. Other Zulu, co-operating in large groups which always had sufficient male labour, said 'it is all right for the woman or girl to drive the cattle if there is no boy and provided she is not menstruating. When the men went to the military barracks in the past, girls had to milk and herd the cattle.' Clearly, then, every change sets up repercussions which run, on paths set by the institutions, through all the institutions. But I must emphasize that Malinowski has not indicated any techniques of analysis by which these repercussions can be broken into smaller units to allow of scientific generalization. Our account above remains purely descriptive. The professional anthropologist can claim that his descriptions are likely to be more accurate and comprehensive than those of amateurs, and here Malinowski's contribution, in field-work techniques, is notable. But must we remain on the descriptive plane, or can we pose, in more general terms, problems arising from the impact of institutions and from changes running through a system of institutions? This Malinowski has failed to consider, and it remains one of our major problems. The Americans have grappled with it.

If we examine the field-work of students in modern Africa, almost all of whom have been influenced by Malinowski, we find that on the whole they produce more or less good, accurate, and comprehensive descriptions of what has happened, is happening, and may happen in the future. Correlations are just deeper than description. For example, Richards concludes that the Bemba have not adopted the use of money in European ways because they had no material property, as the cattle-owing southern tribes had, to give them ideas of quantity, accumulation, and exchange value. Even if this be extended, it is little more than description. Thus I suggested that the Lozi use money in European fashion more than the Zulu do, though both have cattle, because, unlike the Zulu, they had considerable trade in their internal economy for which money was a boon. I also drew attention to Richards' statement that the Bisa fishermen of Bembaland have a better appreciation of money than the pure Bemba, because they trade a lot. Similarly, anthropologists say that the dying of the ancestral-cult weakens the chief, that labour migration gives a man a chance to escape from the authority of his elders, that the increase in situations of conflict has been met by an increase in charges of witchcraft. In detailed analyses of this type we have added greatly to general knowledge of developments. We are even able to predict what will be found in areas not yet studied. Thus on the basis of work by Evans-Pritchard and Stayt I anticipated that the Government's ban on open reaction in witchcraft situations would produce, in the tribes I studied, an increasing use of magic against witchcraft, and we may assume that this is likely to be true of every tribe in Africa.

There is little doubt that the anthropologist, with his training and techniques and background of knowledge, can know far more about an unstudied area than the people who live in it. Certainly, he can in a very short time acquire a more accurate complete knowledge. Our relative skill will increase as we gain wider knowledge, refine our techniques, and use statistics more. But while we must be prepared to recognize the possibility that the description of real events and surface comparisons in mainly similar fields, with a few generalizations at a low level of abstraction, may be the limit of our achievements, we can still try to develop our discipline into a science able to correlate the universal aspects of events, independent of a particular cultural reality.[3] For this attempt we must discard Malinowski's 'theoretical' analysis as sterile. His own work remains an invaluable code for field-research.

7. *Malinowski's Charting of the 'Three Cultural Realities'*
Malinowski produces charts to enable us to study changing Africa. He projects 'the three cultural realities each with its own determinism' – a concept which he does not clarify – on to three

columns. He allows another column for the 'reconstructed past', another for 'new forces of spontaneous African reintegration or reaction', and later suggests a sixth to cover European culture outside Africa. This multiplication of columns is significant.

Specimen chart to be used for the Analysis of culture contact and change

	A	B	C	D	E
Europe	White influence, interests and intentions.	Processes of culture contact and change.	Surviving forms of tradition.	Reconstructed past.	New forces of spontaneous African reintegration or reaction.

What is the value of the scheme? Malinowski gives the chart an almost autonomous methodological merit in the posing and solving of problems. This it has not. For in practice what he does is to examine the reality of modern Africa, and fit what he observes into the various columns. There is no indication that an entry under 'A' automatically poses problems under 'B' and 'C'. In my opinion, the chart might serve at best as a check on the comprehensiveness of field-work, but not as a tool of analysis.

I take an example covered to some extent by his notes on African warfare.

A	B	C
1. European conquest and political control.	1. The new political system as affected by loss of military sovereignty of the African tribe or monarchy, and resultant changes in African organization.	1. African resistance and political submission in tribal memory and reaction.

That is only one of his horizontal columns but it illustrates the type of entry he makes. The chart, if it has universal effectiveness, should cover all problems. I pose one from Zulu history.

In the 1830's Boer trekkers under Retief came to Dingane, King of the Zulu, to ask for land. They did not then wish to wrest land from the Zulu by force, but to get Dingane's permission for them to take up land in the parts of Natal which Shaka's wars had depopulated. Dingane agreed to allow this if Retief's party attacked another chief and recovered for him cattle he claimed. Retief did this, but Dingane murdered the Boer party and killed many of the Boers in Natal. Another group of Boers later that year attacked and defeated the Zulu, and confined them north of the Tugela River. Meanwhile, Dingane was ruling tyrannously, and his brother Mpande was able to lead his own following over to the Boers, who assisted him to defeat Dingane and installed Mpande as king. Let us fit these events, or the institutions behind them, into the columns:

A	B	C
1. Boer desire for land, temporary wish to come to peaceful terms with the Zulu.	1. Dingane uses Boers against enemy chief and they agree to be used to gain favour. Dingane murders Boers, and other Boers avenge.	1. Zulu independence and military power, hostility to neighbouring chiefs.
2. Boer military power, and readiness to use enemy fifth column, Mpande v. Dingane.	2. Mpande gets Boer power to support him and rebellion against Dingane is successful.	2. Zululand divided into segments under king and brothers. People use segmentation in rebellions against bad king: support Mpande against Dingane. Mpande ready to use outside power to help him.

Has the sorting-out added to our knowledge and understanding? To some extent it has, for we have simplified the set of historical events which we are attempting to analyse, and they do stand out more clearly. But the sorting-out itself does not give us the interpretation of data, which has been made prior to the sorting: nor, when put together, does column 'B' alone give an analysis of the dynamics of the whole situation. In horizontal row 2, all personalities, Boers, Dingane, and Mpande, appear in every vertical column. There is no major distortion, but I consider that the all-important interconnexions of the columns, which are relationships between social groups and social personalities, as operated on by social forces, are better covered by the concept of the social field. Here we have a numerically powerful Zulu military state in hostile relations with another less-powerful African state (the enemy chief). The Boers, numerically less powerful than the Zulu but technically better-armed (400 of them defeated the Zulu army because of mounted mobility and guns), cross the Drakensberg. A social field is established which consists of unlike territorial states – though the Boers, having as yet no territory, are only the outliers of an incipient state. Dingane uses the unlike Boer state as a weapon to defeat his like enemy, Sikonyela, just as Shaka employed the stabbing-spear to overcome the javelin. Then he wipes out the Boers, thus attempting to restore the previous balance. Other Boers (and English) react to avenge: Dingane is defeated and the Boer power establishes in Natal a system of unlike territorial states, Boer and Zulu, opposed to each other. A cleavage in Zululand enables one of the parties, Mpande, to find Boer support, as he might have found support from another chief. So the deposed Lozi king, Mwanawina, came with a party of *Mazungu* (it is not even known if they were Portuguese, Arabs, or half-castes) to regain his throne from Lewanika. The Boers use the Zulu cleavage to weaken the Zulu state further and install a friendly rather than a hostile king. It is forty years before the whites are powerful enough to subjugate the whole Zulu state.

It seems manifest to me that it is most profitable to treat the situation in Natal in 1836–40 as a single social field in which there is mutual interaction throughout, e.g. in Dingane's use of the Boers against his external enemy Sikonyela; in Mpande's use of the Boers in his internal rebellion, based on a cleavage in Zulu social organization; and in the advantage taken by the Boers of that cleavage.

I have temporarily isolated Natal at 1836–40. Clearly, a full analysis requires consideration of the drives which brought the Boers to Natal: so that the field of reality in which these events occurred is extended in space-time to the Cape with its own conflicts which produced the Great Trek. Similarly, a full analysis would refer in greater detail to the history which produced the war between Dingane and Sikonyela and the cleavage of Zulu in attachment to Dingane and Mpande: so that the field of reality in which these events occurred is extended in space-time to the whole creation of the Zulu nation under Shaka. Thus in reality, events in the Cape are brought into interaction with events in Zululand and with its history: for the legislative measures which precipitated the Great Trek enabled Mpande to get Boer help to rebel success-fully against Dingane. But though these legislative enactments helped to give victory to Mpande rather than to Dingane, they are sociologically irrelevant to the cleavage of Zulu society into potentially hostile segments attached to brothers of the royal family, and to the process by which Zulu used this segmentation to get rid of a tyrant king and install a brother in his place; i.e. the process by which they defended the values of kingship in rebellion against a bad king. For in this analysis it is partly irrelevant who won the battle. To that extent, Malinowski would be justified in classifying the cleavage under 'C' rather than 'B', though in practice I am certain he would have put these events under 'B'.

I hope I have indicated how much more fruitful it is to con-ceive this set of events as a single field, rather than as 'three cultural realities'. We have seen that this also applies to the estab-lishing of industrial enterprise in Africa. The three columns have as little value as the extra flanking ones he adds. It is significant that not one of his pupils has published an analysis in these terms.

One advantage of the concept of the single field is that it does away with sterile disputes about whether or not an administrator is an integral part of modern political organization. We have seen that Malinowski rejects the concept in a distorted form and then frequently uses it himself, as when he discusses divination in an urban slum-yard. I have analysed the political structure of modern Zululand[4] to show that though chief and administrator co-operate in routine administration, and under the pressure of the force of government, in many ways they are opposed. The administrator stands for one set of values, some of which are desired by many Zulu, the chief for another set. The chief represents tribal history and values; he is related by kinship to many of his people; he lives his social life with them. Above all, he leads their opposition to European innovations and rule. Under Malinowski's scheme, the routine co-operation is classified under 'Contact', and the kin-ship-links and opposition under 'tribal reaction'. But all form a coherent complex about the chief. The Zulu express this by the antithesis: 'The administrator has only the prestige of his office; the chief has the prestige of blood.' The value of the chief's position in the kinship system comes also from the fact that the administrator has not got any position in the system and lives across the colour bar. But many individual Zulu turn to the administrator to gain personal advantages, and, as we have seen with the runaway youth, by some values prefer him to the chief. From the point of view of the individual Zulu the administrator has no place in the kinship system and little in social life, though he enters these in, e.g., law cases. The chief has a place in both.

I break off the analysis abruptly, for I cannot here elaborate other theoretical frameworks. I have tried to indicate that whatever our ultimate abstractions may be, we may best conceive the situation to be studied as a field of interdependent events, on the lines set out in African sociology by Fortes, Schapera, and others. We may isolate zones of the field for analysis, but we have to allow for the operation in one zone, of events emerging from all others.

8. *Conclusion*

This is a bad book. That is its only merit, on the principle stated by Descartes. It is a tragedy that it should have been published to spoil Malinowski's well-merited reputation, based on his own field-work and his general contribution to social anthropology. His 'theory' does not bear examination from any point of view. It is analytically sterile, and it ends in the worst kind of practical anthropology: welfare work without morality, based on naïve over-simplification. The problems become: Is there enough land? Is there enough food? Are there more prostitutes? We need no discipline of social anthropology.

It is also a humbling book. For if, on the positive side, Malinowski's thesis remains descriptive, no social anthropologist has yet put forward an alternative. The Marxists have a theoretical framework. Among ourselves the Wilsons have tried to formulate one. American anthropologists have worked on the theory of 'acculturation'. But we have still to establish a right to maintain that we are more than good recorders of contemporary events.

Chapter Nine

MALINOWSKI'S CONTRIBUTION TO SOCIAL ANTHROPOLOGY

THE late Professor Malinowski's contribution to social anthropology is manifold. His influence in specializing social anthropology and its field research methods, his own field reports, and the school of able and eager students whom he created about himself, have affected for the good every school of anthropology in the world. In this review of a posthumous book I do not consider these in detail, but attempt to assess his statement of his 'functional theory'.

Three things struck me as most significant in this book.* The first is that not only are the concepts basically the same as those set out by Malinowski in his essay on 'Culture' in the *Encyclopaedia of the Social Sciences* (1931), but also that in so far as he has developed his analysis it is proportionately more on the psychophysiological rather than on the sociological side, i.e. he deals more with the processes by which the human organism is conditioned so that purely biological, cannot be separated from cultural, behaviour, while his discussion of the interrelations within culture itself has made no analytical advance. This is despite the fact that the years 1931–41 saw marked progress in the quantity and quality of professionals' field-reports. Second, we have collected here three essays which are more or less repetitive and polemical statements of the same thesis. In his *Sir James George Frazer: A Biographical Appreciation* (1942) he leads from a survey of Frazer's theories to an almost word-for-word re-statement of his *A Scientific Theory of Culture* (1941) and *The Functional Theory* (1939). This is a posthumous book, but I infer from the Preface that Malinowski himself made the initial preparations to publish these three almost identical essays together.

* *A Scientific Theory of Culture and Other Essays* by Bronislaw Malinowski, with a preface by Huntington Cairns. Chapel Hill, The University of Carolina Press, 1944. vii + 228 pp., index. 18s. 6d. (English price.)

Finally, the essay on Frazer ends in an overpitched statement of what anthropology must contribute to the solution of the world's problems. This leads to a most naïve set of proposals, which he makes seemingly unaware of the complicated forces involved, for ending war. Malinowski's tendency to slip almost unconsciously from analytical into practical problems is present in the other two essays: it dominates his recent *The Dynamics of Culture Change*.

These three facts all point to the main weaknesses of Malinowski's 'functional theory' of culture. It is true and obvious enough, as he stresses, that human beings have biological needs and that they satisfy these indirectly through culture, which creates new needs. As an anthropologist, I am incompetent to assess this part of his thesis, which I assume summarizes the findings of certain behaviouristic schools. This has to be evaluated by physiologists and psychologists. Chappel and Coon in their *Principles of Social Anthropology* have used different behaviouristic findings in what appears to be as illuminating and unilluminating a way as a foundation for social anthropology. In my opinion, anthropologists should take these biological needs as given, save in so far as they are transmuted into moral, jural, and ritual norms and values. As such, they fall into the field of sociological study, which I would define as the search for invariable relations in the behaviour of individuals and groups in a social system. There appears to me to be little point in sending an anthropologist trained expensively and living at some cost in the field, to Africa to find out that some Bantu tribe has a complex organization to satisfy the need of its members for food, just as we have a complex organization for this purpose. That statement adds little to our knowledge, though the description of the tribal organization adds a lot.

The excessive development of Malinowski's thesis on the 'conditioning' side implies a definite failure of his theory on the 'intra-cultural' side. I see this as reflecting the fact that the 'function' of an institution is its satisfaction of a need: and needs are common to all societies. Therefore all problems beyond the descriptive plane are answered at once, as witness: 'I am not quite certain whether my brief indication of what the function of each institution is, will remain final' (p. 175). I note here that it might be difficult to pin Malinowski on this point, since he gives at least four different definitions of function. Some pliability in the use of words is necessary, but pliability should not degenerate into sloppiness. Thus: (*a*) 'for function cannot be defined in any other way than the satisfaction of a need by an activity in which human beings co-operate, use artifacts, and consume goods' (pp. 39, 83 and III); (*b*) 'We would have to assess the position of such a group with relation to the community as a whole, that is, to define its functions' (p. 45); (*c*) 'the concept of function, by which we see that distribution and consumption are as much dependent upon the total character of a culture as on the productive organization itself' (p. 50); and (*d*) 'finally, we have introduced the concept of function, that is, the integral result of organized activities, as distinguished from charter, that is, the purpose, the traditional or new end to be gained' (p. 53).

From the next use of the word I got no meaning: 'And it is the solution of these problems, that is, the function of the various institutional types, that provides the primary determinism' (p. 66).

This carelessness in writing and inconsistency in thought is typical of many passages and arguments in the book. Nevertheless, it seems to me that Malinowski gives a good description of the process of cultural conditioning and also re-states well the universal occurrence of certain human institutions – as under the chapter-heads in Tylor's *Primitive Culture*. This justifies his assumption of common basic needs, but is no new contribution.

The best part of the book, and it is valuable though only a repetition of what he wrote many years ago, is his analysis of 'the structure of institutions as integrals' [!]. This, largely as developed by Malinowski, is a significant contribution to the humanistic disciplines. 'Function' in his principal sense is merely a limiting factor in the sociological field. though it presents a real psycho-physiological problem. It has little value as a sociological concept. There is a myth among anthropologists that one of Malinowski's students ended a long thesis: 'Our survey of the facts has forced us to conclude that the function of leadership in primitive societies is to initiate and organize activities.' Is this much more of: 'There's ne'er a villain, dwelling in all Denmark, but he's an arrant knave' than Malinowski's (pp. 115–6):

We could state that the function of the tribe as a political unit is the organization of force for policing, defence, and aggression . . . the function of age-groups is the co-ordinating of physiological and ana-tomical characteristics as they develop in the process of growth, and their transformation into cultural categories. In occupational groups we see that the carrying out of skills, techniques, and such activities as education, law, and power, constitute the integral function of the group.

The concept of institutions is a valuable and enduring one. Here Malinowski's valid and enduring contributions to social anthropology are many. First he helped it emerge as a specialized subject from physical anthropology, archaeology, technology, and linguistics. Even more he helped develop it as a subject specialized beyond ordinary ethnography. He did this partly by his own magnificent field-research, and partly by setting out explicitly what he calls 'the integral structure of institutions'. He states that every human activity is carried out by an organized group of human beings with a particular material apparatus, under moral and jural rules, with a means of transmitting knowledge, and a charter of tradition. He stressed that accurate and comprehensive description entailed a report on personnel, material apparatus, charter, norms, etc. Moreover, he showed that description of a single item of culture could lead to an account of the whole culture; or, from another point of view, a whole culture could be viewed from a number of aspects, each involving a one-sided description of the totality. Malinowski developed a system of charts to enable the field-worker to be sure that he had collected all this information. He stressed the importance of balancing Native statements of what ought to be with data on what actually occurs. I need not elaborate his contribution here: his analysis is well-known – and accepted.

But the very strength of this conception, leading to a complete collection of facts, contained a restricting weakness. Because Malinowski insisted on the 'integrality of institutions', he was unable to break them up for further analysis: and analysis can only proceed by comparing abstracted isolated events or aspects of events. Therefore in his attempts to proceed beyond the descriptive level Malinowski retreated more and more to the biological side, away from cultural problems. At times he sees this, and immediately after the circular statements quoted two paragraphs above, he writes: 'It probably also is clear, to the reader acquainted at the same time with cultural studies and with scientific principles, that the concept of function is primarily descriptive . . . a new heuristic principle in laying stress on the absolute necessity for an additional type of research.'

He goes on to define this additional type of research in the next sentence:

This consists primarily in a consideration of how certain devices, forms of organization, customs, or ideas enlarge the range of human potentialities on the one hand, and impose certain restrictions on human behaviour on the other. In short, functionalism is the consideration of what culture is as a determining principle, in terms of the addition which it provides to the individual and collective standard of living. (pp. 116–17).

This is Malinowski's second line of retreat from the impasses he has created: he slips from analytical into practical problems. Unable to pose comparative analytical problems, because he cannot break up the 'integrality of institutions', Malinowski says: by describing how each culture satisfies the basic and derived needs of its bearers we can set up a standard of comparison, of relative satisfaction between societies. He proceeds:

This might, perhaps, dispose of the oft-repeated criticism that the function of a cultural phenomenon always consists in showing how it functions. As a statement of fact this criticism is absolutely correct. As a methodological indictment it simply discloses the low level of epistemological intelligence among anthropologists. The functionalist, to take a simple example, would insist that in describing a fork or a spoon we also must supply the information on how they are used, how they are related to table manners, to convivialism, to the nature of cooked viands and dishes (p. 117)

– and then he slips into a tirade against an imaginary 'anti-functionalist' and then against historians, which I forbear to quote.

It is quite clear that his example takes him back to description, and he admits and defends this: 'Explanation to the scientific thinker is nothing else but the most complete description of a complex fact'. This is incorrect. For the scientific thinker, adequate description of a complex fact consists in a complete account of the whole history of that fact and of all the scientific laws of all types which have operated through that history. In this sense, there can hardly be anything in reality even approaching adequate description off the astronomical scale, except in the isolation of a minute series of events, as in factory or laboratory. It is worth noting against Malinowski's obsession against history that the experimenter describes the history of the events he is relating,

239

for he must record the setting-up of his experiment. What Malinowski means here by adequate description is as full an account as possible of all the particular and unique realities which centre in a spoon: if it is in England, of all English culture; if it is an African's spoon, of tribal culture; if it is a Sheffield spoon used by an African, presumably of both. It is as if a zoologist had adequately to describe the parturition of a whale and the parturition of a sheep by describing the 'whole' of each animal; and could not class both as mammals because they share a number of characteristics, while differing in many others.

I appreciate that we may yet find that this is little less than the utmost which sociology as a discipline will be able to achieve: accurate and comprehensive descriptions of particular realities. If so, let us at least be clear that this is what we are doing, and not delude ourselves by sprinkling tautological and teleological 'functions' about our analysis. Even as such, sociology already makes a valuable and new contribution to the ordered body of human knowledge. I repeat, Malinowski himself has contributed greatly to our techniques for achieving this aim. His analysis of the *kula* in *Argonants of the Western Pacific* is the most notable example. In Africa, I cite our understanding of witchcraft and magic, of marriage-payment, of lineage-structure, of the role of the mother's brother, of political systems, though these flow chiefly from Radcliffe-Brown and those he has influenced. But many of them used the field-techniques of Malinowski. A comparison of field-monographs written in the last twenty years shows indeed considerable advance here. On this view social anthropology is a craft with specific ordered techniques practised with various degrees of skill, thoroughness, art, and inspiration.

However, I believe that social anthropology may yet proceed beyond that level, and that it has already produced generalizations of scientific description, i.e. statements of invariable interdependence of events, which can be further developed. I cite the first example which comes to my mind, Van Gennep's concept of *rites de passage*. The examples cited in the previous paragraph also fall into this category. I do not consider that we can make any progress in this direction within the framework of Malinowski's functional 'theory'. As we have seen, his major units, the institutions, by definition cannot be broken up for analysis, and he constantly stresses this.

The three significant facts I set out in the second paragraph of this review are indications of this weakness of the 'functional theory'. Malinowski retreats to the conditioning process and biology because, with his concepts, he cannot formulate comparative problems on the cultural plane. For the same reason, we find three essays in one book stating the same thesis in almost the same words. Had his formulation been more fruitful, Malinowski would not slip into a re-statement of 'functionalism' every time he tries to pose a comparative problem, as he does in his essay on Frazer. We may contrast this with Evans-Pritchard's analysis of Frazer and Tylor's theories in his *The Intellectualist (English) Interpretation of Magic*[1] where he discusses the weaknesses of the theories in the light of modern research, the type of data which Frazer used and how this affected his generalizations, and attempts to show how far the theories still stand and what further problems they pose. Finally, we should have expected Malinowski to set out some means of comparing the institutions of different societies otherwise than 'in terms of the addition [they provide] to the individual and collective standard of living'. His essay on Frazer ends in naïve proposals to end war. Always an attempt to follow up a theoretical suggestion, leads to a practical problem and a facile solution. This last weakness dominates Malinowski's *The Dynamics of Culture Change* (1945), for his whole thesis breaks down in this field. He cannot fit his concepts to the facts of modern Africa.

I cannot in this short review indicate in what forms I think we should pose our problems. *A priori*, there must be very many possible ways in which this can be done. Whichever are the most fruitful, they will have to take account of Malinowski's development of the 'organized institution' concept. I consider this one of the major problems of anthropological methodology, which should be tackled as soon as possible.

Malinowski's contribution goes beyond a mere provision of a framework and technique for fieldwork. His own books are most vital contributions to the whole body of our knowledge, in their facts and their fruitful hypotheses, suggestions and implications. They will always remain classics of method and stimulus. Many younger social anthropologists, directly and indirectly influenced by him, have done excellent fieldwork and made notable theoretical contributions.

Malinowski developed the idea of fieldwork whose originator in England was Haddon though Boas had already begun field research in America. When Haddon took the Torres Straits expedition into the field he began the specialization which established social anthropology in it own right. We may seem now far advanced from the reports of Haddon himself, the Seligmans, Rivers, and of those whom indirectly they influenced (Junod, Van Wing, Smith and Dale, Rattray, Meek, Codrington, Lind-blom), but this advance is the measure of their achievement. Malinowski's contribution to this advance was notable perhaps owing to the historical accident which in the 1914–18 war kept him so long among the Trobrianders and made him learn the language. Nevertheless, his contribution here is lasting.

His own experience led him to insist on long-term fieldwork and this had marked effects, not altogether good ones. Cairns in his preface to this book says that Malinowski's 'own practice was in strictest accord with contemporary standards which require a meticulous knowledge of the whole life of individual tribes'. We have seen there are dangers in this, and Malinowski over-emphasized the need for it. The romantic device 'fieldwork' became a slogan: everybody rushed to primitive areas, and later to more civilized ones. On the other hand, everyone who had ever been to a primitive field was able to contribute something, instead of being regarded as, generally, fit only to be an informant. Once 'the new jargon' was learnt, he could rank as a professional. Worst of all, the 'fieldwork' cry carried a sneer at those who had not done it: better a missionary who'd seen an African, than a Lévy-Bruhl who had not; better an African himself, than a Frazer.

I am the last the decry fieldwork, and I consider that every social anthropologist should have studied at least two social systems. But when I reflect on the broad generalizations that have emerged in the history of our science, I find that the most stimulating have come on the whole from armchair students, who saw no tribe though they studied European society: Van Gennep's analysis of *rites de passage*, Lévy-Bruhl's of prelogical collective representations, Durkheim's of division of labour, Hubert and Mauss' of sacrifice and offering, and the many works of Tylor, Frazer, Marett, Engels, Freud, Pareto. When I consider the type of data with which they worked, I can only wish that they might be here again to use the data provided by modern field-research in even more fruitful hypotheses. This is not to deny that some modern fieldworkers have produced as stimulating hypotheses: but, if we are to learn from our history, I hope that some of them will forsake the field for the study. Should they succeed in advancing the work of their predecessors, it will be on the basis of modern field-research, with all that it owes to Malinowski.

As one who saw even a little of Malinowski's brilliance at work, aside from my reading of his works, I cannot help asking why it was he became tied in the very structure of his institutions. I do not attempt a psychological interpretation, but, as an anthropologist, make a sociological suggestion: Malinowski was the only specialized social anthropologist of his 'generation' in Britain after the 1914–18 War. He had done his fieldwork during the war and came to London with its wealth mated with his intelligence. Haddon, Seligman and Marett belonged to an earlier 'generation'. Radcliffe-Brown was the only contemporary of Malinowski's who could have created a rival school in Britain, but he was to do so in South Africa, Australia, and America. Save for the hiving-off of dissident pupils, the rebellious of whom were in practice mostly engaged in field-research outside of England, Malinowski stood as solitary king. He is noted for his distortions of the views of preceding or foreign or filial rivals. Power corrupts. Subject only to criticism from his juniors, Malinowski quarrelled with them or absorbed their views in his original thesis. This remained to the end, in his own words, 'primarily descriptive': outside of his own stimulating field-reports, especially *Argonauts of the Western Pacific*, I doubt strongly if any of his 'theoretical' statements will have the survival value of his *Baloma: The Spirits of the Dead Among the Trobriand Islanders* (Journal of the Royal Anthropological Institute, 1916). And this stands as a classic statement of the problems of field-research. The present book is at best a more convenient reference for the thesis set out in the *Encyclopaedia of the Social Sciences*.

I have criticized Malinowski's theoretical framework which I believe to be a stultifying one, but I have tried to indicate his very real contribution. I do so deeply conscious of what I, as a fieldworker and would-be comparative student, owe to his work, and deeply regretful of how often I failed in the field to collect the complex data for which he rightly pleaded.

Chapter Ten

MALINOWSKI—FIELDWORKER AND THEORIST*

SOME NAMES fix the scientific climate of their time, in that whole periods are known by them or whole ways of looking at the world. In physics there are Galileo, Newton, and Einstein; in zoology and biology, Darwin and Mendel; and Freud's name covers a whole approach to the human personality, even when particular theories within this approach do not agree with his formulations. In the social sciences there are perhaps only Marx and Keynes; but in the 1920s and early 1930s, it seemed that Malinowski might rank with these giants. He had a dominant fertilizing influence on his own subject, anthropology, and on all the social sciences and psychology; philosophers, novelists, students of linguistics, every kind of intellectual, was affected by his writings. Yet since the last war, he is hardly mentioned in intellectual discussion. I find it difficult to convey to my own students how important he was when I studied at a South African University, for even at that distance, far from his personal influence as a teacher, he seemed to offer a new way of understanding the life of men in society.

I have often wondered why his reputation, except in narrow academic circles, has lasted so short a time. I am encouraged to speculate further by Professor Firth's book,[1] in which twelve of Malinowski's pupils have tried to evaluate his contributions to the social sciences. We were surely not mistaken in supposing that Malinowski opened our eyes; nor, to any great extent, has time falsified his findings. The answer is likely to concern ourselves as much as Malinowski, and I believe it is most of all

* Broadcast on the B.B.C. Third Programme twice in 1959; reproduced in a shorter version in *The New Statesman and Nation*, lix, No. 1514 (26 March 1960) under the title 'Malinowski Reassessed'.

concerned with what has happened, since his time, to the study of society.

At the beginning of the First World War, Malinowski, then a lecturer at the London School of Economics, went to live among and study the Trobriand Islanders, at the South-east tip of New Guinea. One of the legends of social anthropology is that he was in Australia for a meeting of the British Association when the war broke out; as he had been born in West Poland, he was an Austrian citizen, and was due to be interned as an enemy alien; but on the grounds that he was also a Pole, and therefore an enemy of the Austrians, the Australian Government was persuaded by British anthropologists to agree to intern him on the islands. It may be a myth, though Mrs B. Z. Seligman assures me it is not, for the Australians allowed all enemy scientists at the meeting to go home: but if it is a myth, like all myths, the story stresses an important element of truth. In this case it is that Malinowski stayed among the people he was studying, as no previous anthropologist had done. Some Americans, like Boas, had spent years studying individual Red Indian tribes; but I believe it is true to say that before Malinowski no professional anthropologist had lived so long with any one tribe, or, in consequence, observed so closely the whole process of its social life. Moreover, he learned and worked with the Trobriand language, and not with interpreters. This situation had a profound influence on Malinowski's work: it was the source of his strength and his originality, and yet, I believe, it eventually stifled him.

To understand this paradox, you have to remember that anthropology had developed, from about 1854, partly in museums, and partly through the work of scholars from other disciplines who were interested in the evolutionary development of human society. For example, in Britain, Sir Edward Tylor was Curator of the Pitt-Rivers Museum at Oxford, Sir James Frazer was a classical scholar, Robertson-Smith started life as a theologian, Sir Henry Maine and Vinogradoff were lawyers, Viscount Bryce was a political scientist. So above all, anthropology was dominated by an evolutionary outlook, drawing inspiration from the Darwinian movement: as zoologists reconstructed the evolution of animals from fossils, deposited in rocks, so anthropologists came to see customs as fossils, relics from a former stage of society. Secondly, in so far as anthropology was based in museums, scholars felt they could move customs about, isolated from their part in general social life, in very much the same way as implements and other material goods of tribal societies could be moved from case to case. Thirdly, those who elaborated theories about the development of human society depended for their facts on all sorts of books about life among the tribal peoples. And these books – written by travellers, traders, missionaries and colonial administrators – were (then as now) biased in several ways, and in recurrent ways, so that they seemed to give a convincing picture.

A traveller passing through a remote area is always liable to be impressed by the exotic and the romantic, the striking and the bizarre; it makes his book more readable, and therefore more profitable, if he gives undue space to the rôle in tribal life of ceremonial, war, witchcraft beliefs, and so forth, as against a humdrum account of daily life. This bias persists even into the books written not by travellers but by traders, missionaries and administrators who live for far longer periods in any one tribe. Moreover, particularly in the last century, missionaries and administrators had gone to the colonial areas very consciously to raise and improve the local people, and many of them in their reports emphasized the darkness and barbarity and savagery of tribal life. There were, of course notable exceptions, like David Livingstone, but the bias is apparent in nearly every book of that period – and many of this. In addition few of these Westerners, if literate, lived among the people: and on their occasional intrusions into local life, they were drawn by interest in spectacle, or their very presence led to the performance of set behaviour. Finally, they questioned the people, often through interpreters, about their customs and way of life. And if you try it yourself, you will find it much easier, let alone less embrarassing, to describe your wedding ceremony, than to tell your questioner about how you live with your spouse from day to day.

So the records providing the facts for the scholarly anthropologists at home were biased towards whatever was ritualistic or exotic, and these scholars themselves were chiefly interested in problems such as the evolution of religion and magic, and of forms of the family, in how so-called primitive men thought, often with a carry-over from the past of assumptions about the noble savage, or the brutish life of men who lived in trees.

The extent to which the bias of the facts affected anthropology can be seen even in a study which still ranks as a great classic of observation and analysis, the description of the Tsonga tribe of East Africa by a Swiss missionary, Henri A. Junod, who had switched his interests from insects to men under the stimulus of Lord Bryce. Junod had lived among the Tsonga more than a score of years. But this is how he allocates space in his chapters on 'The Evolution of a Man from Birth to Death'. Birth ceremonies take up fifteen pages, with a few remarks on the handling of infants. The whole of childhood is five pages, followed by twenty-six pages on the circumcision ritual at puberty. Love charms and marriage ceremonies occupy twenty-one pages, and mature age and old age only seven pages. Death ceremonies are compressed into thirty-four pages: and these lead in the second volume to no less than fifty-five pages on the ancestor-cult. And the emphasis on ritual is even greater if you look at the life cycle of a woman.

When professional anthropologists began to go into the field, as notably in the 1891 expedition to the Torres Straits led by Haddon of Cambridge, they collected data more systematically, but the same bias is present in their work as in Junod's. On this expedition also they worked through interpreters, questioning in set formuae. These were then the types of facts with which professional anthropologists dealt at the beginning of the twentieth century, and the bias in their data affected sharply the types of theories that were presented. There were rather mechanical evolutionary theories, and even more mechanical theories of how culture spread from place to place, such as Elliott-Smith's thesis that all developed cultures sprang from Egypt. This was notably true in Britain: in France the school of Durkheim was handling the data in a far more fruitful way, though still with the same bias. And this was the situation when Malinowski went to live among the Trobrianders.

The very manner of his work among the islanders forced Malinowski to collect facts quite different in type from those his predecessors and colleagues were using. I am sure too that his personality influenced the way he reacted to his situation. The fact that he was a foreigner living in Britain may have been important, for neither Radcliffe-Brown in the Andaman Islands, nor W. H. R. Rivers among the Todas, had collected the same detail of what went on in everyday life. The English did not produce a great sociologist at a time when there were many on the Continent and in America. It is true that the British, to quote George Homans of Harvard, 'have always regarded the study of savages as O.K.'; but for many years most of the leading anthropologists in Britain have come from the Continent and from the Dominions, from regions where the break-up or building of society focuses attention on what makes a society. Even most British-born anthropologists, till recently, had some foreign connection, or were Scots, Welsh, Irish or Jews. English society itself has been perhaps too homogeneous and stable – dare I say too smug and complacent? – for its members to become empirical thinkers about social life.

Because of his situation, and perhaps because of his personality and foreignness in his adopted home, Malinowski became aware of the complexity and intricacy of social life among his islanders. He saw the life of the individual not as just moving from a wedding to a funeral, but he studied men and women of all ages, living together in various stages of a marriage cycle. He saw boys and girls growing up to a culturally determined adulthood; and always he saw individuals living within culturally set customs and norms, trying to exploit these for their own ends, using and yet rebelling against their society. He showed that magic was not a set of ideas, as in Frazer's treatment, but a real and vital part of love-making, agriculture, trading, politics – of living. Nor was myth merely an intellectual response by man to the universe. The passage in Malinowski's work which brings out most vividly for me the illumination of his approach, occurs in the Riddell Memorial Lecture of 1935 on *The Foundations of Faith and Morals*. He tells there how when he was collecting myths from Trobrianders, one man kept boasting of his right, and the right of his clan, to tell a particular myth. Malinowski continually told him to stop boasting and to get on with the myth. He says that it took him some months to see that this boasting was an essential part of the myth; and how this led him to formulate his theory that myths were neither an intellectual response by men to explain the nature of the universe, nor an emotional response to helplessness in the face of awe-inspiring natural phenomena, but a present important 'social charter' for the existing form of society, with its distribution of power and privilege and ownership. Something like this had been said before by thinkers in other subjects, but Malinowski elaborated the point in telling detail and built it into his theory of institutions.

In this example we can see the main lines of how Malinowski's field data produced a revolution in anthropology. Against the simple views of his predecessors, working as they were with biased and inadequate data, he stressed, from the richness of his data, that tribal life was far more complex. Almost every one of his books is constructed in this way. His first great book, *Argonauts of the Western Pacific*, shows how, in order to understand the ceremonial trade of the *kula* ring, the anthropologist must look carefully at complex motives, at property holding and canoe building, at magic and language. This book is a tilt against simple views about primitive economics. In *Crime and Custom in Savage Society* he attacks the simple views on primitive law held by Rivers and Hartland, and even distorts the views of Maine and Durkheim in order to attack them. 'Law and order' in a tribe is a complex business, in which savages try to evade their duties just as Christians do, and are restrained by the obligations of reciprocity imposed on them, as well as by more open pressures. In his essay on 'Magic, Science and Religion' he opens with backhanded compliments at some colleagues, and attacks on the simple extremism of others.

There is, of course, an element of caricature in my summary: but I think it is true to say that he stressed always that primitive society was extremely complicated, and he did so with considerable animus against those who thought otherwise. In short, Malinowski's great contribution was to give the Western world its first, fully informed, rounded description of the so-called savage and his society, in a professional book. Pictures of this sort had been given before: again Livingstone's reports on Africans are notable examples. But Malinowski, with far richer details and with deep sympathy, as well as professional scholarship, established the savage as a man among men, living in a society among societies. In the 1920s he disposed of numerous naïve ideas about primitive man, as either good or bad, ridden by mystical notions and magic, or matter-of-fact and lazy, or ground to the dust by brutish work.

This supreme contribution of Malinowski's is stated in detail by all the essays in the book Professor Firth has edited. And they point out how, in the course of establishing the savage as a man, living in organized society, Malinowski produced insight after insight, analysis after analysis, which others built, later, into more systematic theories of society than he ever achieved himself. For I consider that the best of these essays are also united on one point: he was never able to see either social life or the human personality as a system. As Professor Fortes puts it, in considering Malinowski's contribution to the study of kinship: 'What is inadequately stressed is that kinship relations have to be seen as a system, within the framework of the total social structure.' Professor Firth virtually says the same of Malinowski's shortcomings in economic analysis, despite his important contributions to it. Professor Talcott Parsons, indeed, emphasizes that it was very difficult for Malinowski, at the time when he worked, to see in social life a set of interdependent regularities as constituting a social system, capable of empirical analysis – the approach which has stimulated all important later research in Britain. Instead Malinowski more and more became involved in stating how men were conditioned by their upbringing in particular cultures. He ended, theoretically, with behaviourist psychology.

I myself agree with Fortes' view of what led Malinowski into the blind alley which 'warped his work. He could not shake off the compulsion to present his theories and his ethnographic discoveries in the form of an assault on the *ancien regime*.' More than this, I believe that, whether from habit or from personal conflicts, he carried this war on his predecessors forward against his successors – his pupils. His own data enabled him to demolish earlier anthropologists, or sometimes the straw figures he made of them. When he began to use a similar technique against the pupils whom he had trained, and who had collected data as he had done, all he demonstrated was that he had ceased to be capable of learning. This is most marked in his essays on the study of social change in Africa (see Chapter VIII). Impelled to attack, he lost the chance of learning from his younger colleagues: he failed to appreciate – or perhaps he resented – that they had data as complex as he. And they had the advantage of all pupils over their teacher, of starting where he left off.

I learnt from Malinowski's writings; and when my first Zulu started to tell me a myth, I could rebuke him: 'Cut out your silly old myth. Start boasting!' He was a great and stimulating teacher: but since he lacked a teacher's most important qualification, the ability to learn from his pupils, some of them had to break from him; and he attacked even those who remained faithful to what he called the 'functional school of anthropology'. He could not accept Walt Whitman's moral from the teacher of athletes:

> He that by me spreads a wider breast than my own proves
> the width of my own.
> He most honours my style who learns under it to destroy
> the teacher.

Anthropologists today have to learn a great deal from other disciplines; and with one notable exception, Malinowski seemed unable to do so. Professor Firth, an economist in origin, says that 'the defects in his approach to economic problems were partly due to his lack of knowledge of economic literature, and partly to his failure to scrutinize economic concepts with the same care which he gave to many other ideas.' I came into anthropology out of law, and I feel, as Professor Schapera implies in this book, that Malinowski failed to scrutinize legal concepts with the same care he gave to many other ideas. Malinowski helped to break social anthropology's links with inappropriate subjects – the studies of man as an animal, of prehistoric remains, of primitive tools and so on. But as social anthropology developed associations with other social disciplines, he contented himself largely with saying how misguided were the views of these disciplines on primitive man, instead of going to them for aid in systematic analysis.

There was one discipline from which he took in great measure: Freudian psychology. The extent to which he did so is fully documented by Professor Fortes. It is most striking, for I would say that in many ways Malinowski's contribution to human knowledge was similar to Freud's. Freud gave us a view of human personality, previously accepted by novelists and playwrights but not touched by academic psychology, in which all of man is included: physiological drives, sex urges, hunger, unconscious and conscious hate and aggression, perversion, and so on. All theories of human personality, however they differ from Freud, draw inspiration from him. Malinowski gave us a similar view of man's life in small societies, previously glimpsed by novelists and playwrights and historians, but not handled by academic anthropology. This made a new discipline of anthropology, and affected other social sciences.

But Freud went further than Malinowski. He produced a systematic theory. In detail it has been criticized: its main emphases are accepted still, so that, as Auden wrote,

> To us he is no more a person
> Now but a climate of opinion...

One can see from this book that Malinowski failed to produce a theory, in the way that Freud did: and perhaps this is one reason why his legacy is known by his name to so few. His great contribution was the presentation of a rounded savage in place of a series of lay-figures. In achieving this, he defeated himself, because he never rose above his first book. But in detail he made point after point of the greatest insight.

Of course, psycho-analysis makes an appeal to the search for health, as modern social anthropology does not. This is perhaps why Margaret Mead is far better known in this country than Evans-Pritchard or Firth, on whom among British anthropologists Malinowski's mantle fell. For Mead, widely read and quoted, deals with the emotional doubts and ill-health of men and women and of nations. It is also true that the savage whom Malinowski established among men is now taking his place among men as a trade unionist and an independent citizen of the world. The interest and attention of intellectuals today is focused far more on the political consequences of this than on the cultural shifts and changes which accompany it. Whatever the failings of this great man, there is also a real sense in which his outstanding contribution has been too harshly dealt with by time.

NOTES

INTRODUCTION

[1] My italics.

[2] They also shared a common culture, and kinship links between villages.

[3] 'Moral density' is presumably used here in Durkheim's sense: *De la Division du Travail Social*, 1893, Book II, Chapter II.

[4] I acknowledge gratefully the stimulus here of S. Andrezejewski's *Military Organization and Society* (1953).

[5] 'Social Aspects of First-Fruits Ceremonies among the South-Eastern Bantu', *Africa*, xi (1938), pp. 25 f.

[6] I need only footnote for the record the following: '. . . The magical potency of this concept [of social solidarity] has now been expanded to the point at which Gluckman finds it sensible to explain warlike deviation from customary behaviour as itself a form of custom which has the purposive [*sic*] function of enhancing social cohesion. This kind of double-talk can be made very persuasive but it is purely scholastic argument; it has no more scientific value than the comparable double-headed dogmas of psycho-analysis' (Leach E. R., *Pul-Eliya: A Village in Ceylon* (1961), p. 298).

[7] For the first type of misinterpretation, see Spiro M. E., *Rural Sociology*, xxi, 1956, p. 335–6, and Kaplan I., *American Anthropologist*, lix, 1957, p. 175; for the second, Frank A. G., *American Journal of Sociology*, lxiii, 1957–8, p. 108, and Richards A. I., *Man*, xlviii, 1958, No. 164, and Bose N. K., *Man in India*, xxxiv, 1934, p. 13. The quoted phrase is from Richards.

[8] My present italics, not in the original.

[9] My italics, not Reay's.

[10] Cf. E. J. Hobsbawn's description of 'The City Mob' in *Primitive Rebels* (1959), with his stress on their tendency in pre-industrial cities to support the ruler while attacking his advisers, and note his phrase (p. 119): '. . . for an unjust king is the negation of kingship'.

[11] See Worsley P. M., 'The Kinship System of the Tallensi: A Revaluation', Curle Bequest Essay Prize 1955, *Journal of the Royal Anthropological Institute*, lxxxvi, 1956, Part I, pp. 37 f.; and Smith M. G., 'Segmentary Lineage Systems', Curle Bequest Essay Prize, 1955, ibid., Part II, pp. 39 f.

[12] See my *Analysis of a Social Situation in Modern Zululand*, op. cit., p. 54.

[13] The point is well made by Bateson G. in 'Bali: A Steady State' in *Social Structure: Essays presented to A. R. Radcliffe-Brown*, edited by Fortes M. (1949). See also *Cambridge Papers in Social Anthropology*, 1 (1957), on the cycle of domestic groupings (edited by J. Goody).

[14] See my *Custom and Conflict in Africa*, op. cit., p. 96. As this finally goes to press, I can draw attention to M. Fortes's Henry Myers Lecture in which he shows how 'Pietas in Ancestor Worship' is related to this situation (*Journal of the Royal Anthropological Institute*, Vol. 91, Part 2 (July–December 1961), pp. 166 f.)

[15] See also Cunnison I., *History on the Luapula*, 1951, and *The Luapula Peoples of N. Rhodesia: Custom and History in Tribal Politics*, (1960). I have not space to set out more fully what we now understand by 'structural time', a concept first developed by Evans-Pritchard in *The Nuer* and by Fortes in *The Dynamics of Clanship among the Tallensi* and in 'Time and Social Structure: An Ashanti Case-Study' (*Social Structure: Essays Presented to A. R. Radcliffe-Brown*).

[16] I draw attention in a last-minute footnote to A. I. Richard's discussion of these conditions in 'African kings and their royal relatives' (*Journal of the Royal Anthropological Institute*, Vol. 91, Part 2 (1961), p. 144.)

[17] Cf. the independent statement by Richards that '. . . the survival rate of African kingdoms is inevitably low' (op. cit., p. 136.)

[18] See further my paper on 'The "Case" Method in Modern British Anthropology', in the Transactions of the Fourth International Congress of Sociology, held at Stresa, 1959, and in *The Sociological Review*, ix, 1961.

[19] In the series of 'Case Studies in Cultural Anthropology', published by Stanford University, apparently for beginners in anthropology.

[20] Published in the journal of the Institute, Vol. 91, Part 2 (July–December, 1961), pp. 135 f. I note that Richards says against my own analysis of Bemba succession, reprinted below, that no woman who has not been awarded one of two royal titles has borne a queen (at p. 142). This is contradicted by her own genealogy (in *African Political Systems*, op. cit., p. 102), though a woman Nakasafye who bore two kings probably died before she could succeed to a title. I lack space to cite other articles on states in Africa, but most of these seem to me also to show a basic interest in these 'bureaucratic' problems: e.g. P. M. Kaberry and E. M. Chilver, 'An Outline of the Traditional Political System of the Bali-Nyonga, Southern Cameroons', *Africa*, xxxi (October 1961), pp. 355 f. I find the same interest in Chilvers' demonstration that it is inappropriate and misleading to call the Interlacustrine Bantu kingdoms 'feudal' (*East African Chiefs*, pp. 378 f.), an interest which leads her away from examining similarities and differences in the working of political process, though I am pleased to see that she insists that if any comparison is appropriate, it is with the 'pre-feudal' systems of Europe (Cf. my *Essays on Lozi Land and Royal Property*, 1943, p. 28, and my essay on the Lozi in *Seven Tribes of British Central Africa*, 1951, p. 66).

[21] See various essays in *African Political Systems*, and e.g. Mair, L. P. *An African People in the Twentieth Century* (Ganda) (1934) and Richards A. I., 'Tribal Government in Transition' (Bemba), Supplement to *Journal of the Royal African Society*, xxxiv, October, 1935. I myself at the request of the Provincial Commissioner compiled a report on *The Administrative Organization of the Barotse Native Authorities, with a Plan for Reforming them*, Communication No. 1 of the Rhodes-Livingstone Institute (this is to be discussed in the light of later changes by Heath F. M. N., *Administrative Developments in Barotseland* (in press) (Mr Heath is a District Commissioner in Barotseland).

[22] But contrast Fortes M., 'The Ashanti Social Survey' in *Human Problems in British Central Africa*, VI (1948), pp. 1 f.

[23] J. Van Velsen, 'Labour Migration as a Positive Factor in the Continuity of Tonga Tribal Society', in *Social Change in Africa*, edited by Southall A. W. (1961). For a summary of the general theoretical development referred to here, see my essay on 'Anthropological Problems arising from the African Industrial Revolution' in that book and 'Tribalism in Modern Central Africa', *Cahiers D'Etudes Africaines* 1 (1960), pp. 15 f., as well as the more sophisticated essay by Mitchell J. C., 'Tribalism and the Plural Society: An Inaugural Lecture' (1960). Watson has an illuminating essay on the whole problem in his 'The Social Background' to 'The Impact of Federation on Africans' in *A New Deal in Central Africa*, edited by Leys C. and Pratt C. (1960), pp. 138 f.

[24] In her essay in *East African Chiefs* (pp. 386–7), Chilver touches on the crucial difference between types of weapons and fighting in the European feudal societies and in the Interlacustrine Bantu states, which must alone call in question any designation of these latter states as feudal.

[25] I have concentrated above on British and British-trained American anthropologists, because my brief in this *Introduction* is to put my own work into context, and not to analyse the full development of 'political anthropology'. French and Belgian anthropologists have worked in a tradition till recently independent from our own tradition. Happily the traditions are coming together, but I lack space to deal with recent French and Belgian work (see G. Balandier, 'Structures sociales traditionelles et changements économiques', *Cahiers D'Etudes Africaines*, 1 (1960), pp. 1 f.). I note as of special interest in this connection Biebuyck D. and Douglas M., *Congo Tribes and Parties* (1961).

[26] The conclusion to a preliminary account, 'A Muslim Passion Play: Key to a Lebanese Village', in 'Perspective on the Arab World', Supplement to the *Atlantic Monthly*, edited by W. R. Polk (1956), pp. 58 f.

CHAPTER ONE

[1] The Nuer: Tribe and Clan, *Sudan Notes and Records* (1933–5); *The Nuer* (1940); and *Some Aspects of Marriage and the Family among the Nuer*, Rhodes-Livingstone Institute, 1945 (reprinted from *Zeitschrift für Vergleichende Rechtswissenschaft*, 1938).

[2] e.g. it is taboo for a Zulu or Pedi to anticipate the chief in eating first-fruits, but a breach of the taboo mystically threatens the chief, not the transgressing subject.

[3] See e.g. Nadel S. F., *A Black Byzantium* (1942); Kuper, H. *A Black Aristocracy: Rank among the Swazi* (1946); and my own 'The Kingdom of the Zulu of South-East Africa' in *African Political Systems* (1940), and *Analysis of a Social Situation in Modern Zululand* (1958).

[4] In a different form, this occurs in conquered territories in South and Central Africa.

[5] *Marriage and Family among the Yakö of South-Eastern Nigeria* (1942).

[6] The Tallensi do not appear to have the custom by which a woman can marry a wife and be pater to the latter's children. This occurs among Nuer, Zulu, Lovedu, Dahomey, and various other tribes in South, North-East, and West Africa. Cf. Herskovits M., 'Women Marriage in Dahomey', *Africa*, x (1937).

[7] I agree that this is a better term than *extended*.

[8] Hunter M., *Reaction to Conquest* (1936), p. 233.

[9] See my 'Zulu Women in Hoeculture Ritual', *Bantu Studies*, ix (1935).

[10] Kuper H., 'A Ritual of Kingship', *Africa*, xiv (1944).

[11] Evans-Pritchard first emphasized this most significant difference, beween the levirate proper where the husband is still the dead man, and inherited-marriage which constitutes a new union. Leviratic marriage occurs in such widely separated societies as Nuer and Zulu, and, Fortes tells me, in essence occurred among the Tallensi.

[12] Refer Hoernlé, A. W., ' The Importance of the Sib in the Marriage Ceremonies of the South-Eastern Bantu', *South African Journal of Science*, 22 (1928).

[13] See my 'Zulu Woman in Hoeculture Ritual', op. cit.

[14] As I read these ties, there is a mistake in the red lines of the diagram facing p. 108. In the left-hand corner the red line linking Kpataar B and Bunkiuk B is a link in the cult of the External Ancestral-shrine and should be dotted, not continuous.

[15] 'Kingdom of the Zulu of South-East Africa', *African Political Systems*, op. cit.

[16] See Fortes' 'Ritual Festivals and Social Cohesion in the Hinterland of the Gold Coast', *American Anthropologist*, 38 (1936).

[17] This hypothesis to explain why mystical values attach to the units of social organization was put forward by Fortes and Evans-Pritchard in their *Introduction to African Political Systems*, op. cit. Fortes here expounds it in greater detail.

[18] Namoos bury each individual in his 'gateway', non-Namoos bury in 'cemeteries'. The Namoos sacrifice separately at each grave to show links with the chiefship, the Talis forget these separate graves and sacrifice to all ancestors, for all men have the same ritual bonds with the Earth.

[19] In practice clanship ties do change within the pattern (see book reviewed, pp. 40, 43–4, 84–5).

[20] See *African Political Systems*, p. 83.

[21] See *African Political Systems*, p. 39.

[22] Cf. Richards criticized Evans-Pritchard's *The Nuer* because he 'arbitrarily' excluded all groupings below the village, specifically relations between families in the village, from his analysis: 'A Problem of Anthropological Approach', *Bantu Studies*, xv (1941).

[23] See their *Introduction* at p. 3, where they themselves assert this. Radcliffe-Brown A. R. made this point in his *The Andaman Islanders* (1922), p. 230.

CHAPTER TWO

[1] *African Political Systems* (1940), pp. 11–14, and p. 5.

[2] Op. cit., pp. 39–40.

[3] Gluckman, 'Analysis of a Social Situation in Modern Zululand: B. Social Change in Zululand', *Bantu Studies* (June 1940), pp. 152–3 (reprinted as Rhodes-Livingstone Paper No. 28, 1958). See also *African Political Systems*, Introduction, p. 13.

[4] *The Nuer* (1940), and *The Political System of the Anuak of the Anglo-Egyptian Sudan*, (1940). *The Nuer* also in *African Political Systems*, in which see Fortes on the Tallensi.

[5] Evans-Pritchard, *African Political Systems*, p. 284.

[6] Evans-Pritchard, *Political System of the Anuak*, pp. 134–5.

[7] Fortes, *African Political Systems*, p. 271.

[8] *A Black Byzantium* (1942).

[9] Subsequently published as *The Succession of Bemba Chiefs: a Guide for District Officers*, Government Printer, Lusaka (1948).

[10] Richards (at p. 101) says that Kanyanta (D1) claimed the throne on the grounds that he came of an older line (which legally seems a sound argument) and that MWAMBA always became king (which from the table is clearly incorrect).

CHAPTER THREE

[1] *Adonis Attis Osiris: Studies in the History of Oriental Religion* (1907), second edition, pp. 3–6.

[2] Professor H. Frankfort has recently argued that Frazer neglected many significant differences, for 'the gods as they confront us in the religions of the ancient Near East express profoundly different mentalities': 'Excursus: Tammuz, Adonis, Osiris', in *Kingship and the Gods* (1948), at pp. 286–94. See also his

Frazer Lecture for 1950, *The Problem of Similarity in Ancient Near Eastern Religions* (1951).

[3] I have published an analysis of others' descriptions of these ceremonies: see 'Zulu Women in Hoe Culture Ritual', *Bantu Studies*, ix (1935).

[4] Samuelson, R. C. A., *Long, Long Ago* (1929), p. 303.

[5] Bryant, A. T., *The Zulu People as they were before the White Man Came* (1949), pp. 662 f.

[6] op. cit., pp. 194 f. (my italics).

[7] See Frankfort's warning, cited footnote 2.

[8] Junod, H. A., *The Life of a South African Tribe* (1927), ii, p. 441.

[9] For an analysis of how a ban on certain persons attending a ceremony may be their positive contribution to it, see my 'The Role of the Sexes in Wiko Circumcision Ceremonies', in *Social Structure: Studies presented to A. R. Radcliffe-Brown*, ed. M. Fortes (1949).

[10] See my 'Zulu Women in Hoe Culture Ritual', op. cit.

[11] This fact is strongly emphasized in Tsonga ceremonies at the building of a new village: Junod, op. cit., i. pp. 320 f.

[12] Many of these beliefs and customs occur also in matrilineal societies: but women are involved in different types of tensions (see below) arising out of their reproductive rôle: see my comparison of 'Kinship and Marriage among the Lozi of Northern Rhodesia and the Zulu of Natal' in *African Systems of Kinship and Marriage*, ed. A. R. Radcliffe-Brown and C. D. Forde (1950).

[13] Older women, as mothers of grown sons, had securer positions.

[14] On this theme see Evans-Pritchard, E. E., 'Some Collective Expressions of Obscenity in Africa', *Journal of the Royal Anthropological Institute*, lix (1929).

[15] For examples of these ceremonies see footnote 19 below. Dr H. Kuper informs me that the Swazi have no developed ceremony for the Princess of Heaven, though it has been reported to me by Dr P. J. Schoeman (personally) and by Dr B. Marwick in *The Swazi* (1940), p. 230, where it is said she sends disease, and naked girls herd cattle to get rid of an insect pest. It is possible that they recorded the ceremony among Zulu settled in Swaziland. Dr Kuper writes that obscenity, transvesticism, and other features of the *Nomkubulwana* ritual appear in a Swazi ceremony to drive away an insect pest; and that *Umlendagamunye*, the messenger of the Swazi High God, has some of *Nomkubulwana's* attributes. I refer to the Tsonga and Transkeian ceremonies in my paper on 'Zulu Women in Hoe Culture Ritual', op. cit. Zulu girls of a neighbourhood also went naked, singing lewd songs, to attack a man who had impregnated one of them.

[16] In Chapter XIII, 'The Drama of Kingship', of *An African Aristocracy: Rank among the Swazi* (1947). I have analysed the material on the Zulu in 'Social Aspects of First-Fruit Ceremonies among the South-Eastern Bantu', *Africa*, xi (1938), but Dr Kuper's observations show that there were serious mistakes in the records of Zulu ceremonies. There are a number of important differences between Zulu and Swazi political structures, of which the most relevant is the existence of a dual monarchy in Swaziland under the king and the queen-mother. The queen-mother has an important and essential role in the ceremony, though she does not take the same leading role as in the earlier rain ceremony (see Kuper, 'The Swazi Rain Ceremony', *Bantu Studies*, ix (1935)). She links the king to his male ancestors, as shown in the discussion of the *Nomkubulwana* ritual. But I lack time to deal with her place as it deserves, and concentrate on other themes. Similarly, I do not stress the role of the king's ritual queen, mated to him by blood. Dr Kuper, writing in comment on this paper, stresses the queen-mother's role: 'Both aspects – female and male – are

joined together for national unity; one cannot be complete without the other. Throughout the ceremony there is this ambivalence between the sexes and stress on their complementary rôles which overcomes hostility'. I may add that in this period many societies have a taboo on marriage, to emphasize this theme. This stresses the strains that marriages, which in simple societies link independent sets of kin, create. (See discussion of the *Nomkubulwana* ritual.) Like quarrels, marriages should not occur in the period of ritual unity between firstfruits and harvest.

¹⁷ Dr Kuper considers that this act strengthens the second interpretation: I do not agree.

¹⁸ *Kingship and the Gods*, op. cit., pp. 82 f. The standard books on the classical ceremonies are full of information which suggests that these ceremonies were possibly thus organized, but it seems that there are not data to answer adequately the critical questions: who did what, when, where, how, with what? See, e.g., Harrison, J., *Prolegomena to the Study of Greek Religion* (1922, 3rd edition) and *Themis: A Study of Greek Religion* (1912); Farnell, L. R., *The Cults of the Greek States*, 5 vols. (1896–1909); Cumont, F., *Les Religions Orientales dans le Paganisme Romain* (1906); Toutain, J., *Les Cultes Païens dans L'Empire Romain* 2 vols. (1907 and 1911); Nilsson, M. P., *Greek Popular Religion* (1940); Murray, Gilbert, *Five Stages of Greek Religion* (1925). I have not here considered analyses of cults in regions where, as in West Africa, small independent political units are linked together in politico-ritual unity by a cycle of ceremonies at different shrines to single 'deities'. If sacrifice at each shrine is to be successful, sacrifice must be offered at all shrines: yet the rites emphasize independence and hostility. Nevertheless a system of overlapping circles of 'ritual peace' is this established: see Fortes, M., *The Dynamics of Clanship among the Tallensi* (1945) and 'Ritual Festivals and Social Cohesion in the Hinterland of the Gold Coast', *American Anthropologist*, xxxviii (1936). This type of analysis might clarify the interrelations of cults of the gods and goddesses of city-states at some periods of Greek history, and other rituals. I suggest that it might be worth trying to apply these types of analysis to the classical material.

¹⁹ I cite a few examples of similarly organized ceremonies in Africa to show how widespread is this cultural mechanism: (*a*) The Harvest Festivals of the Gold Coast Tallensi – Fortes, *The Dynamics of Clanship among the Tallensi* and 'Ritual Festivals and Social Cohesion in the Hinterland of the Gold Coast', op. cit.; (*b*) Forde, C. D., 'Intergrative Aspects of Yakö First-Fruits Rituals', *Journal of the Royal Anthropological Institute*, lxxix, (1949); (*c*) every ceremony described in Junod, op. cit.; (*d*) Hoernlé, A. W., 'The Importance of the Sib in the Marriage Ceremonies of the South-Eastern Bantu', *South African Journal of Science*, xxii (1925); (*e*) Gluckman, M., 'The Role of the Sexes in Wiko Circumcision Ceremonies', op. cit.; (*f*) the installation of a Ngoni headman – Barnes, J. A., in 'The Village Headman in British Central Africa' (with Gluckman, M., and Mitchell, J. C.), *Africa*, xxix (1949), (fifth essay in this book); (*g*) the installation of a Shilluk king – Evans-Pritchard, E. E., *The Divine Kingship of the Shilluk of the Nilotic Sudan*, The Frazer Lecture, (1948).

²⁰ *Kingship and the Gods*, op. cit., pp. 9 and 51–2 et passim.

²¹ 'Analysis of a Social Situation in Modern Zululand', *Bantu Studies*, xiv, 1 and 2 (March and June, 1940), (reprinted as Rhodes-Livingstone Paper No. 28, 1958).

²² I suggest that G. Bateson did not fully appreciate this point in his analysis of *Naven* (1936), an analogous ritual process among the Sepik of New Guinea.

²³ Evans-Pritchard in his Frazer Lecture, 1948, *The Divine Kingship of the Shilluk*, op. cit., at p. 36, has discussed this situation.

[24] See my essay 'The Kingdom of the Zulu of South Africa' in *African Political Systems*, and the Editors' *Introduction* at p. 13. See also my 'The Lozi of Barotseland in North-Western Rhodesia', in *Seven Tribes of British Central Africa* (1951).

[25] See e.g., Kern, F., *Kingship and Law in the Middle Ages* (1948), translated from the German by S. B. Chrimes. Kern emphasizes the constraint of Law on the king and the subjects' right of resistance, rather than the role of rebellion in the political process. See Jolliffe, J. E. A., *The Constitutional History of Medieval England*, (1948), pp. 155–65.

[26] See on the points in these last paragraphs: Nadel, S. F., *A Black Byzantium* (Nupe) (1942), pp. 69 ff.; Schapera's 'The Political Organization of the Ngwato of Bechuanaland Protectorate', Oberg's 'The Kingdom of Ankole in Uganda', Richards' 'The Political System of the Bemba Tribe', and Gluckman's 'The Kingdom of the Zulu of South Africa', all in *African Political Systems*, op. cit.; Gluckman, 'The Lozi of Barotseland in North-Western Rhodesia', op. cit., pp. 23 f., and 'Succession and Civil War among the Bemba', Rhodes-Livingstone Journal, 16 (December, 1953) (reproduced above as Essay II); Kuper *An African Aristocracy*, op. cit., pp. 88 ff.; Kern (*Kingship and Law in the Middle Ages*, op. cit.) also stresses 'the lack . . . of a strict claim to the throne for any individual member of the ruling line' in the early Middle Ages, especially in Germany. This raises the problem whether there are any systematic social changes associated with the emergence of a single clearly defined heir to the throne.

[27] This problem is analysed at length in my 'Social Aspects of First-Fruits Ceremonies among the South-Eastern Bantu', op. cit. Dr Kuper also stresses this important point: *An African Aristocracy*, op. cit., p. 224. See also Junod, H. A., op. cit., ii, p. 10 – 'Although no taboo prevents any owner of a field from eating the green mealies whenever it suits him, Mboza asserts that people who have obtained green mealies before the other inhabitants of the village, do not precede them in an enjoyment of this much appreciated food: "It would cause jealousy amongst them". This reason is perhaps at the bottom of the luma taboo. Moreover they fear lest they might have to share their good luck with all their friends!'; and Richards, A. I., *Land, Labour and Diet in Northern Rhodesia* (1939), pp. 374 f.

[28] N.B. The Swazi queen-mother takes the lead in the rainmaking ceremony, with the king attending on her; he is leader in the first-fruits rites.

[29] Dr S. Kark, who ran a Health Centre in Southern Natal, reports this in unpublished manuscripts; Lee, S. G., 'Some Zulu Concepts of Psychogenic Disorder', *South African Journal for Social Research* (1951), pp. 9–16; Kohler, M., *The Izangoma Diviners*, Ethnological Publications of the South African Department of Native Affairs, Pretoria: No. 9. (1941); Laubscher, B. J. F., *Sex Custom, and Psychopathology* (1937).

[30] 'Introduction' to *African Political Systems*, op. cit., pp. 16 ff.

[31] See my 'The Lozi of Barotseland in North-Western Rhodesia', op. cit., pp. 45–6, on this theme generally.

[31a] [See my 'Les Rites de Passage' in *Essays on the Ritual of Social Relations*, ed. M. Gluckman, 1962.]

[32] Ibid., pp. 23 f.

[33] A fairly free translation from Delegorgue, A., *Voyage dans l'Afrique Australe*, 2 vols. (1847), ii, p. 237.

[34] See quotation from Delegorgue above. Cf. the way in which an African sacrificial gathering is the appropriate occasion for people to vent their grievances and confess their ill-feeling; indeed, they must do so in order to be in that amity

with their fellows which the ritual requires: see, e.g., Fortes, *The Dynamics of Clanship among the Tallensi*, op. cit., p. 98, and Junod, op. cit., i, p. 160.

[35] See the reference above at footnote 31, to the absence of these rituals among the Lozi, who have an elaborate arrangement to express oppositions in the state.

CHAPTER FIVE

[1] The most important published anthropological studies of the region by students who were not officers of the Rhodes-Livingstone Institute are: Smith E. W. and Dale A., *The Ila-speaking Peoples of Northern Rhodesia*, (1920); C. M. Doke, *The Lambas of Northern Rhodesia*, (1931); Melland F., *In Witch-bound Africa* (1923); Richards A. I., *Land, Labour and Diet in Northern Rhodesia* (1939) and *Bemba Marriage and Modern Economic Conditions* 1940) as well as many papers; and Wilson G. and M., *The Analysis of Social Change: Based on Observations in Central Africa* (1945), *Land Rights of Individuals among the Nyakyusa*, (1939), and *The Constitution of Ngonde* (1940), as well as several papers; Brelsford V., *Fishermen of the Bangweoulu Swamps* (1946). Institute officers have studied and have published on: Broken Hill township (the late Godfrey Wilson, first Director); Barotseland, Tonga of Mazabuka and Lamba (Max Gluckman, formerly Assistant Anthropologist, then Director, now Lecturer in Oxford University); Ngoni of Fort Jameson and Lamba (Barnes J. A.); Tonga of Mazabuka (Elizabeth Colson, now Director); Yao and Lamba Mitchell J. C.); Hera tribe among the Shona of Southern Rhodesia (Holleman J. F.). Cunnison I. was beginning a study of the Lunda of the Luapula Valley. The present symposium was worked out in close collaboration with our colleagues, Dr Colson and Dr Cunnison. We are grateful to the Institute of Social Anthropology, Oxford University, for its stimulating criticism of our field reports [footnote written 1948]. [Mitchell's preliminary analysis here was expounded fully later in *The Yao Village* (1956), and Barnes' in *Politics in a Changing Society* (1954)].

[2] Elizabeth Colson, 'Rain-shrines among the Plateau Tonga of Northern Rhodesia', *Africa*, xviii (1948).

[3] See my *Economy of the Central Barotse Plain* (1941) and *Essays on Lozi Land and Royal Property* (1943).

[4] Allan, W., Gluckman, M. Trapnell, C. G. and Peters, D. U. *Land-holding among the Plateau Tonga of Mazambuka District* (1948).

[5] G. Wilson, 'An Introducton to Nyakyusa Society' in *Bantu Studies*, x (1936), at p. 276.

[6] Cf. Richards, A. I. 'The Political System of the Bemba Tribe, North-Eastern Rhodesia' in *African Political Systems* (1940), at pp. 103–4.

[7] All proper names in this paper are fictitious.

CHAPTER SIX

[1] My observations on modern Zulu politics were made especially in the districts of Nongoma, Mhlabatini, and Hlabisa, and to a lesser extent in Ngotshe, Vryheid, Ingwavuma, and Ubombo. Certain observations have also been made in towns, on travels in more southerly districts, and at gatherings of chiefs and Zulu with Mshiyeni, the Regent of the Zulu royal house.

[2] I lack space to discuss historically the way in which Government rule has been accepted, but have tried to make this implicit in my account of the system today.

NOTES

[3] See Schapera I. (Editor), *Western Civilization and the Natives of South Africa* (1934).

[4] For population figures and maps see van Warmelo, N. J. *A Preliminary Survey of the Bantu Tribes of South Africa* (1935). Magisterial districts comprise about 30,000 people; tribes vary from tens of to a few thousand taxpayers.

[5] These duties are defined by the Natal Code of Native Law, Proclamation No. 168/1932. See Stafford, W. *Native Law as Practised in Natal* (1935).

[6] I lack space to discuss the relations of different Government departments or the role of missionaries, and the reaction of the Zulu to changes, many of which have not been purposefully made.

[7] See Jabavu D. D. T. on 'Bantu Grievances' in *Western Civilization and the Natives of South Africa*, op. cit. These are outlined from the point of view of an educated African.

CHAPTER EIGHT

[1] Hunter (Mrs M. Wilson) completely abandoned this point of view in a later book written in collaboration with her husband: *The Analysis of Social Change*, (1945).

[2] In my 'Analysis of a Social Situation in Modern Zululand', *Bantu Studies*, June 1940, pp. 168 ff.: reprinted as Rhodes-Livingstone Paper No. 28 (1958).

[3] This is what G. and M. Wilson attempted in *The Analysis of Social Change*, op. cit., p. 104, n. 1.

[4] See my essay on the Zulu in *African Political Systems*, op. cit.

CHAPTER NINE

[1] In *Bulletin of the Faculty of Arts of Cairo University*, Vol. 1, Part II, 1933.

CHAPTER TEN

[1] *Man and Culture*, edited by Raymond Firth (1958).

INDEX

abductor: sued for damages, 186.

'absorbent' concepts, 205 f.

adaptation in colour bar, 220.

administrative organization: various authors on, state—, 31; in tribal states, 59.

administrator and Zulu, 233 f; administrator (white): role in colour bar, 218.

adultery: mystical repercussions of, 64.

African disabilities: Kenya, 144.

agnatic descent, social principles of, 63.

agricultural ceremonies: classical, 258 fn. 18.; in ancient Near East and Mediterranean, 111.

agricultural rituals, 132 f.; and priest-kings, 110 f.

allegiance to chief: in tribal law, 22; in mediæval English law, 22.

Alur: Southall on, 30.

ambivalence, 78; of followers to head-man, 152; of social relations, 126; to chief, 123.

ancestor-cult, 72 f, 75; bounded by kinship, 141; of chief, 58; focus of differentiation and cohesion, 73; and kingship, 57 f; shrines, 54.

ancestors: in segmentary vs. state society, 58; power of—in relation to chiefs, 79; relation of chief to, 125, 133.

Andrezejewski, S., 253, fn. 5.

Ankole: inheritance wars, 131; rebellions and revolutions, 9; succession among, 14, 20.

anthropology: behaviourism and—, 236; early field-workers, 242; and lawyers, 185–6; Malinowski on—and government, 210; Malinowski's polemics in, 208; need for comparative work in, 207; practical—,

217; scientific correlations in, 229; specialized social—, 238.

anti-witchcraft movements: in C. and S. Africa, 143.

Anuak: segmentary society, 87; studied by Evans-Pritchard, 15.

appeal courts: in Barotseland, 181, 183.

archeologists: and anthropologists, 41.

archival research: Malinowski's sneer at, 210.

Aristotle: catharsis, 126; on rebellions and revolution, 9 f; on Greek institutions, 6.

Ashton, H., 35.

Azande, 137.

Bacchantic ceremonies: among S. E. Bantu, 114 f; among Tsonga, 114 f.

Bambada Rebellion, 144.

Barnes, J. A.: on Ngoni, 160; changes in anthropological analysis, 41; on Ngoni chief, 43; analysis of Ngoni, 34; on Ngoni rebellions, 30; treatment of power, 46.

Barotse (see also Lozi); description and government of, 180; law of treason, 22; rebellions and revolution, 33; ritual and secular organization, 26; treatment of commoners after civil war, 22.

Barotse law: general and particular rules in, 198; procedure of, 180–1.

Basuto: first-fruits ceremonies among, 35.

Bateson, G.: *Naven*, inspiration of, 44; theory of, 18.

Beattie, J. M.: treatment of political problems, 45.

beer: attitude to, 164.

behaviourism: in Malinowski's theories, 236.

position of magistrate among, 171 f.; pantheon, 112 f., 117; political system, 85; position of women among —, 127; rebellions, 33 f., 86; rebirth nationalism, 82: stability of marriage among, 117; succession disputes, 14 f.; tribal loyalties among, 175 f.; social components of ceremonies among, 112; treatment of commoners after civil war, 22; taboos and restraints on women, 116; transvestite ceremonies, 113, 117 f.; use of money, 229; wage labour, 215; women's rites, 112 f.